Writing with Style

Conversations on the Art of Writing

Writing with Style
Conversations on the Art of Writing

Third Edition

John R. Trimble
The University of Texas at Austin

Prentice Hall

Boston   Columbus   Indianapolis   New York   San Francisco   Upper Saddle River
Amsterdam   Cape Town   Dubai   London   Madrid   Milan   Munich   Paris   Montréal   Toronto
Delhi   Mexico City   São Paulo   Sydney   Hong Kong   Seoul   Singapore   Taipei   Tokyo

Acquisitions Editor: Brad Potthoff
Editorial Assistant: Nancy C. Lee
Associate Managing Editor: Bayani Mendoza de Leon
Production Manager: Meghan DeMaio
Marketing Manager: Sandra McGuire
Creative Director: Jayne Conte
Cover Designer: Suzanne Duda
Project Coordination, Text Design, and Electronic Page Makeup: Jerusha
  Govindakrishnan, PreMediaGlobal
Printer/Binder: Edwards Brothers
Cover Printer: Lehigh-Phoenix Color

Library of Congress Cataloging-in-Publication Data
Trimble, John R.
  Writing with style : conversations on the art of writing / John R. Trimble.—3rd ed.
     p. cm.
  Includes index.
  ISBN-13: 978-0-205-02880-1
  ISBN-10: 0-205-02880-2
  1. English language—Rhetoric.   2. English language—Style.   3. Exposition (Rhetoric)
4. Report writing.   I. Title.
  PE1408.T69 2011
  808′.042—dc22
                                                            2010043524

1 2 3 4 5 6 7 8 9 10—13 12 11 10

Prentice Hall
is an imprint of

PEARSON

www.pearsonhighered.com

ISBN-13: 978-0-205-02880-1
ISBN-10:   0-205-02880-2

For Jan

Contents

A Word About These "Conversations"

> For me, writing is the only thing that passes the three tests
> of métier: (1) when I'm doing it, I don't feel that I should be
> doing something else instead; (2) it produces a sense of
> accomplishment and, once in a while, pride; and (3) it's
> frightening.
>
> —Gloria Steinem

B ooks on writing tend to be windy, boring, and impractical. I intend this
one to be different—short, fun, and genuinely useful.

My chief goal is to take the mystery out of how skilled writers think,
so you can begin thinking like them yourself. But beyond that, I want
to share some practical tips on how to make your prose more readable.
Actually, you'll find scores of tips in the chapters ahead—on everything
from opening strategies to the artful use of semicolons. Along the way, I'll
also be examining some common questions about punctuation, quoting,
usage issues, and stylistic taboos—the tough questions that every writer
needs help with from time to time.

My plan, I confess, was to keep it brief enough to be read over a couple cups of coffee. Alas, it now appears that you'll need a third, maybe even
a fourth, to see you through. For that I apologize. The book became a
friend I was loath to bid good-bye to.

A few readers—teachers mainly—may be disappointed that I've
excluded end-of-chapter exercises, not to mention discussion of research
papers, grammar, syllogistic reasoning, patterns of "paragraph movement,"

and other such things conventionally covered by textbooks on writing. I can only answer that this is not—and doesn't aim to be—a conventional manual.

What I offer here is practical shoptalk for armchair consumption—in effect, an informal four-hour refresher course, with the emphasis on refreshment. The book is primarily geared to those writers who've already been through the textbook mill and who now hunger for helpful tips, inspiration, and a clear, lively synthesis of the essentials. But because it focuses on fundamentals, I hope it may prove useful to others, too.

Preface to the Third Edition

Time has sure been kind to this little book. During its first 25 years it enjoyed 32 reprintings. Then along came the lovely Silver Anniversary Edition, all freshened up, which gained it many more new friends. But barely had I noticed when still another decade had slipped by, bringing with it my retirement from the University of Texas. Wouldn't you know, though, that didn't stop my Pearson editor, Brad (middle name "Persistent") Potthoff, from begging for yet another refresh. Happily, his will prevailed. So for this latest edition, featuring two brand-new chapters—"Critical Analysis: Jousting with Mencken" and "Dramatizing Your Ideas"—I'm sharing some of the fun my students and I had in good old 325M, my Advanced Expository Writing seminar at UT. Meanwhile, throughout, I'm also including a sprinkling of updates—fresh help on taboos, exclamation points, ellipses, and usage manuals, among other things.

Once again, I wish you a smooth read. If you have any corrections to suggest, or comments to make, or sources to offer for fugitive quotations, I'd love to hear from you. Email me here: *trimble@mail.utexas.edu*

Acknowledgments

I've been assisted here by a host of talented teachers, editors, and students. Let me publicly honor their contributions.

My thanks, first, to our six pre-publication reviewers, whose suggestions proved wonderfully smart and generous-spirited: Professors Paul Allen, Greg Barnhisel, Daniel Frick, Susanmarie Harrington, John Hyman, and James L. Ragonnet.

Four of my former colleagues at the University of Texas, all superb teachers of writing, were a source of constant inspiration and joy: John

Ruszkiewicz, Diane Davis, Tom Buckley, and, certainly not least, Linda Ferreira-Buckley. Huge thanks, my friends, for helping to show me the way and for giving me the pleasure of your wonderful company.

Another way-shower, or at least way-reminder, was Professor John Bean, author of the extraordinarily sensible handbook for writing teachers, *Engaging Ideas* (Jossey-Bass Publishers, 2001). Rereading that splendid book, by one of the country's top experts in critical-thinking theory, got me excited all over again about jousting with Mencken. Thank you, John Bean.

I'm also grateful to several former students for their invaluable contributions: Amy Jetel, Jolene Shirley, Matt MacDonald, Cory Jones, Terry Kirk, Emily DePrang, and—drum roll, please, for the Queen of Graphics—Kimberly Selber.

At Pearson Education, too, I've been blessed with superb helpers— Brad Potthoff, senior editor; Joe Opiela, editor-in-chief; Meghan DeMaio, production manager; Sandra McGuire, senior marketing manager; Megan Glavin-Fak, director of marketing; and Nancy C. Lee, editorial assistant. Those last words, "editorial assistant," don't begin to describe Nancy's genius for helping, but she already knows my vast gratitude.

More thanks go to Jerusha Govindakrishnan, of PreMediaGlobal, who served as associate project manager for this edition. Her efficiency, attention to detail, and good cheer, week after week, left nothing to be desired. I was equally blessed to have the eagle-eyed, ever-tactful Cindy Bond as my superb copyeditor. Cindy, we need to clone you.

Still more thanks go to my dear friends and colleagues Bryan and Karolyne Garner, of LawProse, Inc., for all their encouragement and unstinting helpfulness. As with "editorial assistant," the words "unstinting helpfulness" seem almost comically inadequate here, but you two know your value to me.

Finally, I owe a gold medal to Brad Potthoff, whose persistence, care, and wise counsel as an editor and friend proved invaluable. He has made this a far better book—in fact, the book wouldn't even be here without him—so every reader stands equally in his debt.

Once more I dedicate the book, and indeed my life, to my beloved Jan. You rock, darlin'.

John R. Trimble

Fundamentals

1

Thinking Well

The indispensable characteristic of a good writer is a style marked by lucidity.

—Ernest Hemingway

And how is clarity to be achieved? Mainly by taking trouble; and by writing to serve people rather than to impress them.

—F. L. Lucas

Each profession, it would seem, has its own style of thought that must be mastered before one feels at home in it. The law certainly does. So does architecture. And so, too, with engineering, accounting, computer programming, film directing, psychology, carpentry—you name it, they all have a style of thought related to the nature of the profession. It stands to reason that writing would have its own, too. And it does.

What a novice needs more than anything, then, is to plug into the brain of an experienced writer—to understand the assumptions she typically makes, the silent monologue that is occupying her head as she composes, the special effects she is trying to achieve . . . Without that guiding instinct, writing will remain all hit-or-miss—a frustrating repetition of trial and error, over and over again.

A beginning chess player faces many of the same problems. Lacking any kind of "chess sense," as players call it, he sits bewildered at the board, moving first a pawn, then a bishop, then—why not?—his queen, all at random, hoping that something good will come of it but knowing that if it does, it will be a mere piece of luck. He has no idea how seasoned players think at the board. Even sitting across from them, he cannot fathom what they're trying to accomplish with a particular move, what blunders they're trying to avoid, what alternate game strategies they might be considering. He can certainly appreciate the *effects*, but the actual thought process is a mystery.

Unfortunately, the Grandmasters have made it far easier for a novice to acquire chess sense than authors have made it for him to acquire its literary equivalent. They've published book after book explaining how to think chess—what opening gambits to consider, what counterattacks work well, what endgame tactics to use. Authors of writing texts, on the other hand, tend to stress mechanics, perhaps assuming that people either know how to think or they don't.

I hope to repair that neglect. My chief aim, both in this chapter and throughout the book, is to help you develop "writer's sense." You'll find it as indispensable as radar to a pilot. Let me begin by explaining how a novice writer typically thinks so that when I move on to explain how the veteran thinks, you'll have a more vivid sense of the contrast.

The Novice

Most of the novice's difficulties start with the simple fact that the paper he writes on is mute. Because it never talks back to him, and because he's concentrating so hard on generating ideas, he readily forgets—unlike the veteran—that another human being will eventually be trying to make sense of what he's saying. The result? *His natural tendency as a writer is to think primarily of himself—hence to write primarily for himself.* Here, in a nutshell, lies the ultimate reason for most bad writing.[1]

He isn't aware of his egocentrism, of course, but all the symptoms of his root problem are there: he thinks through an idea only until it is passably clear to him, since, for his purposes, it needn't be any clearer; he dispenses with transitions because it's enough that *he* knows how his ideas connect; he uses a private system—or no system—of punctuation; he doesn't trouble to define his terms because he understands perfectly well what he means by them; he writes page after page without bothering to vary his sentence structure; he leaves off page numbers and footnotes; he paragraphs only when the mood strikes him; he ends abruptly when he decides he's had enough; he neglects to proofread the final job because the writing is over . . . Given his total self-orientation, it's no wonder that he fails repeatedly as a writer. Actually, he's not writing at all; he's merely communing privately with himself—that is, he's simply putting thoughts down on paper.

---

[1] Paul Burka, a National Magazine Award-winning journalist and executive editor of *Texas Monthly*, told one of my classes, "The hardest thing a writer has to do is curb his self-indulgence."

I call this "unconscious writing." The unconscious writer is like a person who turns his chair away from his listener, mumbles at length to the wall, and then heads for home without a backward glance.

Basically, all it takes to begin moving from unconscious writing to genuine writing is a few moments' reflection on what the writing/reading process ideally involves. Think about it. What it involves is one person earnestly attempting to communicate with another. Implicitly, then, it involves the reader as much as the writer, since *the success of the communication depends solely on how the reader receives it.* Also, since more than one person is involved, and since all of us have feelings, *it has to be as subject to the basic rules of good manners as any other human relationship.* The writer who is fully aware of these implications—the conscious writer—resembles a person who companionably faces her listener and tries her level best to communicate with him, even persuade and charm him in the process, and who eventually bids him the equivalent of a genial farewell.

The big breakthrough for the novice writer, then, will occur at the moment he begins to comprehend the social implications of what he's doing. Far from writing in a vacuum, he is conversing, in a very real sense, with another human being, just as I am conversing right now with you, even though that person—like you—may be hours, or days, or even years away in time. This breakthrough parallels an infant's dawning realization that a world exists beyond himself.

Actually, since the novice is as much a self-oriented newcomer to his social world as the infant is to his, we might suspect that the similarity doesn't end there. And we're right. Both of them pass through a gradual process of socialization and deepening awareness. The writer, for example, after realizing that a world—a reader—exists out there beyond himself, slowly comes to develop, first, an awareness of himself from the reader's vantage point (*objectivity*); next, a capacity to put himself imaginatively in the mind of the reader (*empathy*); and finally, an appreciation of the reader's rights and feelings (*courtesy*). You can see that the young writer is essentially retracing, in a new context, the same psychic journey he traveled as a child. Even the net result is comparable. Having passed the last stage of courtesy as a child, he achieved the mark of a truly civilized person: social sensitivity. When he passes the same stage as a writer, he achieves the mark of a truly civilized author: a readable style.

The Veteran

The thinking process of a skilled writer reflects how she conceives the writing situation. Let's start, then, by developing a realistic understanding of what that situation involves.

All writing is communication. But most writing hopes to go further. It hopes to make the reader react in certain ways—with pleased smiles, nods of assent, stabs of pathos, or whatever.

So we can say, generally, that *writing is the art of creating desired effects.*

Now for an essay writer, the chief desired effect is persuasion. Suppose you are that writer. You want your readers to buy two things: your ideas and you, their source. That is, you want them to view your ideas as sound and interesting, and to view you as smart, informed, direct, and companionable. (All of these things, of course, are desired effects.) If you don't persuade them to accept you, it's doubtful that you'll persuade them to buy the ideas you're proffering. We buy from people we like and trust—it's human nature.

The big question, then, is how to win readers? Here are four essentials:

1. Have something to say that's worth their attention.
2. Be sold on its validity and importance yourself so you can pitch it with conviction.
3. Furnish strong arguments that are well supported with concrete proof.
4. Use confident language—vigorous verbs, strong nouns, and assertive phrasing.

While that looks like a pretty full recipe for successful writing, it isn't. Even if we exclude sheer artfulness, one thing is still missing—and almost always is. The ultimate way we win readers is by courteously *serving* them—that is, satisfying their needs. An experienced writer knows that to serve well is to sell well; equally, to sell well is to serve well. They are complementary activities. The means are inseparable from the ends.

The writer, for all practical purposes, does not exist without the assent of his readers, who have the power to shut him off at whim. This fact of life makes pleasing them absolutely critical. But that's only fair. If we're going to ask them to give us their time and attention, then we're in *their* debt, not the other way around; we must be prepared to repay their kindness with kindness of our own. Beyond pleasing them simply to square debts and keep them reading, though, there's also the practical necessity of pleasing them in order to persuade them. Samuel Butler long ago remarked, "We are not won by arguments that we can analyze, but by tone and temper, by the manner which is the man himself." I don't wholly agree with that, but it's certainly close to the truth. A pleasing manner surely makes one's arguments themselves seem pleasing because it dresses them in an aura of reasonableness.

All of us, I think, grasp these facts of life perfectly well as readers, but most of us manage to forget them as writers. Being unconsciously self-oriented, we think it's enough simply to lay out our ideas. Experience keeps disproving us, though. Readers will always insist on having their needs looked after, as they have every right to, and if we're heedless, they'll say "Enough of you" and toss our piece aside.

How, then, do you serve your reader? First, you must cultivate a psychological sense. That is, you must sensitize yourself to what wins *you* over—how and why *you* respond, and what makes *you* feel well served—and gradually learn to extend that awareness to your reader. This book, incidentally, is as good a place as any to start sensitizing yourself. As you read along, you ought to be asking yourself such questions as these: "Is his style too complex to be readable, or too plain, or is it just right—and why?" "What is his tone, and how does he achieve it? Do I like it or don't I?" "Why does he use a semicolon here instead of a period?" "Do I like this two-sentence paragraph?" "What effect do his contractions have on me?" A writer eager to improve his psychological sense never simply reads; he reads critically. His mind is always alert to the *manner* as well as the message, for only in this way will he learn what works and why it works, plus what doesn't work and why it doesn't. He's like one musician listening to the chords and phrasing of another. What's special he'll imitate and make his own.

Once you acquire the habit of reading attentively, you'll find that your psychological sense will improve sharply, and with it your tactical sense, too. This will have an immediate impact not only on the effectiveness of your writing but on your attitude toward it as well. You'll discover yourself beginning to relish it as a supreme challenge to your powers of salesmanship. At the same time, you'll find yourself becoming increasingly considerate. Your readers' needs, not your own, will dominate your thinking.

And it will give you pleasure; you'll quickly learn to enjoy the sense of communion, the fellow-feeling it brings, for, as in a friendship, you'll be in warm, imaginative touch with other human beings.

All of this brings me to the second prime way of serving your readers: schooling yourself to be *other*-oriented. You try to understand your readers. You actively think of them, identify with them, empathize with them. You try to intuit their needs. You train yourself to think always of *their* convenience, not your own. You treat them exactly as you would wish to be treated, with genuine consideration for their feelings. And you keep reminding yourself, over and over, that *good writing is good manners*.

There are five specific ways you can serve your readers' needs. Please add them to the list of four essentials that I gave you a minute ago;

and as you read them, note how they apply to conversation as well as to writing:

1. Phrase your thoughts clearly so you're easy to follow.
2. Speak to the point so you don't waste your readers' time.
3. Anticipate their reactions (boredom, confusion, fatigue, irritation).
4. Offer them variety and wit to lighten their work.
5. Talk to them in a warm, open manner instead of pontificating to them like a know-it-all.

Although I'll be following up on all these points in later chapters, I'd like to expand here on #1, the need for clarity, and #3, the need to anticipate your readers' responses. This will give me a chance to explain more concretely the assumptions and actual thought processes of a skilled writer.

Phrase Your Thoughts Clearly

A prose style may be eloquent, lyrical, witty, rhythmical, and fresh as Colorado air, but if it lacks clarity, few readers will stay with it for long. Just as no one enjoys looking at a view, however spectacular, through a mud-streaked window, no one enjoys listening to a symphony of words reduced to mere noise.

Hemingway was right: clarity *is* the indispensable characteristic of good prose. It's the first thing a reader demands, and perhaps the hardest thing to deliver. Not only must the individual thoughts be clear but, even more challenging, they must follow a logical sequence. Since the average human mind isn't accustomed to thinking systematically, trying to write clear prose is as fatiguing as waterskiing. You're using muscles that normally get little exercise, and they soon let you know it.

But in writing, as in waterskiing, progress does come with practice. And it's greatly accelerated by imitating the techniques and attitudes of experts. Clear writers, for instance, vary widely in native intelligence, but they all share several attitudes:

- They assume that their chief job is to *communicate*. They hope to do more, of course—namely, persuade and charm—but they know that communication must come first, especially if they are ever to achieve these other effects.
- They assume, with a pessimism born of experience, that whatever isn't plainly stated, the reader will invariably misconstrue. They keep in mind that she is, after all, a perfect stranger to their garden of ingenious ideas. In fact, to her, that garden may initially resemble a tangled thicket, if not a

tropical rain forest. This being so, their job as writer is to guide her through, step by step, so that the experience will be quick and memorable. This involves alertly anticipating her moments of confusion and periodically giving her an explanation of where she's headed. The writer's Golden Rule is the same as the moralist's: Do unto others. . . .

- They assume that even their profoundest ideas are capable of being expressed clearly. They aren't so vain as to think that their reflections transcend the powers of language—Shakespeare punctures that fantasy—nor so lazy as to ask their reader to double as a clairvoyant. As novelist Somerset Maugham remarked in *The Summing Up*:

> I have never had much patience with the writers who claim
> from the reader an effort to understand their meaning. You have
> only to go to the great philosophers to see that it is possible to
> express with lucidity the most subtle reflections. You may find it
> difficult to understand the thought of Hume, and if you have no
> philosophical training its implications will doubtless escape you;
> but no one with any education at all can fail to understand
> exactly what the meaning of each sentence is.

- They have accepted the grim reality that nine-tenths of all writing is rewriting . . .
- Perhaps most important of all, they are sticklers for continuity. They link their sentences and paragraphs as meticulously as if they might face criminal charges for negligence.

But rather than speak for them, perhaps I should let a few clear writers speak for themselves. Here, first, is the distinguished British historian George M. Trevelyan:

> The idea that histories which are delightful to read must be the work of
> superficial temperaments, and that a crabbed style betokens a deep
> thinker or conscientious worker, is the reverse of the truth. What is easy
> to read has been difficult to write. The labor of writing and rewriting,
> correcting and recorrecting, is the due exacted by every good book from
> its author. . . . The easily flowing connection of sentence with sentence
> and paragraph with paragraph has always been won by the sweat of
> the brow.

And now novelist James A. Michener:

> I have never thought of myself as a good writer. Anyone who wants
> reassurance of that should read one of my first drafts. But I'm one of
> the world's greatest rewriters.

And finally E. B. White, perhaps America's most respected 20th-century essayist, whose consistently graceful style entitles him to have the last word:

> The main thing I try to do is write as clearly as I can. Because I have the greatest respect for the reader, and if he's going to the trouble of reading what I've written—I'm a slow reader myself and I guess most people are— why, the least I can do is make it as easy as possible for him to find out what I'm trying to say, trying to get at. I rewrite a good deal to make it clear.

Anticipate Your Reader's Responses

The chief difficulty with writing is that it seems a one-way process. You can't see your reader's face, you can't hear her, you can't get any feedback from her whatsoever. The novice writer, as we've seen, is oblivious to this handicap. The skilled writer, though, is supersensitive to it. But he overcomes it by actively *imagining* a reader—in fact, imagining many different readers—just as an experienced TV newscaster, looking into the camera's unwinking eye, actively imagines a viewer.

The kind of reader (or readers) that a skilled writer imagines will depend, of course, on the occasion, the type of piece he's writing, and other such factors. But whatever the occasion, he'll assume the reader has a zillion other interesting things to do with her time, is reading at a fast clip, and *is just waiting for an excuse to tune out.* The writer's challenge, then, is to avoid giving her that excuse. The supreme challenge is to make her quite forget the other things she wanted to do.

How does the writer meet these challenges? Chiefly by *empathy*. The whole time he's writing, he's constantly switching back and forth from his own mind to hers. Like a skilled chess player, he makes a dozen mental moves for every actual one. Each of them he tests as to the probable response it will elicit. *Anticipation,* he's learned, is the name of the game. If he can anticipate a response, he has a fair chance of controlling it. So every sentence—yes, *every* sentence—receives a battery of challenges:

- "Am I droning here? Is she ready to silence me? Is there any way I can lighten this up?"
- "How can I get her to see—to *feel*—the urgency of this point?"
- "Is the continuity silky here, or is fatigue blinding me to a bump?"
- "Might she welcome an analogy here, or is this abstract idea clear enough on its own?"
- "Am I treating her as if she were an idiot?"

- "Is there any conceivable way this sentence might confuse her?"
- "Have I just used any of these words in previous sentences?"
- "Will this phrase strike her as pretentious? And, honestly, am I using it to impress her, or is this the only way I can express the thought cleanly?"
- "Will she get the nuance here, or should I spell it out?"
- "Can she jump on me for verbosity here?"
- "Will she hear a strongly conversational, living voice coming through, or am I beginning to sound like a book?"

He's equally watchful about the way he paragraphs. He remembers all too well encountering whale-like paragraphs that left him sinking under their weight, not to mention those mini-paragraphs that had his eye bouncing down the page. Too much or too little in a paragraph, he knows, has the same effect: it wears the reader out. He also watches the continuity between paragraphs. "Is the connection solid?" he asks himself. "Will my reader want an even sturdier bridge between these parts of my argument? Is there any conceivable way she can feel disoriented here?"

And so on, and so on. Writing well is a long exercise in second-guessing and empathizing—even a kind of nonneurotic, self-induced paranoia. It puts a premium on social sensitivity, alertness, and goodwill. It is, in short, a very complicated business. But, like mountain climbing, it's also wonderfully challenging. Rewarding, too. When you've genuinely communicated with another person, when you've persuaded her to accept a new viewpoint, and when the whole learning experience has been fun for her because you *made* it fun for her, that's downright satisfying—hell, it's exhilarating.

Some Concluding Thoughts

1. *Mumbo jumbo* is another word for grunts of the mind. Mumbo jumbo is what comes out in first and second drafts when you're writing basically for *yourself*—that is, when you're still trying to fathom what you think about a subject.
2. Once you've finished writing for yourself and begin writing for the *reader*, your mumbo jumbo will start turning into bona fide prose—i.e., sentences that make sense.
3. If your reader can't get your full meaning in a single reading, however—and *a single reading is all she owes you*—you must face up to the fact that you're afflicted with some residual mumbo jumbo.
4. The best remedy? *Shorter words and shorter sentences.*
5. When you finally think you've finished a piece, reread it twice, first through the eyes of the average reader (for unconscious obscurities) and second through the eyes of your worst enemy (for all other lapses).

This tends to have a nicely chilling effect on overheated and under-thought prose.

6. As a last caution, let the piece stand overnight. Then, in the morning, go at it again—you're bound to have a whole new outlook. Also, do as the professional author does and share it with some candid friends. Tell them, "I'm interested in seeing this thing *im*proved, not *ap*proved"—and mean it. As reinforcement, it might help both you and your friends if you quote them a remark George Bernard Shaw once made to the actress Ellen Terry. Miss Terry had confessed her reluctance to deface the man-uscripts of a play he had sent her for criticism. Shaw wrote back to her:

> Oh, bother the MSS., mark them as much as you like: what else
> are they for? Mark everything that strikes you. I may consider
> a thing 49 times; but if you consider it, it will be considered
> 50 times; and a line 50 times considered is 2 per cent better
> than a line 49 times considered. And it is the final 2 per cent
> that makes the difference between excellence and mediocrity.

2

Getting Launched

Writing is very easy. All you do is sit in front of a type-writer keyboard until little drops of blood appear on your forehead.

> —Walter W. "Red" Smith, Pulitzer
> Prize-winning sportswriter

As for false starts, I'll be honest, 90% of my hard drive is filled with them. The more freedom you have, the more paths to explore, the harder the task becomes. I've always had to cover a lot of ground before I figured out exactly which way to go. My problem is that I'm always tormented by the thought that there's a better idea lurking out there somewhere. That's true of scripts, campaign ideas, and essays.

> —Matt MacDonald, JWT Creative Director

It's generally recognized that most people have highly individual ways of getting words onto paper. Writers themselves, at least, recognize this, even when their writing manuals don't. Some writers love outlines; others gag over them. Some writers dash off their drafts at high speed; others, known as "bleeders," tend to be mentally constipated or perfectionistic, and refuse to move on from one sentence to the next until the first has been mercilessly flailed. Some writers spend the bulk of their time lavishly researching their subject; others spend the bulk of their time revising—which can also mean doing their research after the fact.

Given our quirky methods of composition, I'm leery of recommending any one way as effective, for the question always becomes, "Effective for whom?" Each of us finally does the job in the way that best suits his or her temperament and current deadline.

Still, most of us are desperate enough to be always shopping for alternate strategies, bits of which we might later incorporate into our habitual method. That explains why I'm brashly offering yet another approach in the recommendations below. Even if you find only two or three that are right for you, I'll feel justified.

1. Listen to your feelings

Pick a subject that *means* something to you, emotionally as well as intellectually. As in romancing, so in writing: you're most effective when your heart is in it. If you can't honestly say, "Now *this* is something I really think is important," you're a fool to mess with it. Take a stroll around the neighborhood; find a coffeehouse or park bench and brood awhile; call up a friend and vent. Do whatever you need to do to figure out what you'd *really* enjoy tangling with, because it's going to define your life for a major hunk of time, isn't it? Eventually you'll come up with a subject, or a new angle on the old subject, that ignites your interest.[1]

If you feel in good spirits, you might consider writing what's called an "appreciation"—of a person, an event, a character, a book, a locale, or whatever. Share your sense of delight; let yourself sing. If, on the other hand, you feel combative, consider writing a salty dissent à la Maureen Dowd or H. L. Mencken. Whatever your inclinations, *turn your feelings to account*—work in harmony with them, actively tap them. If you ignore your real feelings, which is perilously easy to do, or if you try to write with just your head, the result will be phony, bloodless prose, and the labor of writing may be excruciating. You'll feel like you're performing an intellectual minuet.

But all this is too abstract. We need examples—models of prose that crackles with emotional electricity. A fount of them was Pauline Kael, the celebrated, late film critic for *The New Yorker*. Ms. Kael was one writer who never failed to turn her feelings to account. She was that rare creature: someone who thinks passionately. Her reviews—always dead honest—smoked with emotion. An excerpt will illustrate the point and perhaps induce you to read the book in which it's collected, *Deeper*

---

[1]Experience speaks here. Late one night, years ago, when I was already some four months into writing my Ph.D. dissertation, I looked up from the typewriter and found myself thinking, "Do you really want to be known as the world's expert on [my chosen subject]?" My instant answer, voiced aloud, floored me: "No!" "Well, then," I challenged myself, fighting panic, "what would you *really* like to work on?" After several minutes I knew, and immediately set to it, charged with excitement and energy. Those two questions changed my life.

into Movies—among 13 she published. Here's one of Kael's patented 500-pound bombs, dropped on *The French Connection:*

> The noise of New York already has us tense. [*The French Connection*] is like an aggravated case of New York: it raises this noise level to produce the kind of painful tension that is usually described as almost unbearable suspense. But it's the same kind of suspense you feel when someone outside your window keeps pushing down on the car horn and you think the blaring sound is going to drive you out of your skull. This horn routine is, in fact, what the cop does throughout the longest chase sequence. The movie's suspense is magnified by the sheer pounding abrasiveness of its means; you don't have to be an artist or be original or ingenious to work on the raw nerves of an audience this way—you just have to be smart and brutal. The high-pressure methods that one could possibly accept in Z because they were tools used to show the audience how a Fascist conspiracy works are used as ends in themselves. Despite the dubious methods, the purpose of the brutality in Z was moral—it was to make you hate brutality. Here you love it, you wait for it—that's all there is. I know that there are many people—and very intelligent people, too—who love this kind of fast-action movie, who say that this is what movies do best and that this is what they really want when they go to a movie. Probably many of them would agree with everything I've said but will still love the movie. Well, it's not what I want, and the fact that Friedkin has done a sensational job of direction just makes that clearer. It's not what I want not because it fails (it doesn't fail) but because of what it is. It is, I think, what we once feared mass entertainment might become: jolts for jocks. There's nothing in the movie that you can enjoy thinking over afterward—nothing especially clever except the timing of the subway-door-and-umbrella sequence. Every other effect in the movie—even the climactic car-versus-runaway-elevated-train chase—is achieved by noise, speed, and brutality.

To summarize: It's impossible to write electric prose like this without strong emotion to energize your thinking, so pick a subject you have a stake in and write about it just as candidly as you know how. Even if the essay you end up with has serious faults, they're likely to seem pardonable. Most readers will forgive much when they encounter prose that breathes feeling and conviction. Why? They so rarely encounter it.

But what if the topic is *assigned*? What if you have no chance to "pick a subject you have a stake in"? Ah, then you have to *create* a stake in it. You do that by learning your subject cold—by going after it aggressively, like an intellectual conquistador, and treating it as a challenge to your powers of imagination, curiosity, and open-mindedness. The deeper into it you go, of course, the more you have to work with, right? And the more in command you get to feel, too. Eventually, you find yourself ready to teach others what you have learned—and to make it downright interesting for them. You can do that in part just by keying on what you found interesting. Maybe that's your angle right there.

I recommend we take a moment here to think about Russell Page, perhaps the finest landscape architect that England has produced, at least in the 20th century. Virtually *all* of Mr. Page's projects were "assigned" (commissioned), and often in the most unpromising locales—a marshland, say, or a windswept highland, or a property far too wide and far too shallow. Yet he managed to turn out one elegant landscape after another— truly gorgeous things. How? Mainly his attitude. "Limitations imply possibilities," he wrote in *The Education of a Gardener.* "A problem is a challenge." Isn't that a beautiful way to view things?

I also recommend that we take a moment to think about my old boss at *The Buffalo News,* the newspaper I worked for during the summer following my freshman year in college. As a cub reporter, I got to start off in the time-honored way—writing "obits" (obituaries), sometimes as many as four a day. After two weeks of this fare, I finally summoned the courage to approach my boss—the silver-haired, rather crusty city editor—and ask him when I was going to get some decent story assignments for a change. "Listen, young man," he growled at me, "nothing you write for this paper will ever get read as carefully as what you're writing right now. The relatives of these folks will notice every single error. You get a date or address wrong, they'll spot it. You get a name misspelled, they'll spot it. And they'll resent it, too, you can betcha. But they'll also be grateful if you do justice to their grandpa or mother or whoever it is. They'll put your prose in *laminate,* son. Look, I don't want to discuss this anymore with you." And with that he picked up his editing pencil and went back to work. So did I—and with an entirely new attitude. I pledged myself to start writing obits that deserved that laminate. And I quickly found that the more I learned about these just-departed strangers—through extra phone calls, extra questions—the more I cared about them, and the more I wanted to honor them. I ended up actually liking to write obits. It was a powerful lesson for me.

2. Start small

Once you've chosen your general subject, trim it down to size. You want something manageable, something of reasonable scope. A small garden well tended is far more comely than a large garden that shows overambition. So, too, with essays. It's better to start small and grow big than to start big and maybe grow overwhelmed.

You'll delimit your subject in part simply by asking yourself how you want to treat it. But at this point everything is speculative because, if you're like most writers, you'll find out what you think—and want to know, and need still to know—only through writing about it. *The process itself is your teacher.* Listen to some pros here:

How can I tell what I think till I see what I say?

—E. M. Forster

Writing is an exploration. You start from nothing and learn as you go.

—E. L. Doctorow

I have never started a poem yet whose end I knew. Writing a poem is discovering.

—Robert Frost

There is always a point in the writing of a piece when I sit in a room literally papered with false starts and cannot put one word after another and imagine that I have suffered a small stroke, leaving me apparently undamaged but actually aphasic.

—Joan Didion

I don't write easily or rapidly. My first draft usually has only a few elements worth keeping. I have to find out what those are and build from them and throw out what doesn't work, or what simply is not alive. . . . I am profoundly uncertain about how to write. I know what I love or what I like, because it's a direct, passionate response. But when I write I'm very uncertain whether it's good enough. That is, of course, the writer's agony.

—Susan Sontag

Sometimes you get a line, a phrase, sometimes you're crying, or it's the curve of a chair that hurts you and you don't know why, or sometimes you just want to write a poem, and you don't know what it's about. I will fool around on the typewriter. It might take me ten pages of nothing, of terrible writing, and then I'll get a line, and I'll think, "That's what I mean!" What you're doing is hunting for what you mean, what you're trying to say. You don't know when you start.

—Anne Sexton

I write in the morning. . . . Then, after all the [dinner] dishes are moved away, I read what I wrote that morning. And more often than not, if I've done nine pages I may be able to save two and a half, or three. That's the cruelest time, you know, to really admit that it doesn't work. And to blue pencil it.

—Maya Angelou

I write to find out what I'm talking about.

—Edward Albee

I am an obsessive rewriter, doing one draft and then another and another, usually five. In a way, I have nothing to say, but a great deal to add.

—Gore Vidal

Delay is natural to a writer. He is like a surfer—he bides his time, waits for the perfect wave on which to ride in. Delay is instinctive with him. He waits for the surge (of emotion? of strength? of courage?) that will carry him along. I have no warm-up exercises, other than to take an occasional drink. I am apt to let something simmer for a while in my mind before trying to put it into words.

—E. B. White

3. Stockpile data

After you've staked out a promising subject and think you know what you want to do with it, you'd be wise to follow E. B. White's example: delay a bit. Let things cook. Meanwhile, though, you can be very productive by stock-piling stuff—facts, quotes, parallels, ironies, puzzlements, gut impressions . . . Principally *facts*, though, because readers like to be *taught*, and they invariably prefer the concrete to the abstract. Here, if I may offer a humble example, is something from a description assignment that I once wrote for my Advanced Expository Writing seminar. It grew out of this very data-gathering I'm extolling. I figured my troops might welcome precise numbers about Hemingway's sentence length, so I performed a few minutes' worth of word-counting—and taught myself something in the bargain:

> Although Hemingway is celebrated for his short sentences, he was equally at home with long ones. In fact, five consecutive sentences in his story "On the Blue Water" run 23, 109, 55, 58, and 60 words, and rank among the best he ever wrote.

That second sentence is mostly data.

Facts, of course, are important to you, too. You know from experience that your best writing occurs when you're confident that you have enough data—particularly enough *solid* data. Confidence and preparation are, practically speaking, almost synonymous. Moral: If you have just enough solid data, you don't have enough; with a big surplus, you're primed to write.

4. Pose some tough questions

To generate facts and ideas, *formulate a variety of questions,* both general and specific, such as a tough examiner might ask—Why? Who? How? When? Where?—and bombard your subject with them.[2] As you do, begin *sketching out tentative answers to them* in the

---

[2]Thomas Griffith, former editor of *Life* magazine and a superb writer, would appear to agree: "I work better professionally when my views are crowded and challenged, for I recognize that out of antagonism comes quality, which is why the best sculptures are of marble, not of soap."

form of mini-paragraphs. For this purpose, especially when I'm away from my computer, I like to use a cheap pad of 5-by-8-inch slips, bought at any stationer's, rather than 8½-by-11-inch standard sheets. Being half as large, they're far less threatening and much easier to flip through later. (Don't confuse 5-by-8 slips with the still-smaller 3-by-5 cards. The slips are sold in gummed pads; the little 3-by-5 cards, made of pricey card stock, are sold in packs and are impractical except for recording bibliographical data.)

Each time you formulate a question, take a fresh slip, write the question at the top, skip a space or two, and jot down whatever ideas occur to you. Use as many slips as you need for each question, but be sure to write out the question at the top of each new slip, and number the slips relating to each question to avoid confusion later.

Suppose you are a psychology major and have decided to write an essay explaining the behavior of Martha in Edward Albee's play *Who's Afraid of Virginia Woolf?* One of your slips might look like this:

How does Martha protect herself from
feeling pain and alienation?

1. She smothers any recognition of her father's lifelong indifference toward her (see p. 225) by vocally worshipping him—a good example of what psychologists term "reaction formation."
2. "I pass my life in crummy, totally pointless infidelities," she confesses (p. 189). Two probable reasons: to reassure herself that she is lovable and to discharge her strong masochistic feelings (e.g., "I disgust me," p. 189).
3. She externalizes that self-contempt—and feeds her insecurity—by loudly ridiculing her husband George.
4. She uses liquor to drown the pain. She's now an alcoholic: George remarks that she "can't get enough" liquor (p. 224).
5. She fancifully invents a child—a son—to bring beauty and meaning into her barren life. The son is one person who is all her own, to use as she wishes: to love and be loved by.

Note that each of the five points could be developed further in later slips and could eventually become a separate paragraph of your essay.

Keep at it until you have formulated and framed answers to maybe 10 questions. Then collect the slips like cards in a pack and mull them over. As you reread them, keep shuffling the sequence of questions, forcing your mind to confront different combinations of ideas. From these different combinations you'll find unexpected contrasts and similarities. These, too, you should jot down, along with whatever new significant details and apt quotations suddenly appear in your brain. Remember, your object is to *accumulate data.* Data function like fuel for the brain. The more fuel you supply, the hotter and easier it will burn.

This system of prewriting, you'll discover, has two major virtues. One is psychological, and pretty clever to boot: it enables you to write much of your paper before you begin writing it. By writing under the guise of doing something else (i.e., gathering data), you aren't so likely to choke. The other virtue is organizational: you have convenient places to store your ideas, plus an easy way to retrieve and arrange them. (Years ago, I witnessed a colleague, Professor Ernest Lovell, write an *entire book* on 5-by-8 slips. It turned out it was the sole method he ever used, and he swore by it.)

5. Get an organizing principle—a thesis

The next step is to decide which of your ideas is the meatiest, the most comprehensive. What you want at this point is an idea to try out as the organizing principle of your essay—something that at least feels like a *thesis.* And what is a thesis? It's a viewpoint, a contention. A good thesis, I would argue, is above all *arguable*—that is, not everyone will agree with it. But please understand that it won't necessarily concern a "right/wrong" issue (e.g., *OK, so which is right? Is New York the greatest American city, or only the new Bedlam?*). Often it will concern whether something is urgent or not urgent, interesting or not interesting, a good way to do something or a not-so-good way to do something, a can-we-achieve-this issue or a can-we-not-achieve-this issue. Whatever your position, it should involve some conviction, preferably bold, that even skeptics will approach with curiosity, if only to see how biased/benighted/boring you'll prove to be. Your job, of course, is to convince them otherwise! That is always the grand challenge in writing, isn't it: *to bring people around*—to teach them, amuse them, inspire them, goad them, charm them, awaken them, convince them.

Remember: Your thesis is *not* your subject. It's your *take* on your subject. And it's what you'd have *us* think and feel about it, too. In the real world, it's a letter to the editor.

You won't know how truly promising your thesis is until you try it out, of course, but you have to start somewhere, so find that provisional organizing principle and then sift through your remaining ideas to find a logical direction for the essay to take. Think of your essay as a *story,* which in a sense it will be. Try to imagine for it a distinct beginning, middle, and end.

6. Imagine a good audience

Even if we're writing for an audience of one—a professor, say, or a firm's supervising partner—we can *choose* how we wish to envision that person. Let's say your audience is Professor Starbird. You already know, or think you know, certain things about him, and it will probably pay you to keep them in mind. For example, if he has, like me, definite expectations about how he likes papers formatted—the title styled this way, the quotes cited that way, etc.—you need to respect those requirements. You'd be crazy not to, especially if he'd made a good case for them.

But after a certain point you need to *create* your audience. You need to envision Professor Starbird in a way that frees you to be the kind of person, on paper, that you want and need to be if you are to write and think your best. In my own writing, I normally try to follow the same advice I'll be giving you later, in the chapter on "Readability": I envision my reader—no matter who it is—as a companionable friend with a warm sense of humor and a love of simple directness. That's how I'm envisioning you right now. But even if I'm wrong, you might *become* that way during this "conversation." (People often act as they're treated.) And even if you won't *ever* become my ideal reader, I still need you (or my image of you) to be that way if I am to be the way *I* need to be in order to write in a way I can respect. Make sense?

7. Freewrite a "zero draft"

Now that your mind is properly primed, you're ready to try a rough draft. That very phrase, "rough draft," draws a smile from me now, for I made a career in college of writing just one draft of everything. But I never took a writing course, either, or got assigned a book like this one, so I had to clear my own path through the woods. If you have time for two or three rough drafts, write them, of course. (This book—in its original edition—went through eight drafts, so it's clear that somewhere I discovered the value of afterthoughts.) But even if you don't have time for them, I recommend you at least make time for a zero draft. A "zero draft" is my term for a throwaway—a piece of freewriting that allows you to warm up, get into the flow, work past your inhibitions, bust through your writer's block, etc.[3] This will take just 20 minutes. Surely you can afford that.

---

[3]Even for many pros, it's essential. Here's the ever-honest Anne Lamott, beloved author of *Bird by Bird*: "For me and most of the other writers I know, writing is not rapturous. In fact, the only way I can get anything written at all is to write really, really shitty first drafts." You'll get to hear more from Ms. Lamott in Chapter 7.

And of course you don't have to throw it away later—you just need to pretend that you will.

Here's what you do:

Take one last, leisurely look at your 5-by-8 slips, get a reasonably clear sense of what it is you think you want to say, then resolutely put the slips out of sight and begin *talking* out your thoughts on paper as if you were explaining a concept to a friend. Imagine that it's me. Imagine I've just said to you, "Now let me hear *your* understanding of it," and imagine you're replying.

Begin anywhere. (The beginning will change later anyway; it nearly always does, even for gifted writers.)[4] *I recommend you use the same starting formula for each zero draft.* Simply write the words "Well, it seems to me that . . ." and go from there. You'd also be smart to put a watch in front of you and set yourself a limit of 20 minutes (which you're free to extend, of course, if you get on a roll). This will force you to scribble freely instead of compose.

Never let yourself pause more than a second or two between sentences, and *don't censor your thoughts.* Just let them come out as they want to—they're all tentative anyway. *The key thing is to keep everything moving.* After a bit of babble you'll find yourself starting to make sense. Even then, of course, you can count on running into new mental logjams, but don't panic. Simply force your pen (or your typing fingers) to nakedly record all the confusion and inarticulateness you're feeling. For example: *"I seem to have stalled out here. The words don't want to come. Where on earth can I go with this point?"* One of three things will happen: the problem will gradually work itself out merely through the act of verbalizing it; you'll stumble on an important new insight; or you'll discover something about your argument that you need to know—for instance, that it doesn't hold up in its present shape. A final point: Use your own voice, your own conversational idiom, not the puffed-up language of academe. If you start reaching for fancy language, you'll defeat the whole purpose of this warm-up exercise.

8. Critique your draft

Once you've finished, take a break—the longer, the better—and then come back and read your draft critically. See whether you still like your thesis—or even believe it anymore. Consider how you might enrich it. Determine which ideas have promise and which look extraneous or fuzzy. Ask yourself

---

[4]For gifted composers, too. Poet Stephen Spender tells us: "Beethoven wrote fragments of themes in notebooks which he kept beside him, working on and developing them over years. Often his first ideas were of a clumsiness which makes scholars marvel how he could, at the end, have developed from them such miraculous results."

whether one of those ideas might be the embryo of a still stronger thesis than your original one. Underline phrases that please you. Try to find places in your argument that need further support. Then go back and ponder your 5-by-8 slips again. Check off points you've made in the paper and underline points you need to incorporate. Mentally file them away for the next draft.

9. Freewrite again for 45 minutes

Now, time permitting, you're ready to begin again. If your writer's temperament permits, follow the same procedure outlined in item #7. Put the first draft and your 5-by-8 slips out of sight—well, most of them, anyway!—and let yourself write a new version. This time allot yourself 45 minutes. Take care that you don't start slowing up, for *rapid writing encourages the mind to function freely*. Remember, many of your best ideas lurk in your unconscious. If you slow down to edit what you've written, you'll put an airtight lid on those thoughts and begin experiencing the agonizing "blocked" feeling we're all familiar with. Blockage occurs when the creative process gets short-circuited by the picky critical process. Experience will teach you that the two involve different departments of the mind and function best when kept separate from each other. I like the way a colleague, Professor Betty Sue Flowers, once put it:

> You have to let the madman out. The madman has got to be allowed to go wild. Then you can let the architect in and design the structure. After that, you can have the engineer come in and put it together. And then you let the janitor in to clean it up. The problem is, most people let the janitor in before they let the madman out.

10. Tinker to get the words right

After you've read through your second draft you'll have a gut feeling as to whether a third is needed. Don't be alarmed if it is—most professional authors regularly count on cranking out a half dozen drafts, or more. They're refining, ever refining. If a third rough draft isn't required, you're ready to begin writing in earnest: this is the *editing* stage, otherwise known as revising. (Or—to the happy reviser, like me—*tinkering*.) By this point you've pretty much answered the Big Question—or you're getting close, at any rate:

> **"What am I really trying to say in this piece?"**

The object now is to find the words that best express your answer—and the organization that gives it the smoothest delivery.

3

Openers

It is in the hard, hard, rock-pile labor of seeking to win, hold, or deserve a reader's interest that the pleasant agony of writing again comes in.

—John Mason Brown

What gets my interest is the sense that a writer is speaking honestly and fully of what he knows well.

—Wendell Berry

Say you're at the doctor's, and you've just picked up a copy of *Time*. You idly browse its pages. With your mind on automatic pilot, your eye checks out one article after another, searching for anything intriguing. Since you're hungry for something good, and you're expecting your name to be called, you're ruthless. You give each story maybe three sentences to prove itself, and that's all, but experience—or impatience—has convinced you it's enough. In that brief span your mind answers probably all of these questions:

"Does this story attract me enough to read on?"
"Is the writing easy, or will I have to work here?"
"Is the style fresh or just so-so?"
"Does the writer seem smart? well-informed? spirited?"

So it goes with everything you read. The problem is, though, you as a writer are subject to the very same testing. You, too, will generally be given only three or four sentences to prove yourself. Granted, if you're writing a school essay, your reader—your instructor—will finish the piece regardless of its merits; but if you have convinced her in your opener that this means *work*, you've probably lost her, just as she'd lose you if the roles were reversed. She's only human, after all, and first impressions prove hard to shake. Instead of looking for the good, she'll look for the bad, if only to justify her initial impression. Besides, she'll know from experience, like you, that the quality of an opener tends to forecast what follows. If, at the very outset, a writer seems bored, unwilling to use his imagination, indifferent to his reader, and unclear in his thinking, he's apt to remain that way. But if his opener reveals passion, a clear, perceptive mind, and a flair for drawing in the reader, the odds are he'll stay true to form.

From the reader's standpoint, then, your opener is critical. But it's equally important to *you*, for openers have a way of governing how the rest of the piece gets written. A good opener gives you momentum, confidence, and an extra incentive to make the remaining paragraphs worthy of the first. There's also a practical explanation. A good opener normally includes a good thesis—bold, fresh, clearly focused. And a good thesis tends to argue itself because it has a built-in forward thrust. It's like a good comedy situation: it ignites.

One way to test an opener is for *directness of approach*. An essay, like a house, can be entered by the front door or the back door. Were you to check the opening paragraphs of a random set of undergraduate papers, you'd find that the most skilled writers usually elect what I call the *front-door approach*. They march into their subject with breathtaking assurance, clearly eager to share their opinions. And you can see why. They know what they think—and why they think it. Let me illustrate. Here's the opener from a super undergraduate essay on Prince Hal in Shakespeare's *I Henry IV*:[1]

> Prince Hal is as hard to crack as a walnut. "I know you all," he says of Falstaff & Co. in his soliloquy ending I.ii, but what friend—what reader even—can speak with equal confidence about Hal himself? His true nature seems finally to be as riddling as Hamlet's or Cleopatra's; indeed, he seems at times to be a hybrid of those two characters: infinitely various, theatrical, cunning past man's thought, loving, brutal, equivocal—the list goes on. It's little wonder that Hotspur, so childishly open and simple, often surpasses Hal as the reader's favorite. It's also little wonder that we are hard pressed to decide whether Hal is actually likable or merely admirable.

---

[1]Here, and in the chapters on "Middles" and "Closers" that follow, my examples of student writing all deal with Shakespeare's plays. I chose these examples partly for their eloquence, partly because Shakespeare is our most universal author, and partly for purposes of continuity.

Less experienced writers, on the other hand, choose the *back-door approach*, the long way in—like this:

> In the second scene of the first Act of William Shakespeare's *The First Part of King Henry the Fourth*, Prince Hal presents a soliloquy which serves as a crux of this play. Although this play would appear by the title to tell of King Henry IV, actually the principal character is the King's son, Hal. The play reveals what seems to be a remarkable change in character for the Prince and follows his exploits in a civil war waged against his father. . . .

This opening paragraph—essentially a plot summary—continues for another four sentences. Would you be eager to read on? Would you even be awake to read on?

It's clear why writers like this one elect the back-door approach:

- They haven't taken the trouble to formulate a point of view, so they have little to argue, hence little reason to argue it. What's the point of coming to the point when you don't *have* a point?
- Because they have little to say, they fear their reader. They know he's apt to expose their bluff. So they instinctively delay a confrontation with him as long as possible—often right down to the last sentence.
- They haven't yet learned to value their reader's time. In fact, they haven't learned even to *consider* their reader, at least in any systematic way, for they're still preoccupied with merely getting ideas on paper.
- They have a vague notion that they're supposed to be writing for the World, not for a well-informed reader. And even though common sense tells them otherwise, they cling to that notion since it lets them rationalize flagrant padding. In the back-door opener above, for instance, our writer gives us the full name of the author (instead of just "Shakespeare"), the unwieldy complete play title (instead of just *I Henry IV*), and the Act and scene laboriously written out (instead of just "I.ii").

Below is another example of the back-door approach, but this one is more sophisticated, more adroit, in its use of a smoke screen. The writer begins with some cautious reconnoitering of the surrounding terrain—a stall known as Establishing the Large Critical Overview—but unfortunately discovers only mists and goblins known as Grand Generalizations. This student grasps how the thing is supposed to *sound*, certainly, but having zero to say, she must content herself with an empty gush—lovely, for sure, but still empty. It's The Art of Saying Nothing Profoundly:

> Shakespeare's *Hamlet*, admired for its poetic style and intriguing characters, has remained a classic for over three centuries. The character of Hamlet is probably one of Shakespeare's most perplexing and most pleasing. He is easily identified with because of his multi-faceted personality and his realistic problems.

When the student came in for a conference, I helped her to read her opener from the reader's perspective. The experience was eye-opening. Gradually she began to realize that an essay is only as good as its thesis, that the first four or five sentences are make-or-break, that a back-door approach is transparently evasive, and that it's a delightful challenge to wake up your reader. She proved an apt learner. Her very next paper showed it. Instead of rewriting the piece on Hamlet, which now sickened her, she decided to start afresh on another character in the play, King Claudius, whom she found interestingly problematic. This is how her new essay began:

> He killed his brother. He married his brother's wife. He stole his brother's crown. A cold-hearted murderer, he is described by his brother's ghost as "that incestuous, that adulterate beast" (I.v.42). The bare facts appear to stamp him an utter moral outlaw. Nonetheless, as his soliloquies and anguished asides reveal, no person in *Hamlet* demonstrates so mixed a true nature as Claudius, the newly made King of Denmark.

Below are some more good openers, all by this student's classmates, most of them written well into the semester after the class had begun to discover what makes an opener click. Note the directness in each case— the front-door approach. Note, too, the concrete detail, the sense that the writer knows precisely where he or she is going, and the salesmanship— the *verve*—in the phrasing. I'll quote the entire first opener, but to conserve space I'll quote only the initial sentences of the other two:

> In *The Taming of the Shrew,* the servant is really a lord, and the lord's wife is really a page, and the schoolmaster is really a suitor, and the crazy suitor is really a wise old fox, and the perfect beauty is really a shrew, and the shrew is really a perfect wife, and things are not as they seem. Even the play itself pretends not to be a play by putting on a production within a production. In it, three characters are being duped by this rampant role-playing. By the examples of Sly, Kate, and Bianca, Shakespeare acquaints us with the effects of wealth, love, and power, respectively, and shows how the emergence of an inner (perhaps truer) character can be said to have been tamed. However, the "taming" occurs only as a result of the manipulation of the supposers by the posers. Moreover, while things are not as they seem because of the dual-roled characters, neither does the "taming" suggested by the title ever really take place.

> The occult element leavens Shakespeare's works with a pinch of the unknown and an implication that it should remain so. His artful but often annoying ambiguity seldom allows more than a fleeting glimpse at a forbidden terrain before it is bulldozed out of sight by convenient

rationales. Several examples of Shakespeare's significant use of the occult immediately come to mind: the witches in Macbeth, the antics of Titania and Oberon in *A Midsummer Night's Dream,* the Ghost in *Hamlet,* and the figure of Owen Glendower in *I Henry IV.*

"He that walketh with wise men shall be wise; But the companions of fools shall smart for it." King Solomon's proverb appears reversed in *King Lear* for it is a wise Fool who accompanies and counsels a seemingly foolish king. In the play, the Fool assumes myriad roles—that of teacher, loyal servant, comedian, and often the punitive voice of Lear's own conscience.

Don't you know these writers had fun?

So much for examples. Now here are a few tips to run your eye over as you sit down to write your next opener. Keep in mind, as you read them, that openers are a challenge for *everybody,* and that even skilled writers will sometimes spend as much as a third of their writing time tweaking their opener into proper shape.

1. Before starting to write, do two things. *First,* ensure that you have a strong thesis. There's a good way to tell if you have one, but it takes courage. Write on some notepaper, "I contend that—" and complete the sentence. Now study what you've written. If somebody else's essay were arguing the same thesis, would *you* be intrigued by it? Is it complex enough, or controversial enough, to allow for lengthy exposition? Have you really stuck your neck out, or are you pussyfooting? *Second,* have on hand a list of concrete details and apt quotations, and be ready to use them. Remember, if you lead off with a string of abstract generalizations, your reader may impatiently mutter "Sheesh" and tune you out. But if you lead off with concrete details, your reader will think, "Hey, this person has really done their homework. What an eye for detail!"

2. Like most writers, you may choke at the very thought of beginning, for writing involves confronting, head on, all of one's verbal and mental inadequacies. You may, as a result, find yourself making a dozen false starts. If so, try doing what a Pulitzer Prize-winning reporter once advised me to do. "Pull yourself back from your desk," he said, "take a deep breath, and say to yourself, 'OK, now, what is it I'm *really* trying to say?' Then simply say it—*talk* it. I got that tip from an old hand when I was a cub reporter many years ago. It works."

3. If you follow this procedure and still feel discouraged with your opener, let it stand as it is, roughed out (if even that), and return to it after you've finished the first draft. There's no rule that says you must write every paragraph sequentially. Remember, writing involves discovery. Once the first draft is finished, you'll probably have found several points that deserve top billing. You may even discover—as I have

demonstrated to many a student through the years—that your *second* paragraph is your real opener.

4. Use the front-door approach. Idle chat will destroy your credibility.

5. Use natural, simple prose—the simpler the better. You can come back later and add grace notes if you have a mind to ("punitive" in the *Lear* example above was doubtless one such afterthought), but initially keep it *simple*. Simple prose is clear prose. And simple prose, if smooth and rhythmical, is readable prose. Let your ideas alone do the impressing. If they look banal to you, there's only one remedy: *upgrade them.* Don't try to camouflage their weakness with razzle-dazzle rhetoric. You'll razzle-dazzle yourself right into a bog of bull.

6. Unless you have good reason to do otherwise, make your opener full-bodied. If it's splinter-sized—a mere two or three sentences long—and lacking point, your reader may conclude that you're short on ideas and are only going through the motions. Experience will have taught her, as it's probably taught you, that those conclusions are usually dead on. (Of course there's always the glorious exception that makes a dictum like this look silly.) On the other hand, if your opener is barnlike, your reader may conclude that you lack a sense of proportion. You can just hear her groan: "Has the author no mercy? Why put *everything* in the first paragraph?"

7. Consider opening with a dramatically brief sentence—say, four or five words long. It will compel you to begin with a bold assertion, give your grateful reader a handle on the sentences that follow, and offer her the enchantment of surprise, since most opening sentences run considerably longer—in the neighborhood of 15 to 25 words.

8. If possible, organize your opening paragraph so that the biggest punch—the strongest statement of your thesis—comes at the *end.* (Note the *Taming of the Shrew* example above.) Such an organization has three advantages: it lets you build toward a climax; it gives you a great entry into your next paragraph, because of the springboard effect; and it saves you from repeating yourself.

4

Middles

My style of writing is chiefly grounded upon an early enthusiasm for [Thomas H.] Huxley, the greatest of all masters of orderly exposition. He taught me the importance of giving to every argument a simple structure.

—H. L. Mencken

When you embark on an essay, you may know exactly what you're supposed to do and how best to do it. If so, you're fortunate. Most people don't. The entire concept of essay writing is fuzzy to them. This chapter is for the bewildered majority. It's an attempt to bring into focus the *what* and the *how* of the business. The *what* of it I'll explain with an analogy. The *how* of it is rather more complicated because it involves the very process itself. For the next few minutes we're going to follow an imaginary student right through the stages of writing an essay. Then I'll show you a model short essay written by a former student, Danny Robbins, now a professional sportswriter, so you can see what the finished product might look like.

What, you may ask, has all this to do with "middles"? Well, you're about to see that the middle section of an essay is inseparable from the opening, since it explains and develops the thesis. And you will see that the middle is also inseparable from the process by which the thesis is arrived at, since it amounts to a coherent retelling of that process.

First, the *what* of it. When you write a term paper, a final examination, or even a lab report, you're engaged in what's called "expository" writing. Expository writing is *informative* writing. Its primary goal is to *explain*.[1]

---

[1] Most of the world's prose falls under the heading of "expository writing." All newspapers, popular magazines, nonfiction books, letters, academic articles, speeches, guidebooks, legal briefs, court opinions, office memoranda—all this and more is expository writing. But poetry, fiction, plays—that's all termed "creative writing," even though it's sometimes far less creative than good expository writing.

Implicit in most expository writing, however, is a second goal: to *persuade*. The two goals almost invariably go together since it's hard to explain something—a political issue, a historical event, a novel, a philosophy—without taking a position on it; and once you take a position, you naturally want others to accept it as sound. That gets you into the realm of reasoning—the realm of persuasion. The whole point, finally, is to have your reader respond: "Yes, I understand now. You've convinced me."

Your situation as an expository writer closely resembles that of a prosecuting attorney, society's professional skeptic-persuader. Let's develop that analogy, for once you grasp it, you'll understand the gist of essay writing.

The Analogy

Even before the trial gets underway, our prosecutor is already going about her important first business—sizing up her audience, the motley jury (analogous to your *readers*). How sophisticated are they? What are their interests, their prejudices, their intellectual capacities? Are they a solemn bunch, or do they smile at her droll witticisms? The answers to those questions will determine the delivery she uses—even, to some extent, the evidence she presents. She lost many decisions in her younger years simply by ignoring the character of the jury, but she's naive no longer. She now takes this preliminary testing-and-probing period very seriously. (You as a writer, of course, must rely on intuition, the laws of probability, and guesswork, making your task more speculative but certainly no less important.)

Now she's ready to begin her presentation to the jury. She could spend six months in Nassau each year if she could simply announce: "Ladies and gentlemen, the defendant, Ivan Isor, is guilty. You can tell it from the mad glint in his eye. The State rests." Unfortunately, the jury will oblige her to *prove* Mr. Isor's guilt, and only facts plus cogent argumentation can prove anything. So she begins by stating the essence of her case (the *thesis*) in carefully formulated language: "The State will prove that the defendant, Ivan Isor, with malice aforethought, attempted to level City Hall with a tank." Then the prosecutor spends the bulk of her remaining time calling forth witnesses (the *evidence*) to prove her case, saving her star exhibit (the tank itself) for last so the impact will be greatest. All the while, though, she's achieving many other important things: foxily anticipating and defusing the contentions of the defendant's lawyer; demonstrating her own mastery of the facts of the case; clarifying what's really at issue and what's not; defining her exotic legal terms so the jury can grasp them; supporting each new charge with a wealth of factual proof; quoting authorities either to buttress her case or to freshen her eloquence; underscoring the logical sequence of her evidence; and providing the spellbound jurors with a running summary of how the pieces of the case interconnect.

Finally, she makes a closing appeal to the jurors (the *conclusion*) in which she neatly recaps the high points of her case—she knows they have short memories—and explains in the clearest possible way why her version of the case is the only one a reasonable person could accept. She ends on a note of triumph: "And last, ladies and gentlemen, you have Ivan Isor's stolen tank before you, his fingerprints on its wheel, the plaster of City Hall still clogging its treads, and 'Down With All Burocrats' blazoned on its sides—misspelled *exactly* the way he always misspelled it!" The prosecutor has followed the age-old formula of debaters: "Tell 'em what you're going to tell 'em, tell it to 'em, and then tell 'em what you've told 'em."[2] By following this formula, she has not only made it easy for the jury to grasp her argument, she has made it almost impossible for them not to.

The Checklist

Virtually everything our prosecutor did finds an exact correspondence in successful essay writing. I'll stress only the major points.

At the top of the list is *a sure sense of the audience*. If you ignore the special character of your audience—your jury—you might as well not even begin. It would be like telling a locker-room joke to your grandmother.

After a sure sense of audience come five other essentials, which I recommend you memorize. You'll find them in every successful essay:

1. A well-defined thesis
2. A clear strategy
3. Strong evidence
4. A clean narrative line
5. A persuasive closing

To understand their importance, you must see them in action, so let's now follow our imaginary student through the stages of writing an essay. This will give you the added advantage of seeing the kind of preparatory work out of which strong openers and middles are born.

---

[2]The formula works, of course, only when it's kept discreetly veiled. The trick is to follow it without appearing to; otherwise your presentation sounds mechanical.

The Hypothetical Case

Suppose the student's assignment is: "Write a 1,500-word essay discussing your views on capital punishment." What position should he take? Well, this particular student thinks he already knows—he happens to be against it[3]—but since he is now an experienced college senior, he resolves to suppress his notions until he has thoroughly researched the subject.

It's partly a matter of pride: he doesn't want the facts to end up embarrassing his intelligence. In addition, though, he wants his essay to reflect that he has open-mindedly investigated the issues—the pros as well as the cons. He knows that if he doesn't do this, he won't be able to anticipate and defuse his reader's objections to his contentions—a crucial element in persuasive writing, just as it is in the courtroom.

So he studies the subject, *recording all the evidence* he discovers: examples, statistics, quotations from authorities, arguments. That's step one. Step two is to *organize his facts*. For this he uses lists. Eventually he comes up with some 20 arguments favoring the abolition of capital punishment and another 20 favoring its retention. Having done the necessary homework, he now arrives at step three: *weighing* these arguments. This enables him finally to decide which of the two positions is most convincing to him.

That decision, though, is still mainly intuitive and unconscious rather than rational. While he's now convinced that the case against capital punishment is the stronger one, the actual proof of that position hasn't yet crystallized in his mind. And there's the rub. Until he can prove it to himself, using a coherent line of reasoning, he knows he won't be able to prove it to his reader. The shotgun approach—a blast of unconnected reasons—is out of the question. His essay must be able to say, in effect, "Here's my position, and this is why any sensible person would accept it." In practical terms, this means showing precisely *how* he reached his position, step by step.

So he goes back to his list of arguments to work out a blueprint. The arguments are already roughly organized, but now he must *classify them into major groups*—moral reasons, economic reasons, political reasons, legal reasons—and analyze how they all add up, how they interconnect. This is a crucial part of the writing process, he knows, for his reader will expect the proof of his thesis sorted into neat, logically developing *stages*, and this is precisely what he is doing now.

---

[3]The views and arguments I'll attribute to the student are "his," not mine. I've never truly researched this subject myself, so my own views on it, which feel maddeningly fickle, are as unformed as they are uninformed. Alas, the poor student may suffer the consequences of my ignorance. The whole point of this fictional recreation, though, is to show how an essay might be generated and structured. The arguments themselves are hypothetical.

A related task, while he's classifying his arguments, is to decide the *sequence* in which to present them. This is a tactical decision. Some of the reasons, he realizes, are clearly more persuasive than others. Should the most persuasive ones all come first, or should he build his arguments from least persuasive to most persuasive, or should he mix them? Or would he be wiser to eliminate most of the marginally persuasive reasons and go for quality rather than quantity? He puts himself in the reader's shoes and decides that if *he* were reading this essay cold, he'd be most convinced by quality, not quantity, and also by an increasingly persuasive order of arguments. Such an order would be agreeably climactic.

He's ready, he thinks, to begin writing now. He's got the *arguments* he needs, the *support* for these arguments, the *coherent grouping* of them, and the most *tactical sequence* in which to present them. In addition, during the ordering process he has weeded out (he hopes) all that is either irrelevant or marginally persuasive, so that what he is now going to give the reader is a trim digest of his case.

One important thing remains, however, and that is to get clear in his mind *the nature of his audience.*

Two years ago it never occurred to him to size up his audience, for two years ago he wasn't writing expressly for his reader; he was writing simply for himself. Now, though, persuasion is vital to him, so it's become part of his standard procedure to second-guess his reader's needs, taste, and level of sophistication. He knows that this will determine, among other things, his choice of *tone* (serious, bantering, ironic, indignant), his *diction* (elegant, informal, tempered, blunt), his *sentence structure* (complex, occasionally complex, simple), and his *mode of argument* (technical, nontechnical, objective, subjective). All these decisions are crucial, for they define the "voice" and posture he thinks are most appropriate for the occasion.

In this case his audience is well defined: it will consist solely of Professor Buckley, a bright, amiable fellow who is always warning his students, "Be polemical, but be practical."

With Professor Buckley clearly before him in his imagination,[4] our student finally starts writing.

---

[4]A clarification here: I am not endorsing the practice of "writing for the teacher"—i.e., giving the teacher (or any reader, for that matter) what you presume he wants to hear at the expense of what you genuinely believe. That's a sellout. I *am* recommending, though, that the writer remember who his reader is in order to communicate with him in a manner that is likely to be understandable and winning to him. For example, you don't talk to a three-year-old the way you talk to an adult, although you may be saying essentially the same thing to both. You use language that the child can understand; you work from where his head is, not yours. Similarly, a lawyer doesn't argue a case before a rural jury the way she'd argue it before the Supreme Court. That's not dishonesty; it's common sense and good manners (consideration). The argument remains the same, but the presentation changes to suit the audience.

He opens with a brief, fascinating history of capital punishment and its relevance as a social issue. This consumes most of two paragraphs. Then he ends his introduction with a firm position statement:

> This gradual trend toward the abolition of capital punishment reflects a growing awareness that such extreme punishment doesn't make sense—economically, morally, or pragmatically.

This thesis sentence provides him (and his reader) with an immaculately simple structure for his essay. It lets him plunge right into explaining the economic reasons in his next paragraph:

> Considered from a coldly economic point of view, capital punishment is a waste of human resources. Instead of killing a man, society should take advantage of his ability to work and pay restitution.

The next sentences in this paragraph develop support for that contention—part of the support being an example of a country that has tried this plan successfully. His next paragraph develops other economic reasons buttressing this one, with the strongest reserved for last:

> Nor let us overlook the staggering court costs. With capital punishment, a single, speedy trial is unheard of. Almost invariably a case will be retried repeatedly as the condemned person exhausts every possible appeal and delay.

He ends the section with a brief summary of his arguments up to that point.

With this stage of his argument completed, he moves on to the next, the moral reasons. These, he knows, are stronger. New paragraph:

> But beyond the mere economics of the issue, capital punishment is a moral outrage. First, it is a basic violation of the Judeo-Christian ethic, the cornerstone of our democratic society.

He supports this contention by quoting authorities such as Jesus, Clarence Darrow, and George Bernard Shaw, all of whom argue that compassion rather than merciless revenge is the most civilized form of justice. (Here he takes the opportunity to counter a probable objection—the Old Testament notion that "an eye for an eye" is just—with the Old Testament commandment superseding it: "Thou shalt not kill.") Then, in a new paragraph, he moves on to his second argument in this group:

> Furthermore, capital punishment—which is essentially a lynch mob by proxy—lowers the standards of public morality. In effect, it encourages

barbarism by the state—indeed, it brings society down to the level of a ruthless murderer. Once the state has the power to murder with the grace of the statute book, historically it loses all sense of proportion. We have seen this happen in Great Britain in the 18th century, when even the pettiest crimes were thought fit for punishment at the gallows.

After developing this point, he's ready for his third and strongest moral argument, which he sets off in another new paragraph:

Finally and most seriously, capital punishment strikes at the very basis of morality itself. Morality rests upon the fact that we are mortals, frail and imperfect in our understanding, not infallible. By contrast, capital punishment presumes that man can set himself up as God, and that juries never make mistakes. The moral presumption in this is surely as great as that of the criminal who takes the life of his victim.

Now he begins his main attack—the pragmatic reasons. With the gusto of Churchill on D-Day he opens a new paragraph:

Both economically and morally, then, capital punishment simply doesn't make sense. But the most damaging indictment against the practice is pragmatic: it fails to achieve its purpose, which is the deterrence of crime. Now why does it not deter a criminal? Because it rests upon a false assumption: that murder or rape, for example, is committed consciously, is premeditated. But this is patently not so. Most capital crimes are crimes of passion, committed unthinkingly in the heat of the moment. The criminal never considers punishment.

To support that reasoning, he cites statistics to show that the vast majority of murders are committed within the family, and that murder rates in states with the death penalty are no lower than in states without it. He also cites once more the example of Great Britain, where public execution of pickpockets did not prevent the spectators from being deprived of their wallets.

Moving to a new paragraph, he next argues:

So capital punishment doesn't work. But when we try to force it to work, we find that we can't even administer it fairly. First, there is the economic bias: the rich can always pay their way out, while the poor will die. Second, the meting out of the death penalty often depends upon *whom* you kill, for human life is not valued equally.

Here he gives examples of criminals who were executed for killing public figures, while fellow criminals who killed people of lesser renown were paroled in three years.

This brings him to his conclusion. He succinctly recapitulates his chief arguments and draws out their full implications—and perhaps especially the implications of *ignoring* them. He's saying, in essence, "Here's what follows if you don't buy these arguments." Then he ends with a sentence neatly summarizing his case:

> The evidence all in, the conclusions are inescapable: economically the proponent of capital punishment is a waster, morally he is a bankrupt, and pragmatically he is a fool.

The Model

What follows now is an actual essay written by a student named Danny Robbins, who was a college junior at the time. It's a splendid example of all five points on our earlier checklist, but especially of #2: a clear strategy. This is about as well-organized an essay as you are likely to see. It also illustrates the truth of George Bernard Shaw's observation: "Effectiveness of assertion is the Alpha and Omega of style. He who has nothing to assert has no style and can have none; he who has something to assert will go as far in power of style as its momentousness and his conviction will carry him."

The Character and Purpose of Caesar

Octavius Caesar in Shakespeare's *Antony and Cleopatra* embodies all the ideals of ancient Rome. His pursuit of world power at any cost is consistent with the militaristic, male-oriented society of which he is a part. The Roman spirit, it seems, is so deeply ingrained within Caesar that there is absolutely nothing else in the world of any importance to him besides strength and conquest. In fact, he seems so one-dimensional a character that he may not be a true character at all. I think he is merely a symbol—a voice that recurs in the play not to capture the imagination or make one learn something about human nature but rather to provide a measuring stick by which one can calculate change in Mark Antony.

Certainly there are aspects of Caesar's character that cry out for further development by Shakespeare. He is so young, yet acts so old. And nowhere does Caesar show the sensitivity, curiosity, or frivolity one might expect from a 23-year-old. It seems that if Shakespeare really wanted to make Caesar a provocative character, he could have done something with these qualities. But he doesn't. It appears that Caesar is so typecast, so stereotyped as a Roman, that the reader or spectator must view him for what he stands for rather than for what happens to him in the play. No matter what the situation, his actions are perfectly Roman. And in this manner, it appears that his function is like that of a "constant" in a mathematical equation, a figure of never-changing value. Antony would be the "variable" in the equation. He is changed by the passion of Cleopatra, and Caesar's function is to provide contrast for this. Caesar, then, must not change. Three instances, covering the entire time span of the play, bring this out.

In Act I, Caesar criticizes Antony behind his back for the good times Antony has in Egypt. The play has just begun, and Caesar is already telling Lepidus that

> From Alexandria
> This is the news: he fishes, drinks, and wastes
> The lamps of night in revel; is not more manlike
> Than Cleopatra, nor the queen of Ptolemy. . . .
> You shall find there
> A man who is the abstract of all faults
> That all men follow.   (I.4.3–10)

This is Caesar's very first speech, and in it one finds a 23-year-old man condemning pleasure. Caesar cannot understand why Antony does not take up arms with the triumvirate, why pleasure comes before duty. This opening speech is a clear disclosure of Caesar's personality. But perhaps more importantly, Antony's values are being compared to Caesar's. Not only do we see the things that Caesar values—masculinity, work, ambition—but it is significant that Antony is the subject of Caesar's first lines. In the total scope of the play Antony is the "subject" of all of them, whether he is mentioned by name or not.

Then in Act II there is another, more telling glimpse into Caesar's character. He and Antony are trying to patch up their damaged relationship, but Caesar pursues reconciliation in a purely utilitarian manner. He is a Roman first, a friend second. Caesar acts purely as a soldier. And he is concerned with Antony as merely a once-famous soldier who can help him defeat Pompey. Caesar is so wrapped up in his quest for world power that he will sell his sister "whom no brother / Did ever love so dearly" (II.2.150–151) to Antony to get Antony's support. Antony seems to go along with Caesar to appease him for the moment and end the conversation. Nevertheless, the end result is that the shallowness of Caesar's nature is exposed again. He, unlike Antony, shows no regard for the beauty of human relationships. He is concerned only with using people to advance his military goals. The fact that Caesar shows no love or compassion— not even for his sister—highlights the relationship between Antony and Cleopatra.

Caesar acts no differently in the final Act of the play. In fact, he appears more ruthless. After Antony's death, Cleopatra seeks mercy from

Caesar. Caesar—who in the war against Antony has just slaughtered many men in his own self-interest—says:

> She [Cleopatra] shall soon know of us . . .
> How honorable and how kindly we
> Determine for her. For Caesar cannot live
> To be ungentle.   (V.1.58–61)

This is, of course, a joke. Caesar has murdered Pompey, Lepidus, and Antony. The "mercy" Caesar plans for Cleopatra is to use her as a public display of his "generous heart." Proculeius lets slip this notion: "let the world see / His nobleness well acted" (V.2.44–45). For the first time Caesar is making an outward show of pity and kindness and, true to his nature, he is sincere about none of it. Furthermore, the sparing of Cleopatra's life has a military purpose—to make him look good in the eyes of his subjects—just like everything else he does.

Thus Caesar's character never changes from beginning to end. He is not to be pitied or even contemplated to any great extent by the audience. Caesar acts simply as a standard by which one can study the effects of Cleopatra's love on Antony. Shakespeare seems to be using Caesar as a symbol of Roman society, a yardstick by which Antony's deviance from Roman ideas can be measured. There is nothing deep or stimulating about the man. His traits are negative and obvious, so obvious that I think Shakespeare made them this way on purpose. Caesar is supposed to be a model Roman, whereas Antony is supposed to be—and is—a richly complex human being.

The Model Analyzed

To help you consolidate what you've learned so far, I'll critique this essay in terms of the five-point checklist:

1. *A well-defined thesis:* Like our earlier imaginary student, Danny did the necessary headwork before actually beginning to write. All that preparation gives him two advantages: he can write boldly, because he really knows his stuff; and he can set forth his arguments lucidly, because he understands exactly how they interconnect. The opening paragraph illustrates both advantages.

His thesis is clear and deliciously controversial:

> I think he is merely a symbol—a voice that recurs in the play not to
> capture the imagination or make one learn something about human
> nature but rather to provide a measuring stick by which one can calculate
> change in Mark Antony.

It's also placed right where it ought to be for greatest effect—at the climactic end of the opening paragraph. He leads into it with *I think,* which primes us for a major assertion (this is the first appearance of *I*) and which also discreetly implies his recognition that the assertion may be considered debatable by the reader. We are to know, in other words, that he isn't arrogantly advancing this notion as a statement of fact, but rather as an opinion. Nonetheless, it's a firmly held opinion, and we admire his courage for stating it so unequivocally. He's not waffling with us; instead, he's boldly crawling out on an interpretive limb, just as I'll advise you to do in Chapter 9. The entire opening paragraph, in fact, is refreshingly direct in manner—another example of the front-door approach in action.

   2. *A clear strategy:* Basically the opening paragraph is asserting three things, each one leading to the next:

   A. Caesar embodies the Roman ideal.
   B. In fact, he is *nothing but* the Roman ideal—that is, he is one-dimensional, a walking symbol.
   C. From *B* we must infer that his dramatic function is to serve as a yardstick by which we can measure the change in his fellow Roman, Mark Antony.

Danny knows that if he can prove points *A* and *B*, he can persuade us that his thesis (*C*) is, at the very least, probably valid.

   In the second paragraph, he contents himself largely with amplifying on points *A* and *B* (chiefly *B*). But when he says, "No matter what the situation, his actions are perfectly Roman," we can feel ourselves being primed to *view* these concrete situations, for this is where the proof obviously lies. And, sure enough, here it comes: "Caesar, then, must not change. Three instances, covering the entire time span of the play, bring this out."

   The plan of attack could hardly be more explicit—or more beautifully simple: three major examples, one per paragraph. This is what Mencken had in mind when he spoke of "the importance of giving to every argument a simple structure." Note, too, the fine positioning of this curtain-raising sentence. Like the earlier thesis sentence, it rounds off its paragraph, thus providing its own transition directly into the proof (paragraphs 3–5). Not a word is wasted.

   Danny's parallel structure in the opening sentence of each of his three supporting paragraphs makes his strategy even more transparent:

   a. "In Act I, Caesar criticizes Antony . . ."
   b. "Then in Act II there is another, more telling glimpse . . ."
   c. "Caesar acts no differently in the final Act of the play. In fact, he appears more ruthless."

What reader isn't grateful for such clear signposting of the argument? We notice, too, a progression in the persuasiveness of the examples. Each is stronger than the last, thus building toward an intellectually and aesthetically satisfying climax.

3. *Strong evidence:* Danny has chosen representative examples "covering the entire time span of the play." He quietly draws this to our attention to defuse the possible objection that the evidence is stacked (for example, all from the first half of the play). In addition, on four occasions he has quoted actual lines, which greatly enhances the concreteness of the examples. Many students would simply argue by generalization, assuming that the reader will supply the appropriate textual support. Danny properly does the supporting himself. All the reader need do is read and enjoy.

4. *A clean narrative line:* There are no bumps in this essay. Each sentence, each paragraph, is hinged on the one that precedes it. Danny was able to achieve this fine continuity because he had a clear plan of attack: he knew what he wanted to say and what he had to prove. When you know precisely where your essay has to go, you can "tell" your argument as simply and coherently as if it were a story, which in a sense it is.

But the continuity is also the result of careful craftsmanship. Note, for instance, all the parallel structuring: the way paragraph 2 repeats the pattern of paragraph 1; the way each of those paragraphs ends with a key sentence; the way paragraphs 3–5 all begin alike; the way the closing paragraph looks back to the opening paragraph, and so forth. We have *patterns* here. They organize the ideas for us; they silently tell us how the pieces of the argument relate to one another.

5. *A persuasive closing:* The final paragraph is a beautiful wrap-up: succinct, bold, and complete enough to gather in all the major points the essay has been making. We feel them now fixed in our memory.

The Importance of Continuity

What follows is really part of the "Final Tips" section that concludes this chapter, but since it's both lengthy and vitally important, I want to discuss it separately.

> Good writers are sticklers for continuity. They won't let themselves write a sentence that isn't clearly connected to the ones immediately preceding and following it. They want their prose to flow, and they know this is the only way to achieve that beautiful effect.

But how are these connections to be made? The better the writer, the less need he has for mechanical means of connecting his ideas, too many of which tend to clutter an argument. Instead, he relies chiefly on a coherent understanding of what he wants to say, a simple style, the occasional repetition of key words, and the careful use of pronouns such as *this* and *that*. In manner he resembles a furniture maker who uses interlocking tongues and grooves to do the work of nails and screws.

Sometimes, though, a situation will require a more explicit connective—such as when the direction of the argument is turning or when an idea is to be paralleled or contrasted with an earlier idea. In these situations, the writer will call upon a conjunctive adverb or brief transitional phrase to signal the kind of thought that's coming next. I call this "signposting" an argument. Here he has choices within choices. As Rudolf Flesch points out in *The Art of Plain Talk*, some conjunctive adverbs are bookish—that is, used chiefly in print—whereas others are conversational and for that reason less stuffy. In the list below, the bookish ones are followed in parentheses by their conversational equivalents. Keep in mind, though, that the equivalence in each case is approximate, not perfect. Note, too, that the bookish adverbs can afford you greater variety *and* precision of meaning—which is doubtless why we encounter them more often in books than in conversation:

above all	in particular
accordingly (and so)	instead
admittedly	in summary
again	likewise (and)
also	moreover
besides	more specifically
but	(for example)
certainly	nevertheless (but)
consequently (and so)	nonetheless
finally	on the other hand
first	rather (however, instead)
for example	second
for instance	similarly
furthermore	so
hence (therefore)	still
however	then
in addition	therefore
(besides, also)	though
in conclusion	thus (therefore, so)
indeed (in fact)	to sum up
in fact	yet

It's a rather overwhelming list, isn't it? (And it's only a partial one.) But the sheer number of transitional words indicates, among other things, just how important signposting an argument really is. Continuity doesn't magically happen; it's *created*. The surest way your reader will know how your ideas connect is by your telling her. These are the words you tell her with. I suggest you keep the list propped up before you the next few times you write an essay. It will remind you to give your reader the directional signals she needs; it will save you word-hunting; and (a nice bonus) it will suggest an occasional new avenue of thought simply by tempting your mind to explore other directions of argument—a "nevertheless" thought, perhaps, or a "consequently," or a "for example."

Final Tips

1. *"Well, what does it finally add up to?"* This is the reader's invariable question. Your essay is the reply: *"It finally adds up to this, in my opinion. . . ."* Don't begin writing a final draft (there may be more than one!) until you have asked yourself the reader's question and understand your intended reply. If your reply contains an original perception, if it's debatable, and if you've been able to state it in one sentence, it's a good thesis. Now go ahead and prove it.

2. Think of yourself as a prosecuting attorney, think of your essay as a case, and think of your reader as a highly skeptical jury.

3. To prove your case, you'll generally have to substantiate several things. The prosecutor, for example, must substantiate that the defendant had the motive, the means, and the opportunity to commit the crime. So determine what things you must substantiate, classify your evidence according to those things, and then substantiate them, *one at a time*. This is called "dividing up the proof." If you follow this procedure, you'll find that structuring your essay is relatively simple.

4. Signpost your argument every step of the way. If you have three important pieces of evidence to support a particular contention, *tell* your reader so she can understand precisely where you're going. For instance: "Three examples will bear this out. First, the original treaty of 1923. . . ." Similarly, if you have three arguments and if one is stronger than the others, save it for last and *label* it as the strongest. For instance: "Finally and most seriously, capital punishment strikes at the very basis of morality itself."

5. Assertions are fine, but unless you prove them with hard evidence, they remain simply assertions. So, assert, *then support;* assert, *then support;* assert, *then support*—and so on throughout your essay. Remember, *examples* and *facts* are the meat of it. They do the actual convincing; they also have their own eloquence.

6. Some paragraphs, like transitional and one-sentence paragraphs, are special-occasion devices and follow their own rules. (I'll be speaking

more about them later.) The normal paragraph, though, resembles a good essay: it has unity by virtue of being organized around a single major point. Several examples may be brought in to support that point, and several ideas to qualify it, and several sentences to illuminate its implications, but there's still only a *single major point*. "One main contention per paragraph"—it's a sensible guideline to follow. If you don't follow it, your points will tend to get lost, and so will your reader.

7. Instead of viewing the opening sentence of each paragraph as a topic sentence, as you've probably been taught to do, try this:

> View each paragraph opener as a *bridge sentence* aimed at smoothing our way into the new paragraph.

More than one student has said that's the single best tip they've carried away from their writing conferences with me. I say this only to underscore the difference it can make in your prose style. Below are a number of paragraph openers from a famous *Atlantic Monthly* article by Bergen Evans called "But What's a Dictionary For?"—a review of Merriam-Webster's revolutionary *Third New International Dictionary*. They will illustrate the bridging technique graphically:

    a. What underlines all this sound and fury?
    b. So monstrous a discrepancy in evaluation requires us to examine basic principles.
    c. Yet wild wails arose.
    d. More subtly, but persuasively, it has changed under the influence of mass education and the growth of democracy.
    e. And the papers have no choice.
    f. And so back to our questions: what's a dictionary for, and how, in 1962, can it best do what it ought to do?
    g. Even in so settled a matter as spelling, a dictionary cannot always be absolute.
    h. Has he been betrayed?
    i. Under these circumstances, what is a dictionary to do?
    j. An illustration is furnished by an editorial in the *The Washington Post* (January 17, 1962).
    k. In part, the trouble is due to the fact that there is no standard for standard.

Even out of context, these sentences suggest how skillfully Evans is guiding his readers—building bridges for us, persuading us. We never come to a new paragraph wondering, "Where am I? How did I get here?" To repeat a point I made a few moments ago: Continuity doesn't magically happen; it's *created*.

5

Closers

The most emphatic place in a clause or sentence is the end. This is the climax; and during the momentary pause that follows, that last word continues, as it were, to reverberate in the reader's mind. It has, in fact, the last word. One should therefore think twice about what one puts at a sentence-end.

—F. L. Lucas

What's going on in the mind of a skilled writer as he approaches his final paragraph? Let's revisit our capital-punishment student just as he reaches that juncture. Perhaps we can listen in . . .

Oh-oh, he looks bad—eyes glazed, body leaden. We appear to be catching him at a very low moment:

"This is ridiculous—my brain's turning to mush. Maybe I'll just stop here. The piece is virtually done anyway—I've made my main points. Besides, who's going to know the difference?"

(Enter Conscience and Common Sense. They beat back Fatigue.)

"No, I guess I can't quit yet. Buckley wouldn't accept an argument that merely stops. He'll want to see the thing *end*, to enjoy a sense of closure. He once said that's a basic aesthetic desire in all of us. 'Every reader wants his final reward.'

"Then, of course, there's the matter of what he'll be able to recall. Since *my* memory certainly has its limits, I'm sure his does, too. If that's the case, his sense of this piece is bound to be colored by the last sentences he reads. My opener may have disposed him to read eagerly, and my middle paragraphs may have sustained his interest, but my final graf may well be the chief thing he carries away with him. That's certainly the way it is with the last minute of a basketball game, or the last kiss at the door. Hmm. I can see that I *have* to make it memorable—as powerful as my opener, if I can.

"But I wonder how I should slant it toward him? I suppose, if he's anything like me, by the time he's gotten this far, he'll be tired. He's bound to welcome a final gathering up of my argument in a form that can be grasped handily. This would also leave him feeling that my argument really does hang together. He mustn't have any doubts on that score. I want him utterly convinced.

"But I imagine he'll be bored if my closer simply recaps earlier points, and especially if I repeat my earlier phrasing. He'll feel I'm merely going through the motions. He'll also feel that he's stopped learning things. I've *got* to keep him hooked to the very end. I've got to leave him convinced that my mind is still blazing with ideas."

The closer our student finally devises is half-summary, half-conclusion, similar to a prosecutor's closing appeal to the jury. He neatly sums up the high points of his evidence, reexplaining why his argument is reasonable. He also takes care to point out its important implications, so that the reader will be convinced that the argument is substantial. He makes the whole paragraph self-contained and packed so that it could serve as a fair substitute for the essay itself, as indeed it may in his reader's overworked memory. And he finishes off with a sentence that has such satisfying finality that his last period feels unnecessary.

For a long paper—say, 10 pages or more—this formula for a closer is ideal. In fact, it's obligatory, since you will have given your reader a volume of ideas to digest. Unless your presentation has been unusually coherent, he's apt to be left seeing trees but no forest. He really *needs* a systematic wrap-up.

With shorter papers, though, you should take liberties with this formula, particularly if your next-to-last paragraph has already gathered up many of the threads of your argument. You certainly don't want to insult your reader's intelligence.

There remain, however, three imperatives, no matter how brief your essay.

1. **Focus on your main point (which may be your final point).**
2. **Gratify us with at least one last new twist or phrase to make your point memorable.**
3. **End with emotional impact.**

The four closers quoted below satisfy these imperatives beautifully. All are from short essays written for the same upper-division Shakespeare course, and all deal with the same subject, *King Lear*. This, I should point out, is no coincidence. It wasn't until these students got to their last essay assignment of the semester—on *Lear*—that any of them learned to write a powerful closer. When you read them, you may find this hard to believe. Each seems the product of a truly natural talent. Appearances deceive, though. What looks so natural is really the effect of repeated practice, careful revision, and considerable reader feedback, not just from me but from their classmates as well. I suspect that a semester spent with Shakespeare also had something to do with it. As you read these closers, remember to read for manner as well as message:

> After his defeat and capture, Lear's transformation of character is complete. To be a prisoner of his daughters should be the most humiliating experience in a king's life, yet we find Lear expressing real happiness. Because he is with Cordelia, the longing for power and loyalty has been replaced with a desire for love and compassion. At last Lear sees a love without price and power. He actually looks forward to being a prisoner with Cordelia:

> > Come, let's away to prison.
> > We two alone will sing like birds i' th' cage.
> > When thou dost ask me blessing, I'll kneel down
> > And ask of thee forgiveness. So we'll live,
> > And pray, and sing, and tell old tales, and laugh
> > At gilded butterflies . . .   (V.iii.8–13)

> The kind of love he now wants is the antithesis of the worship that his other daughters promised him. Lear has discovered a human love based on sharing and feeling, and found that it is worth far more than crowns or kingdoms. The tragedy of King Lear is that Lear's ideal universe discovers itself in a prison rather than in a kingdom. For when Lear had the power to preserve love he could not see it, and when he had the wisdom to see love he could not preserve it.

> So, by a series of occurrences very close to the core of the man, Lear, this king becomes aware of life just as it is lost to him forever. The only non-static character in the play, Lear becomes the tragic one. The tragedy is one like saving a man's life so that he may be executed. But, in that saving, Lear is, if only briefly, whole, magnificent, wise.

> Even though Lear changes into a wise, compassionate, and fit ruler, his sorrows begin anew. The sentimentalist's phrase "poetic justice" holds no meaning for Shakespeare. Ruin wrought in the old king's heart and brain is irreparable, and the tornado that whirls him to his doom carries with it the just and the unjust. Lear's little golden pause of peace, when he

and Cordelia reunite, followed by the intolerably piercing scene in which he bears her dead body out of prison muttering that they have hanged his "poor fool," shows that even the virtuous suffer—not at the hands of the gods, who are indifferent, but at the claws of beastly humans. In *King Lear*, the consequences of imprudent action were never followed out to a grimmer end.

It seems we can really only speculate as to what Shakespeare is trying to say about life in *King Lear*. There are no religious morals or Elizabethan motifs jumping out at us like handy crutches. Perhaps Shakespeare is trying to convey in Lear an inner human dignity in suffering. Lear, the exalted, suffers with the common. He shares with all of his brothers the ability to suffer. Suffering is *his* bond. His ability to feel the pangs of rejection, defeat, and total disillusionment enables Lear, who has "ever but slenderly known himself," to achieve a spiritual stature in death denied him in life.

What F. L. Lucas said at the opening of this chapter about a sentence-end is probably even more true of an essay-end. A weak sentence-end can always be recouped by a strong following sentence; a weak essay-end cannot. Knowing this, many experienced writers take the precaution, during the early drafting stage, of setting aside a couple of choice ideas or phrases for use in their closer. That's a smart policy.

6

Diction

Less is more, in prose as in architecture.

—Donald Hall

In composing, as a general rule, run your pen through every other word you have written; you have no idea what vigor it will give your style.

—Sydney Smith

Conciseness

Most of us write as if we're getting paid a dime a word. We've been conditioned, I suppose, by school assignments calling for more words than we have ideas. That gets us into the habit of phrase-stretching—a hard habit to break. Then, too, it's easier to think in long, ready-made phrases, which have the added attraction of sounding elegant. What secretary or bureaucrat doesn't feel indebted to the coiner of "please be advised," "enclosed please find," "thanking you in advance," and "in reference to yours of . . ."?

This habit of thinking in prefab phrases slowly dulls our sensitivity to words as words. It's inevitable. We may hear someone say "at this point in time" and pride ourselves on recognizing the phrase as a cliché, but we'll probably not notice that it's also redundant. (What does *in time* say that *at this point* doesn't already say?) If we think in terms of months, we're only half-conscious of days. If we think in terms of phrases, we're only half-conscious of words.

Good writing starts with a profound respect for words—their denotations, their connotations, their force, their rhythm. Once you learn to respect them, you'll develop a passion for using them thriftily. Why use three or four words if one says the same thing? Why say "in the event that" when you can say "if"? Or "in order to" when you can say "to"? Or "for the reason that" when you can say "since"? Why write "They speak with great bitterness" when you can write "They speak bitterly"?

A skilled writer writes as if she were paid a dime for each word she *deletes*. Her prose is concise. Every word of every sentence works at maximum efficiency; the total effect suggests power, purpose, and speed.

Let's look for a moment at some far different prose. Here's a marshmallow from a fairly typical student paper:

> His bold and brash temper has been replaced by a careful and prudent manner.

When the student came in for a writing conference, I had him stare at this sentence. "What words aren't pulling their weight here?" I asked him. After studying the sentence hard for a minute, he saw that *bold* and *brash* are synonyms here, so he deleted *bold and*. Then he realized that *brash temper* could be replaced by a single strong noun—say, *brashness* or *impetuosity*. He chose the latter for its freshness.[1] Then he saw that *careful and prudent* was redundant, so he struck *careful and*. Finally he went to work on *prudent manner*, trying to get a single strong noun that would parallel *impetuosity* and tighten the contrast here. The answer brought a smile, for it was simplicity itself: *prudence*. The revised sentence now looked like this:

> His impetuosity has been replaced by prudence.

The original sentence had 14 words; the revised one, 7. (It can be revised even further, as I'll show in a minute when I discuss verbs.) There's no question, is there, which version has the greater vigor and pleasing directness.

Less *is* more. A good writer will tinker like this with every sentence, going back over each of them laboriously, even obsessively, until satisfied that she cannot make them any more succinct without sacrificing clarity. Which perhaps is why Hemingway could say, "Writing must be a labor of love or it is not writing."

What's the chief difference between a skillful writer and a mediocre one? The skillful writer is prepared to take many more pains to

---

[1] Here's a reason for owning a good thesaurus. Use it to be *reminded* of words, not to learn them, for if you learn them there, you'll learn them out of context and risk misusing them. An old standard is *Roget's International Thesaurus*, 5th ed. (HarperCollins), edited by Richard Chapman. For a free online dictionary/thesaurus, try Dictionary.com.

say it cleanly. What looks like greater brainpower is usually just greater persistence. My student demonstrated the point to himself. On that day he became a convert to conciseness and went on to become one of the top writers in his class.

Vigorous Verbs

Active: Bill climbed the mountain.
Passive: The mountain was climbed by Bill.

The typical English sentence will tell us "X does Y," in that order. Thus, "Bill climbed the mountain," not "The mountain was climbed by Bill." Why is "X does Y" the normal word order? It's simpler. Plus it gives us first things first. What most of us want to know first is who or what is starring in the story (the sentence). If the actor appeals to us, we'll want to learn more—namely, what that person or thing has done. So the "X does Y" pattern respects the natural path of our curiosity. But there seems still another reason for our preference: We find it easier to process a story when the *grammatical subject* and the *actor* are the same. In "Bill climbed the mountain," the two certainly are: "Bill" is the grammatical subject as well as the actual subject, or actor—the person who did the climbing. But in "The mountain was climbed by Bill," we have two subjects. The grammatical subject is "mountain," while the actor—the *real* subject, many of us would say—is "Bill." And we don't learn his identity until the end, which is way late. Hence our sense there of indirectness, of backing in. That's a typical feeling with passive constructions.

All of this commonsense theory is useful to know if we are to make proper sense of the "active" versus "passive" verb question. Let's get the definitions clear. We call a verb "active"—short for "active voice"—when its grammatical subject is doing whatever the verb describes. We call a verb "passive" when its grammatical subject isn't doing anything; instead, it's being *done to*. So the action of the passive-verb sentence is actually reversed, with the actor/doer showing up only at the end: "The mountain was climbed *by Bill.*" Here, then, are two important ideas to remember:

> **Active verbs move us forward; passive verbs move us backward. Active verbs give us the actor up front; passive verbs make us wait to learn the actor.**

And sometimes we *never* learn the actor, either because the writer forgets to add a "by Bill" or because he chooses, for whatever reason, not to add one. That can be exasperating. Here's another important point to remember:

> **A passive verb always includes some form of the verb** *be—is, are, was, were, has been,* **or** *have been*—**plus a past participle (typically a verb ending in** *–ed*). **Contrary to popular belief, "is" alone isn't passive. Inert, yes; passive, no.**

Curiously, even if we've learned all this, most of us overuse the passive voice anyway. Let me explain more of the advantages of the active voice and why we often fall into the passive despite ourselves.

Good prose is *direct, definite*. Like a firm handshake, it betokens and inspires confidence. It tells the reader: "You're in good hands with me. I have worked out my views on this subject and believe they make sense, so I'm giving it to you just as I see it. I respect you too much to waste your time with hedged prose, and I respect myself too much to come across as wishy-washy. Sure, we'll probably disagree here and there, but at least we'll both know where we disagree."

Weak prose, conversely, is *roundabout, vague*. Like a limp handshake, it betokens insecurity. It implies to the reader: "You probably should have chosen a different guide. See, I'm truly afraid of you. And afraid of being me, too. I'm not even sure what I think about this subject, so I can't give it to you straight. Being vague is the only refuge I have—my smoke screen, you might say. Vagueness lets me get by with sort-of-understanding, and it also disarms you a bit since you'll have difficulty knowing where you disagree with me."

Many style elements contribute to these impressions, but probably none more than the choice of verbs. Why? *Because the verb acts as the power center of most sentences.* If a writer's verbs are active, fresh, and definite, her sentences will have snap; they'll impress us with her spirit and conviction. But if her verbs lack oomph, or if she backs into her ideas with a lot of passives, her sentences will sag; they'll convince us of her dullness and diffidence. *Because every sentence normally has at least one verb, the aggregate effect of a writer's verbs is huge.*

Theodore Bernstein makes this point well in *The Careful Writer*, using America's Declaration of Independence as an example. Its authors wanted to do two things, he says: justify the colonists' claims to independence and galvanize them into open rebellion. Both ends they accomplished with superb effect. How? Mainly by using vigorous, unequivocal verbs. Of the 1,500 words in the document, Bernstein points out, only a dozen or so are passive constructions. The others have zing, like these: "[King George III] has plundered our seas, ravaged our Coasts, burnt our towns, and destroyed the lives of our people."

Sometimes, to be sure, the passive voice is actually desirable. You may want to emphasize the effect of a particular action: "Charles alone was injured in the accident." Or you may want to soften the phrasing of an idea: "You'd be advised to leave now." Or you may be ignorant of the agent performing the action: "The ransom note was left in the mailbox." And sometimes it doesn't matter who performed an action: "Our stadium was rebuilt in 2010."

Generally, though, the active voice is preferable. You can prove this to yourself by taking an old piece you have written and converting every unnecessarily passive verb into the active form. You'll be astonished at how much this alone invigorates your style. You might try something else that has a similar effect: recast as many *is* and *are* constructions as possible—especially the expletives (*there is, there are, there were*) and impersonal constructions (*it is, it was*), which allow you to amble past the subject and verb positions of a sentence without having said a thing.

Note, in these examples, the difference in conciseness:

1. His impetuosity *has been replaced* by prudence.
   Prudence now *tempers* his impetuosity.
2. It *is said* that power is *corrupting*.
   Power *corrupts*.
3. Meaning *was found* by Freud in everything.
   Freud *found* meaning in everything.
4. *There were* 200 guests *in attendance* at the party.
   Two hundred guests *attended* the party.
5. It *was decided* to destroy the evidence.
   [?] *decided* to destroy the evidence.

That last example illustrates another problem with the passive: it lets the writer avoid assigning responsibility for an action to a specific agent. Who actually made the decision to destroy the evidence? We aren't told. The buck is passed, the position hedged. The passive voice thus serves as a dodge for someone who either lacks specific knowledge of something or wants to hide it.

Unfortunately, recognizing the superiority of active verbs in a set of examples is easier than using that awareness in our own writing. Why?

Our "choice" of verb forms is seldom an actual choice at all. Rather, it tends to be automatic since it reflects an *attitude*—toward ourself, our reader, and our subject. If we're blessed with confidence, whether innate or earned through hard work and achievement, we'll almost instinctively assert what we know—and assert it straight out.[2] But if we feel insecure about our ideas, we'll unconsciously turn to the passive voice as a refuge.

Knowing how telltale our verbs are can be a decided help. When we're editing, it lets us spot weak passages we might not otherwise notice. We only have to read our piece once through looking exclusively at our verbs.

You ought, in fact, to do this with every piece you write. The small investment of time will pay rich dividends.

Freshness

The difference between the almost right word and the right word is really a large matter—'tis the difference between the lightning-bug and the lightning.

—Mark Twain

"There is no deodorant like success," writes Elizabeth Taylor. We read that and stop in our tracks, smiling with amusement, perhaps even chuckling aloud. What captivates us? The answer is clear: the perfect freshness and whimsical aptness of the image.

Each time we write we have opportunities to delight our reader with arresting phrases like that one. Here's another, from critic John Aldridge, demolishing a piece of current fiction: "the drama, which develops at about the speed of creeping crab grass. . . ." And yet another, by novelist Kurt Vonnegut: "He had an upper-class Hoosier accent, which sounds like a bandsaw cutting galvanized tin." And one more, this one from T. S. Eliot as he reaches the end of several paragraphs of highly theoretical speculation: "Have I been toiling to weave a labored web of useless ingenuity?" Ah!

Each of these authors instinctively understands one of the chief secrets of artful writing: you have to keep the reader in a state of near-perpetual surprise. Not suspense, but *surprise*. It's like baseball. A skilled pitcher mixes up his pitches. He'll throw a fastball, then a curve, maybe a change-up, then a knuckleball. Skilled writers work the same way.

---

[2]"Writing is, above all, an act of confidence, an assertion of the importance of what has gone on inside the writer, an exhibition of his thoughts or experiences." —Mina Shaughnessey

They're constantly feeding our appetite for novelty, be it with a fresh idea, a fresh phrase, or a fresh image. And if they're naturally witty, they'll also serve us up the amusingly offbeat—the literary equivalent of a knuckleball. Woody Allen's brilliant *New Yorker* pieces, collected in his book *Getting Even*, provide classic examples of the latter. So do Steve Martin's hilarious romps published in that same magazine.

I think you might find it instructive to listen to a few professionals talk about their art. The agreement among them is remarkable. Here, first, is master storyteller Theodor Seuss Geisel (Dr. Seuss):

> We throw in as many fresh words as we can get away with. Simple, short sentences don't always work. You have to do tricks with pacing, alternate long sentences with short, to keep it alive and vital. Virtually every page is a cliff-hanger—you've got to force them to turn it.

Next, science-fiction writer Ray Bradbury:

> Creativity is continual surprise.

An anonymous critic reviewing another writer's book:

> Best of all his style is laced with little surprises of diction or structure and the small shocks of well-made metaphors.

Supreme Court Justice Oliver Wendell Holmes:

> I find the great charm of writing consists in its surprises.

Novelist Ford Madox Ford:

> Carefully examined, a good—an interesting—style will be found to consist in a constant succession of tiny, unobservable surprises.

To write creatively—to come up with "a constant succession of tiny . . . surprises"—we must *want* to. We all have imaginations; the trick is to use them. And it's in the using of them that writing suddenly becomes a labor of love—an intensely creative, pleasurable activity. Each time we set down a sentence we must ask ourselves, *"Now how can I express this more memorably?"* Occasionally, just adding a choice adjective is all that's needed:

> He wrote with a *surgical* indifference to feelings.
>   —William Nolte

More frequently, adjusting the verb—the engine of the sentence—will bring the desired effect:

> A prig is one who delights in demonstrating his superiority on small occasions, and it is precisely when he has a good case that he *rises* to the depths of prigocity.
>
> —Dwight Macdonald

(Actually, this last sentence works its magic on us by two surprises, not one—first through the witty substitution of *rises* for *sinks*, and second through the wonderful nonce word *prigocity*, which converts mere priggishness into a complete and seemingly even fussier state of being.) But perhaps the best way, as the earlier examples showed, is through an image—a simile, say, or a metaphor.[3] Both are pictorial analogies that can explain and delight at the same time.

Unfortunately, memorable analogies seldom come unsought. Usually we must go out beating the bushes of our imagination to scare them up.

A good tip: *Always be thinking in terms of "like."* Such-and-such is like—what? Challenge your imagination. What *is* it similar to? Do this with every sentence you write. Make it part of your writing habit. Charles Ferguson, in *Say It with Words*, offers another tip that will help you actually cultivate these metaphors and similes. I confess I was initially dubious, but after trying it I found it wonderfully fruitful. Here's his recommendation:

> Let a person think, and as far as possible speak, for one day a week in the terms common to some particular profession or trade. In his reflections let him pick images from this vocabulary, and let him by this process see how many can be carried over into common speech and writing. On Monday it might be that he would choose his images from cooking; on Tuesday from engineering; on Wednesday from railroading; on Thursday from nuclear science; on Friday from agriculture; on Saturday from sport. And by Sunday he could certainly need a rest, but if he continued the process he might choose his terms from the wealth of language in the field of religion.

Sometimes, when an analogy suggests itself, you can simply tack it right on to the end of your sentence—like this:

> A professor must have a theory, as a dog must have fleas.
>
> —H. L. Mencken

---

[3]A *simile* compares two things using *like* or *as* ("That dorm is like a zoo"); a *metaphor* makes the comparison implicitly ("That dorm is a zoo").

Sometimes you can even frame the entire thought in terms of the comparison: you just drop the explicit *like* or *as* and develop the analogy metaphorically. Here, for example, is an excerpt from John Mason Brown's review of *Death of a Salesman* that brilliantly illustrates the use—and effect—of a great metaphor:

> Mr. [Lee J.] Cobb's Willy Loman is irresistibly touching and wonderfully unsparing. He is a great shaggy bison of a man seen at that moment of defeat when he is deserted by the herd and can no longer run with it. Mr. Cobb makes clear the pathetic extent to which the herd has been Willy's life.

The beauty of that metaphor is that it allows us to *see* Cobb's portrayal of Willy Loman. We are given a visual—even an emotional—correlative of the bare abstract idea, and so that idea comes alive to us, and haunts our imagination with its poignancy.

You can understand now, I think, why novelist Joseph Conrad could proclaim the following as his artistic mission: "My task which I am trying to achieve is, by the power of the written word to make you hear, to make you feel—it is, before all, to make you *see*. That—and no more, and it is everything."

Occasionally we'll run across a passage that seems the very quintessence of fresh, visual writing. Such a one, I believe, is the vignette below, by novelist/essayist John Updike, appearing in his *Assorted Prose*. Read it twice, please:

> We recently had a carpenter build a few things in our house in the country. It's an old house, leaning away from the wind a little; its floors sag gently, like an old mattress. The carpenter turned his back on our tilting walls and took his vertical from a plumb line and his horizontal from a bubble level, and then went to work by the light of these absolutes. Fitting his planks into place took a lot of those long, irregular, oblique cuts with a ripsaw that break an amateur's heart. The bookcase and kitchen counter and cabinet he left behind stand perfectly up-and-down in a cockeyed house. Their rectitude is chastening. For minutes at a stretch, we study them, wondering if perhaps it isn't, after all, the wall that is true and the bookcase that leans. Eventually, we suppose, everything will settle into the comfortably crooked, but it will take years, barring earthquakes, and in the meantime we are annoyed at being made to live with impossible standards.

Note the seeming inevitability of the phrasing, the rightness of each word. Note, too, the originality of perception, the "small shocks of well-made metaphors," the fine wit (especially the pun on "rectitude"!), and the sense of perfect wholeness it achieves. Updike knows how to break an amateur's heart himself.

Let me share one more beauty. It's from Paul Gallico, America's best sports writer of the 1920s and '30s. In this excerpt from a *Vanity Fair* piece called "A Large Number of Persons," an essay on various sports crowds, he pays homage to the immortal golfer Bobby Jones and his army of adoring fans. Gallico's spoof of golf galleries is the funniest—and truest—I've ever read:

> The golf gallery is the Punchinello of the great sports mob, the clown crowd, an uncontrollable, galloping, galumphing horde, that wanders hysterically over manicured pasture acreage of an afternoon, clucking to itself, trying to keep quiet, making funny noises, sweating, thundering over hills ten thousand strong, and gathering, mousey-still, around a little hole in the ground to see a man push a little ball into the bottom of it with a crooked iron stick. If the ball goes in they raise a great shout and clap their hands and sometimes slap one another on the back, crying "Oh, boy!" and "Beautiful, beautiful, magnificent!" And when the white pellet just sneaks past the rim of the orifice or twists out of it, or goes up and looks in and sticks on the edge, a great mass murmur of pity runs through the group and they sound their "Oh's" like a Greek chorus greeting the arrival of a new set of catastrophes. Then it is that they make their absurd clucking noises and shake their heads, some in unison, some in antiunison, like mechanical dolls all set off at once.
>
> The golf gallery is closest of any to the game that is being played. Every individual in the stampede is familiar with the implements used and the problems that arise from tee to green. They are really vicarious players, and the crass outsider who rattles a toy movie camera at one of the artists just as he is about to apply a delicate brush of his poker against the side of the quiescent ball, is given the hissing and glaring-at of his life. The Jones galleries were something to see, up and away over the hills before the master had completed the poem of his follow-through, running, crowding, tearing, galloping, hustling—men, women and children, in sunshine or in cloudburst, their tongues hanging out, their faces red, their sports clothing disheveled, elbowing one another in the wild route over the lea to secure a momentary vantage point from which to bear witness to the next miracle.

7

Readability

When we encounter a natural style, we are astonished and delighted; for we expected to see an author, and we find a man.

—Blaise Pascal

Sentences are not different enough to hold the attention unless they are dramatic. No ingenuity of varying structure will do. All that can save them is the speaking tone of voice somehow entangled in the words and fastened to the page for the ear of the imagination.

—Robert Frost

A readable style is one that invites reading. That circular definition I think we can all agree on. But when we ask what makes a style readable, we move into personal taste. Here it's everyone for himself. Let me take a moment to state my own views on the subject. If you agree with them, you might find the tips that follow both sensible and helpful.

Basically, I require two things of an author. The first is that he or she have something fresh to say—something that will either teach me or amuse me. If he doesn't, I stop reading. The second requirement is that he not waste my time getting out what he has to say. If he idles, I figure I'm better off reading someone else.

But beyond these bedrock requirements, what I find most appealing in a writer is an authentic manner. I like to see him or her come across as a vital, companionable human being, not a stuffed shirt or emotionally unfeeling. I like an author to *talk* to me, unbend to me, speak right out to me. If the prose has a natural, conversational rhythm to it, if it's forged out of homespun English rather than highbrow English, if it's stamped with the mark of a quirky personality, if it carries the ring of honesty and passionate conviction, then the writer has captured my attention. I like an author to be natural, warts and all. It shows me that he or she trusts me enough to show vulnerability and not be afraid of me.

Below are examples of what I mean—examples, too, of what Pascal and Frost doubtless had in mind in those remarks of theirs that I quoted at the head of this chapter. The first pair of passages, a couple of pages apart, come from novelist/memoirist Anne Lamott's *Bird by Bird: Some Instructions on Writing and Life*, a book at once wise and funny—but, best of all, real. Here she's disclosing part of her writing life and the demons she battles, especially her fear of rejection and her perfectionism. In fact, we get to see her battle her perfectionism right in front of us as she reminds us—and no less herself!—of its high costs:

> What I've learned to do when I sit down to work on a shitty first draft is to quiet the voices in my head. First there's the vinegar-lipped Reader Lady, who says primly, "Well, *that's* not very interesting, is it?" And there's the emaciated German male who writes these Orwellian memos detailing your thought crimes. And there are your parents, agonizing over your lack of loyalty and discretion; and there's William Burroughs, dozing off or shooting up because he finds you as bold and articulate as a houseplant; and so on. . . . Quieting these voices is at least half the battle I fight daily. . . .

> Perfectionism is the voice of the oppressor, the enemy of the people. It will keep you cramped and insane your whole life, and it is the main obstacle between you and a shitty first draft. Perfectionism will ruin your writing, blocking inventiveness and playfulness and life force (these are words we are allowed to use in California). Perfectionism means that you try desperately not to leave so much mess to clean up. But clutter and mess show us that life is being lived. Clutter is wonderfully fertile ground—you can still discover new treasures under all those piles, clean things up, edit things out, fix things, get a grip. Tidiness suggests that something is as good as it's going to get. Tidiness makes me think of held breath, of suspended animation, while writing needs to breathe and move.

And here's another pair of riveting paragraphs, from the novelist Dorothy Allison. Whenever I think of intellectual and emotional honesty, I think of paragraphs like these, ringing with conviction, passion, and integrity:

> I have always passionately loved good books—good stories and beautiful writing, and most of all, books that seemed to me to be intrinsically important, books that told the truth, painful truths sometimes, in a voice that made eloquent the need for human justice. That is what I have meant when I have used the word *literature*. It has seemed to me that literature, as I meant it, was embattled, that it was increasingly difficult to find writing doing what I thought literature should do—which was simply to

push people into changing their ideas about the world, and to go further, to encourage us in the work of changing the world, to making it more just and more truly human.

All my life I have hated clichés, the clichés applied to people like me and those I love. Every time I pick up a book that purports to be about either poor people or queers or Southern women, I do so with a conscious anxiety, an awareness that the books about us have often been cruel, small, and false. I have wanted our lives taken seriously and represented fully—with power and honesty and sympathy—to be hated or loved, or to terrify and obsess, but to be real, to have the power of the whole and the complex. I have never wanted politically correct parables made out of my grief, simple-minded rote speeches made from my rage, simplifications that reduce me to cardboard dimensions. But mostly that is what I have found. We are the ones they make fiction of—we queer and disenfranchised and female—and we have the right to demand our full, nasty, complicated lives, if only to justify all the times our reality has been stolen, mismade, and dishonored.

What permits such miracles of literary authenticity to happen? The answer, I think, is either a religious reverence for truth at whatever cost—this is proverbially the case with major artists—or else genuine self-acceptance. If a person accepts herself, she will be herself, and will speak her mind in her own idiom without inhibition. She won't be engaged in posturing with her reader, or counterfeiting her real personality and feelings, because she'll have no wobbly idealized self to defend.

Achieving such self-acceptance is a difficult proposition, though. The fear of rejection straitjackets most of us from early in life. Instead of learning to discover our own writing voice, we learn to mimic the voices of others. In fact, we do a pretty good job of learning to smother all traces of individuality.

The Godlike Pose

If we're honest with ourselves, most of us can see this defensiveness operating every time we're asked to produce a piece of serious writing—an essay, for example, or a report. At such times, fear compels us to try to appear godlike: wise, rational, authoritative. But since, beyond a certain point, we can't become more rational and authoritative, we instinctively—and often unconsciously—compensate in our writing style by donning the trappings of pure rationality and authority: studied "objectivity," impersonality of address, elevated diction, a grave manner, elaborate sentences, and the rest. It can be pretty convincing. We can even fool ourselves with our stylistic majesty.

Unfortunately, this is mostly a learned response. What keeps reinforcing it is the popular dogma that only a lofty, formal style is appropriate in serious writing. That dogma not only strengthens our feeling that we must be something we're not, but also teaches us *how* to strike the godlike pose.

How did the dogma originate? Probably through thousands of precedents resembling our own attempts at imposture. After enough people over enough decades donned the trappings of authority, the trappings themselves became part of the established style of serious discourse. At that point, Decorum—not just the individual's ego—began insisting on a standard of stylistic acceptability. From then until now we have had convention reinforcing instinct, and instinct in turn rigidifying convention—in short, a vicious circle.

You can see it operating at every commencement exercise. A speaker has been chosen to give the major address. "My God, what can I say that will be equal to the occasion?" he wails. He thinks and thinks; his desperation grows; his brain begins to freeze. Eventually he bows to tradition and comes up with an impossibly formal Address—a collection of platitudes substituting for genuine feeling and conviction. The audience hears it, yawns, then dozes. Each person leaves with the same unspoken sentiment: "Well, chalk up another boring commencement speech. Why doesn't someone—just once—give a simple, heartfelt talk, something really honest? Why must it always be so pretentious?" Because, as we've seen, convention—and the speaker's scared ego—won't have it any other way. With each new precedent, it becomes all the harder for a new commencement speaker to be simply himself.

The Dogma of Formalism

The only way to break this circle is for each of us to subject the dogma of Formalism to a searching analysis. How solid, in fact, is its rationale? What are its actual effects? What (if any) reasonable alternative is there to it? And what are the stylistic practices of our best contemporary authors?

Let's begin with its rationale. Judged solely by its corrective ends, it makes sense. The teachers who preach the formal style are trying desperately to elevate people's writing standards. More specifically, they hope to teach them stylistic discipline and grace; teach them that talking and writing, while related, are not the same thing; teach them, in short, that when one writes seriously, one must take one's style seriously. In essence, they are reacting against the shortcomings of the informal style adopted unthinkingly by so many students. Since such a style recognizes no difference between writing and talking, it tends to be loose, banal, and imprecise—disadvantages too great to offset its merits of simplicity and ease.

So far, so good. Unfortunately, what these teachers fail to perceive is that the archly conservative formal style has shortcomings of its own. While capable of satisfying the needs for precision and conciseness, it tends to lack ease and freshness, since it inhibits variety of diction, simplicity, and anything offbeat. Its self-consciousness is both its virtue and its limitation.

Which brings me to its actual effects—two principal ones, both negative. First, more often than not, it ironically promotes writing that is as bad in its own way as the very writing it's hoping to discourage—"bow-wow language," Mencken called it, marked by stilted diction, abstract phraseology, frozen sentence rhythms, and so on. Exceptionally literate people may eventually find themselves at home with a formal style, but most writers never will—and their awkwardness will show. Second, and more insidious, it promotes phoniness and empty conventionality—the Standard Way of Thinking. When a person is obliged to write like another person, who was himself obliged to write like still another person, he is invariably going to start adopting that person's neutered style of thought and to stray ever further from what he actually thinks and feels. But that's just the beginning. Teach a person this trick and pretty soon he's formed a lifelong habit. We see the dismaying evidence all around us—in "businessese," "academese," "officialese," "committee prose." Their labels may differ, but not their gobbledygook essence. Each is a form of imitation-writing sterile in its uniformity, opaque in its jargon, and absurd in its pomposity. People don't learn to write this way when they've been encouraged to write simply, directly, and honestly. They learn to write this way only when they've been taught a style which implies that naturalness is unnatural, that informality is unacceptable, and that individuality is unpardonable. (More on this in our next chapter.)

George Orwell discusses something like this syndrome in his classic essay "Politics and the English Language." He observes, for instance:

> As I have tried to show, modern writing at its worst does not consist in picking out words for the sake of their meaning and inventing images in order to make the meaning clearer. It consists in gumming together long strips of words which have already been set in order by someone else, and making the results presentable by sheer humbug. . . .

> In our time it is broadly true that political writing is bad writing. Where it is not true, it will generally be found that the writer is some sort of rebel, expressing his private opinions and not a "party line." Orthodoxy, of whatever color, seems to demand a lifeless, imitative style.

That last sentence says it all.

We might solve the problem, it seems to me, if we stop thinking of style in the simplistic either/or terms that the formalists have taught us to adopt. Typifying their way of thinking is the following entry on contractions in a widely used Freshman English text:

> The use of contractions (I'll, can't, couldn't, didn't, he's, shouldn't) is appropriate in informal and colloquial styles but not in a formal style.

The trouble with such a dictum is that it postulates only two kinds of style, both of them extreme—an informal, colloquial style versus a formal style—and implies that only the latter is legitimate for serious writing.

The "General English" Style

What students are rarely told is that there exists a *middle* style— "General English," language expert Porter Perrin calls it—that is essentially a happy compromise between formal and informal. Being a compromise, it is by far the most palatable of the written styles, and its area of appropriateness, at least in the real world, is virtually unlimited. Why? Because skilled writers can stay within the "General English" style and still satisfy the four essentials of prose: precision, conciseness, ease, and freshness. (Indeed, as I've shown, they'd be hard put to satisfy all four with any other style.) Little wonder that it has been displacing formal English as the prevailing literary style in recent years.

The special character of this style—at least at its best—was caught by novelist Somerset Maugham when he remarked that "good prose should resemble the conversation of a well-bred man." (Or woman, he surely meant to say.) Several illustrations of it appear in this book—most notably the passages by White in Chapter 1, by Kael in Chapter 2, by Updike in Chapter 6, and by both Lamott and Allison in the present chapter. If you revisit those passages, you'll observe that each is conversational in tone—unaffected, idiomatic, straightforward—but also beautifully wrought. The phrasing is tight and precise; the diction, fresh and apt. Considerable labor has been lavished on these sentences, we can be sure, not a little of it on concealing that very labor. They all seem happy accidents—precisely the intended effect.

What makes such a style so appealing to today's reader is its authenticity and graceful informality. What makes it so attractive to writers themselves, I think, is that it frees them to discover their own voice.[1] Moreover, it reinforces their desire to speak the truth as they see it. All of us need that reinforcement—we need as much of it as we can get, in fact. We surely don't get it when we feel compelled by a stylistic dogma to efface our personality, adopt the language of orthodoxy, and pretend to an exalted authority we know we don't possess. Bonamy Dobrée, in his *Modern Prose Style*, summed up the matter well:

> The modern prose writer, in returning to the rhythms of everyday speech, is trying to be more honest with himself than if he used, as is too wreckingly easy, the forms and terms already published as the expression of other people's minds.

Unfortunately, while the "General English" style may be our answer, it doesn't simplify our writing problems. Just the reverse: the more you poke into its subtle complexities, the more you conclude that it's likely to serve only as an elusive ideal we might aim for. Writing an informal style is easy—you just talk on paper. Writing a formal style is pretty easy, too, once you have the knack—you just haul out all the high-sounding, impersonal phrases you've seen other people use. But writing a good "General English" style is hard. It's hard because it requires a sophisticated control of *tone*, which is the most intangible but perhaps most consequential element in a writer's voice.

As I said earlier, "General English" is essentially a compromise between formality and informality. This means it involves a mingling of contraries: formal and informal diction, objectivity and subjectivity, impersonality and directness. All of these things affect tone. Part of the challenge, then—and it's a formidable one—is to get the right mix. That's as tricky as concocting a good sweet-and-sour sauce. The other part of the challenge is to work around the edges of these various extremes without taking a tumble.

When, for example, will a colloquialism lend just the right note of easy informality, and when might it have the effect of cheapening a sentence? Or, to take the opposite problem, when will an unusual word add a nicely piquant effect, and when might it sound merely pretentious? Yet again: when will a personal touch be welcome, and when narcissistic? Guessing right requires a good ear, taste, and tact—all of them intuitive, finally, and acquired only through considerable reading and writing.

---

[1] "In literature the ambition of a novice is to acquire the literary language; the struggle of the adept is to get rid of it." —George Bernard Shaw

The question of style is obviously a large issue—at bottom, a moral issue—and one that we could go on and on with. We will, in fact, pursue it a little further in the next chapter. But to draw the matter to a temporary close, I'll simply tell you what I tell my students when the issue comes up in class and we're just minutes away from the bell:

Closing Thoughts

"Each time we write, we're making a choice as to the kind of person we prefer to be. Since it's so important, let's make that choice a conscious one for a change. Here's what it involves: 'Do I want to be authentically *me*, speaking my own thoughts in my own idiom, or am I content to be a pseudo-self, using borrowed thoughts, borrowed language, and a borrowed personality to gain the approval of a few literary traditionalists?'

"Our assumptions about our readers will condition that choice, of course, since we never write in a vacuum. But instead of automatically assuming that they will reject authenticity, ask yourself this: Is it likely that mainstream readers actually *prefer* to read the highly repressed, orthodox, formal style, or might they, too, not secretly regard it as all too often effete and stuffy?

"Sometimes, of course, stuffy or not, the formal style will seem to be the only one appropriate to the occasion, either because tradition decrees it or because the subject calls for an impersonal treatment. If you're writing a legal brief, for example, or a statement of corporate policy or a scientific paper, your job is to transmit information, not personal reflections; and you'll show readers that you understand that job by adopting a serious, reasonably judicial manner that keeps you offstage.

"But, for heaven's sake, let's not allow ourselves to be slaves to blind convention—or unnecessary pomp, for that matter. Few situations are really so intrinsically formal as we're conditioned to believe. Just because everyone else is standing on ceremony on a given occasion doesn't necessarily mean that it's obligatory, or that they *prefer* to; they may simply be afraid to be themselves, and may be just waiting for some free spirit to come along and give them the courage of their instincts. This holds as true for writing as it does for life in general.

"I suggest you keep in mind the example of Franklin Roosevelt. When he gave his periodic radio addresses to the American people, he could have adopted a lofty, presidential style. In fact, convention almost demanded it. But Roosevelt blithely ignored convention, choosing instead to give what he called 'fireside chats'—personal, down-to-earth talks laced with colloquialisms and jokes. Here was a man who obviously listened to the promptings of his heart. He figured that the average citizen, like himself, would prefer relaxed plain talk to studied oratory. And he was proved right. Those talks helped make him one of the most endearing of modern presidents.

"So I recommend that you be guided by what your own eyes and ears tell you, not merely by the so-called authorities. Just what *is* considered acceptable style today in serious writing? Look at the evidence—magazines such as *The New Yorker*, *Harper's*, *Forbes*, *The Atlantic Monthly*, and *Time*; newspapers like *The New York Times*, *The Wall Street Journal*, and *The Washington Post*; the latest books of Pulitzer Prize–winning nonfiction. You'll find that we're witnessing a revolution in the notion of what constitutes a good style for serious writing—a movement toward greater naturalness, vigor, informality, and individuality. It was bound to happen. We see similar revolutions occurring in lifestyles, religious beliefs, and sexual attitudes. When even *The New York Times* permits contractions in its editorial columns, as it does now, you know that literary Victorianism is on its way out."[2]

Tips for Improving Your Readability

Here are the two best ways I know for promoting an authentic and readable style:

- **View your reader as a companionable friend— someone with a warm sense of humor and a love of simple directness.**
- **Write like you're actually talking to that friend, but talking with enough leisure to frame your thoughts concisely and interestingly.**

If you tack these two tips on the wall by your writing desk and make a habit of practicing them, your readability quotient should soar.

---

[2]Bergen Evans, coauthor of *A Dictionary of American Usage* and, until his death in 1978, one of the country's top usage experts, remarked in 1962: "As written English is used by increasing millions and for more reasons than ever before, the language has become more utilitarian and more informal. Every publication in America today includes pages that would appear, to the purist of forty years ago, unbuttoned gibberish. Not that they are; they simply show that you can't hold the language of one generation up as a model for the next."

Here are 26 more. Occasionally they'll reiterate or anticipate points I make elsewhere, but for convenience of reference I'm including them here as well:

1. As a rule of thumb, whenever you've written three longish sentences in a row, make your fourth a short one. And don't fear the super-short sentence. It's arresting. Sometimes just a single word will be plenty long:

> Many American parents think that today's colleges are veritable breeding grounds for premarital sex. Nonsense. Each year, literally tens of students graduate with their virtue still intact.
>
> —Gregg Hopkins

That last sentence, by the way, illustrates the literary knuckleball I spoke of in Chapter 6. It also illustrates an axiom in aesthetics: "The smaller the sign [i.e., cue,] the greater the pleasure." Hopkins counts on our tendency to read "tens of students" as "tens of thousands." The joke slips through before we realize it, in a double take.

2. Use occasional contractions. They'll help you unbend, let your readers relax as well, and free up your writing voice. The most popular contractions involve *am, are, is*, and *not*, especially these:

> I'm
> you're, we're, they're
> he's, she's, here's
> won't, wouldn't, shouldn't, don't, doesn't, can't

Compare:

> "Why should we not have clean air?"
> "Why shouldn't we have clean air?"

Honestly, which of those two writers would you rather hang out with? Contractions, though, are like kisses: bestowed too freely, they lose their effect, in fact seem cheap. Save them for when you want to humanize some sentence like "Let us start now because I will not be in town tomorrow." My goodness, who ever *talks* like that? Keep your writing voice natural. Let yourself sound like the very person you'd want to read yourself: "Let's start now because I won't be in town tomorrow."

3. Generally, prefer *that* to *which*. The one is conversational; the other, slightly more bookish. I like to save "which" for after a comma, to introduce a nonrestrictive clause: "The bike, which she rode just yesterday, has a flat." The term "nonrestrictive," by the way, simply means that the

clause doesn't restrict the field of reference to one particular object; the clause is contributing only some incidental information, so it functions just like a parenthesis, and could be cut with little damage. Here, because the sentence begins with the words "The bike," our writer has already speci- fied the bike she's talking about, so her "which" clause isn't specifying any- thing, it's just adding some other information. Her commas around it are appropriate. But compare that to this sentence: "The bike that she rode just yesterday has a flat." Here, our *that* clause is clearly restrictive: It nar- rows the reference to a *particular* bike—the one ridden just yesterday. That makes it essential information, so it mustn't be set off by commas. My own practice is this: *If I could cut the clause, I'll use "which" and a comma before it; otherwise, I'll normally use "that."* But note my hedge: "nor- mally." When in doubt, I'll read the sentence aloud, testing it on my ear. And I'll check to see what other *that's* and *which's* may lurk in the area. Sometimes I'll want a "which" purely for variety. Other times I'll want it just because, for whatever reason, it seems to sound better. So much of writing is finally intuitive, isn't it? As Rudolf Flesch has wisely said, "You have to go by feel, not by rule."

4. If you mean "I," *say* "I." Don't wrap yourself in pomposities like "the writer" or "one" or "this author" or "we." Reserve "we" and "our" for those situations where you're referring to both your reader and yourself—i.e., where there really is someone else involved. Reserve "one" for when you mean "a person," as in "One would have to be a CPA to grasp that." When referring to the reader alone, address that person as "you," not "the reader." The printed page already puts enough distance between the two of you. Why add to it? When generalizing about readers or people, and when including yourself among them, go ahead and use "we" and "our." They're simple, conversational, and democratic.

5. Use dashes to isolate concluding phrases for emphasis or hu- morous effect. Pauline Kael is an artist with the dash. By rereading her review quoted in Chapter 2, you'll get an idea of the effects you can achieve with it yourself.

6. Professionals quote, amateurs paraphrase. Pros understand a powerful truth: readers love listening to people talk—love hearing the ac- tual words, not a preemptive digest of them. So use dialogue wherever your context warrants it—it's intrinsically dramatic. And don't be shy about inventing some. *Imagined* thoughts—one of a writer's best resources—let you do just that:

> Events inexorably force Enobarbus to a decision—an impossible one. It
> would seem that he's thinking here something like this: "My mind tells me to
> leave Antony for Rome. My heart tells me to leave Rome for Antony. Both

courses of action are right, and both are wrong. To go either way is to deny a central fact of my existence. I am a Roman, but I am also a man. There seems to be only one solution: death. It will eliminate the need to choose."

Here's another example, this one from my student Matt Darroh, in a paper on John Updike's classic short story "A&P":

> Mr. Lengel offers Sammy some well-intended advice: "You'll feel this for the rest of your life. . . ." In other words: "You'd better get used to keeping your mouth shut when you don't agree with certain things because that's life, and that's what you have to do. If you want to be successful, you need to quit being so idealistic. That's what I did, and that's what you have to do."

And here is the prominent architectural critic Witold Rybczynski, in his fascinating book *Home: A Short History of an Idea*, drolly contrasting the typical high-fashion modern chair, stripped of frivolity and frills, with its well-padded, voluptuous predecessors:

> It exhibits lightness and movability, and it invites admiration for these qualities—just as a well-made camp cot does. But it does not ask to be sat in, or at least not for very long. The Rococo chair invites conversation, and the Victorian chair invites after-dinner naps, but the Modern chair is all business. "Let's get this sitting over with and get back to something useful," it commands. It is about many things, this chair, but it is no longer about ease, leisure, or, if truth be told, about comfort.

And here is Stewart Brand, a National Book Award-winner, sharing with us in *How Buildings Learn: What Happens After They're Built* how building historian Orlando Ridout "reads" the statements that some house styles are making, or trying to make, about their owners:

> "The front facade [says Ridout] is a self-conscious part of the house, where the owner is trying to make a statement to the world about what he is about—whether it's 'I'm a simple man with simple tastes' or 'I'm richer than you are and don't you forget it' or simply, 'I have crossed the threshold of gentility. I can now afford a brick house with a fancy entrance porch.'"

7. The more abstract your argument, the more you should lace it with what I call "word pictures"—illustrations, analogies, vivid quotations, metaphors, similes. These are aids not only to your readers' understanding but also to their memory. In fact, they'll probably remember your illustration or analogy far longer than the abstract idea itself. But if the illustration is a good one, they'll be able to reconstruct the thought fairly

easily, so it will have served its purpose twice over. Here, for example, is Pulitzer Prize-winner Ron Suskind, in *A Hope in the Unseen*, explaining what faces an ambitious African-American youth, Cedric Jennings, at his crime-infested, inner-city high school in Washington, D.C.:

> Cedric's 4.02 grade-point average virtually ties him for first in the junior class with a quiet, studious girl named LaCountiss Spinner. Pride in such accomplishment is acceptable behavior for sterling students at high schools across the land, but at Ballou and other urban schools like it, something else is at work. Educators have even coined a phrase for it. They call it the crab/bucket syndrome: when one crab tries to climb from the bucket, the others pull it back down. The forces dragging students toward failure—especially those who have crawled farthest up the side— flow through every corner of the school. Inside the bucket, there is little chance of escape.

8. Minimize your adjectives. Try to let nouns—especially *accurate* nouns—work alone. This will simplify your style *and* give it more point. Voltaire, who knew something about style, wasn't overstating the case much when he said, "The adjective is the enemy of the noun." Twain echoed him: "As to the Adjective: when in doubt, strike it out." In a charming 1880 letter to a schoolboy named D. W. Bowser, with whom he corresponded for two years, Twain expanded on this advice, saying:

> I notice that you use plain, simple language, short words and brief sentences. That is the way to write English—it is the modern way and the best way. Stick to it; don't let fluff and flowers and verbosity creep in. When you catch an adjective, kill it. No, I don't mean utterly, but kill most of them—then the rest will be valuable. They weaken when they are close together. They give strength when they are wide apart. An adjective habit, or a wordy, diffuse, flowery habit, once fastened upon a person, is as hard to get rid of as any other vice.

9. Minimize your adverbs, too—especially trite intensifiers like *very, extremely, really, clearly*, and *terribly*, which show a 90% failure rate. Compare "She was very upset by the news" with "She was shattered by the news." The use of *very* and its cognates diminishes the word that follows, making it feel weak. Often, that word is actually fine. But when it isn't, "weak" generally means "inaccurate," "inexact." So find another word—there always is one. And note this irony: when you then cut the intensifier, your phrasing usually *gains* intensity. Which sounds hungrier, "very hungry" or "ravenous"? No contest. But I'll concede this: the right adverb, fresh and adroitly placed, is one of life's finest small pleasures.

Here are two proofs, both from Stewart Brand. Again, these gems appear in his *How Buildings Learn: What Happens after They're Built*. In each case, he saves his adverb for the next-to-last word, where it won't get overlooked:

> James Donnelly of Whole Earth inked every page of the manuscript bright red with line-editing corrections, for which I am whimperingly grateful.

> Because of water, houses deteriorate most from the bottom up and the top down. Damage comes from below thanks to what the British call, knowledgeably, "damp."

10. Use the fewest words possible and the simplest words possible. Occasionally, to be sure, the longer word will work best—it may express the idea concisely, or contribute just the cadence and texture wanted, or gratify your reader with the joy of surprise. (Remember *rectitude* and *chastening* in the Updike passage quoted in Chapter 6?) But be warned: the more you surrender to the temptation to write fancy, the further you'll stray from your true feelings and the more you'll write in a style designed to impress rather than serve the reader. Also, oratory can fool us into thinking we're saying something smart, when in fact we may not yet have gotten past a platitude. So follow Henry Thoreau's famous advice, for your own protection: "Simplify, simplify." This sounds easy but isn't, given all the temptations of self-indulgence and vanity. "To write simply is as difficult as to be good," sighed Somerset Maugham. Hemingway agreed: "Writing plain English is hard work."

11. Be sure that each sentence is somehow connected to the ones immediately before and after it. There's no other way to achieve fluidity, or what I like to call a "clean narrative line"—the hallmark, in my opinion, of professional prose.

12. In a long essay or report, summarize your argument every now and then so that readers can keep their bearings. I myself enjoy seeing these summaries cast as brief transitional paragraphs, maybe three or four sentences long. They make a welcome change of pace; they also *show* the steps in a writer's argument.

13. If you like putting questions to your reader, fine. They can add point to a discussion—and, like transitional paragraphs, variety to your style. But answer them promptly. If, for example, you've raised a juicy question at the end of your opening paragraph (which, by the way, is a wonderful strategy), the opening sentence of your next paragraph should start answering it—explicitly. You've created an expectation in us

(*Hmm, what's her answer?*) that you need to gratify, pronto. If, as often happens in that second paragraph, you find you need to explain something else first, fine; but by all means *explain* to us that you have to explain that thing first, so we'll know you haven't forgotten the question. More often than not, young writers will forget to clue in their reader as to what they are about—where they're headed and why they're taking that particular route. They assume it's understood. But the reader isn't clairvoyant; she knows only what the writer remembers to tell her. So share your road map with her. Then she can just sit back and enjoy the trip.

14. Use semicolons to reduce choppiness, particularly when you have several sentences with parallel structures. Also use them for a change of pace. (See the section on semicolons in Chapter 13.)

15. Read your prose aloud. *Always* read your prose aloud. Do you sound comfortable with your own ideas? Do you sound at ease with your reader? Can you read each sentence without stumbling or running out of breath? Does the phrasing sound like you, talking at top form, or does it sound alien, like it's coming out of some statue? Does your prose flow along? Have you managed to avoid unconscious word repeats, especially at the beginning and end of consecutive sentences? Skilled writers will always double-check those two spots. Their paragraph openings, too. It's easy to fall into a rut there.

16. Instead of always saying "first" and "second," occasionally use the numerals themselves in parentheses. (A *pair* of parentheses, please.) It's a superstition that numerals have no place in serious writing. For proof, browse through any major anthology of expository prose.

17. Numbers are tricky. When to write them out? When not to? *Everybody* has a theory on this one—which is a useful reminder of just how variable "rules" can be. Some experts claim that if a number needs a hyphen (e.g., "twenty-two") or a space (e.g., "two hundred"), it must be written as a numeral (e.g., "22" and "200"). Others will tell us, with equal flatness, that if it's two syllables or less, it must be written as a word (e.g., "sixteen" versus "31"). The *Chicago Manual of Style*, ultraconservative here, tells us to write out "whole numbers from one through ninety-nine." Still other experts insist, "Use numerals for everything over twenty." Actually, that last dictum is getting closer to my own taste—and of course it *is* just a matter of taste—since they've made it pretty brainproof. But why write *eighteen* when it's so much simpler to write *18*, and when *18* is easier for readers to remember—not to mention already converted into the numeral they'll actually use? What can possibly be objectionable about *18*? I hear someone answer, "It lacks the dignity of *eighteen*." Such a person doubtless undresses with the lights out. As for

my own practice: For its simplicity and good sense, I go with AP style here—that is, the *Associated Press Stylebook*: "Spell out whole numbers below 10, use figures for 10 and above."[3] But since I always fear forgetting which side 10 goes on, I like to recite their rule this way: "*If it's a one-digit number, make it a word.*" May I confess, though? Sometimes I'll write out a number like 16. And not just at the beginning of a sentence, either, where you have to. More heretical still, sometimes I'll use figures, not words, for numbers below 10. You'll see me do this in Chapter 10, where, in a section on "Attractive Formatting," I offer a word count of several sentences. It just seemed the simpler, more graphic style there, and I was emboldened to employ it by remembering the example of a professor friend who writes for eminent science journals. When citing numbers, he and his peers regularly use figures where non-science writers might fear to. My point is, while I admire consistency in style, I also have learned to respect instinct; and sometimes "sixteen" feels better, or looks better—don't ask me why. The same with "5" or "8." Maybe I'm unconsciously adopting Anne Lamott's aesthetic here: "writing needs to breathe and move."

18. When you begin a sentence with *And* or *But* (and you most definitely should now and then), don't, for heaven's sake, put a comma after it. You want to quicken your prose with those words, and the comma would just kill any gain. Here's Rybczynski again, in *Home: The History of an Idea*:

> The modern kitchen, in which everything is hidden in artfully designed cabinets, looks well organized, like a bank office. But a kitchen does not function like an office; if anything, it is more like a workshop.

The comma is needed *only if a parenthetical phrase follows*. In that case, another comma goes *after* that phrase as well: "But, considering the evidence, she's probably right."

19. *So* and *Yet* also make great lead-offs, though most amateur writers can't believe it, or refuse to, at least in their own prose. They're sure they'd be sinning, even after seeing the practice credentialed in reputable publications, and even after having it explained to them. Maybe this is just something you have to develop nerve for. If you're a skeptic, I suggest you keep watch for such sentences, and monitor your reactions

---

[3]This rule also jibes with the U.S. Government Printing Office *Manual of Style*, which sets the style of all federal government publications, including United States Supreme Court decisions and the *Congressional Record*. It also jibes with MLA (Modern Language Association) style.

to them. Over time, I think you'll come around. Take this example from software developer and essayist Paul Graham:

> Part of what software has to do is explain itself. So to write good software you have to understand how little users understand.

Or take this passage, from Mark Bittman, a *New York Times* food columnist, writing about the lovely Italian coastal province of Liguria:

> The coastline, riddled with natural harbors, made the Ligurians great traders, too. Genoa, the region's capital, was a powerful city-state that vied with Venice to rule the Mediterranean in the 15th and 16th centuries. So food products from all over northern Italy and the world were exported or imported through Liguria.

Could anything be smoother, or simpler, than those little segues? Note that *So* and *Yet*, like *And* and *But*, are normally spared commas because they're so short and brisk. But their polysyllabic kin—*Consequently* and *However*—normally *do* get commas. That's another reason right there to like *So* and *Yet*.

20. As a sentence starter, prefer *But* to *However*. It has two fewer syllables and takes no comma, so it's a cleaner, punchier transition word—especially at the head of a paragraph, where it's peerless. *However* seems to work best internally, positioned right next to the point of emphasis. When it's at the sentence head, it says to the reader, "Here, you go figure out where the stress ought to be." What reader wants that job? Not me.

21. Do you have a good wit? If so, share it—share your sense of verbal play, your good spirits. Let yourself have fun with your prose. What's called "serious writing" need not be solemn writing. F. L. Lucas, in his famous book *Style*, observed with characteristic good sense: "No manual of style that I know has a word to say of good humour; and yet, for me, a lack of it can sometimes blemish all the literary beauties and blandishments ever taught."

22. Paragraphing is hugely important—as much a matter of good style, and good sense, as practically anything else one can think of in writing. Long paragraphs intimidate most readers (*I don't want to go in there!*); lots of short paragraphs can suggest a breezy, Madison Avenue glibness or a refusal to pursue a point home; a succession of cookie-cutter paragraphs—say, two per page—can suggest a tired imagination. Moral: Use variety to keep things alive and vital, as Dr. Seuss advised. But be sure that your lead-off sentence in each paragraph—your *bridge*

sentence—does double duty as a *topic sentence*. It should forecast, if not state outright, the new thought you're now developing there. Go back to the last page of Chapter 4 ("Middles") and study the 11 bridge sentences I quote there from Bergen Evans. Even without having read the article itself, you can tell in each case where the paragraph is heading. That makes for beautifully coherent, fluid prose.

23. Here's a tip on the creative use of white space—a tip I'll have more to say about in Chapter 10. Let's say you need to shift from one large section of your exposition to another large section, but you're stymied as to how to bridge into it and at the same time signal the magnitude of the shift. The solution? Skip four spaces instead of the usual two between paragraphs. Doing this will

- Cue readers *visually* that a major new section is at hand.
- Give them a convenient place to pause.
- Spare you from having to manufacture a real transition. Here, white space substitutes for *meanwhile*, a most convenient pseudo-bridge that pros rely on when all else fails. It says, "OK, enough of that. Now let's move on to. . . ."

24. Choose your title with care. Leave the "teasing" title to writers who are still putting cuteness before communication. Focus instead on making your own title accurately descriptive, which is challenge enough. If possible, try to give it zing as well. Remember, it's our introduction to you as well as to your paper. A pedestrian title is about as welcoming as a burnt-out motel sign.

25. If you've written a paragraph that sounds labored, back off and ask yourself, "How would I *say* this to a friend?" Then go ahead and talk it out loud. Afterward, write down as nearly as you can recall what you said. Chances are, most of your talked-out sentences will shame your earlier, written version of them. Why? When we write, we tend to over-complicate, and our very words get in the way; but when we talk, we instinctively simplify. We need it to be simple just to get it out, it seems.

26. Another tip for the same crisis is this: Take a short break and read some paragraphs of a writer whose style you relish. Try to *soak in* that style; try to feel yourself actually writing those paragraphs as you read them. Then say to yourself, "OK, now how would [Wonderful Writer] write this?" and let yourself try again. This usually works. And even when it doesn't, it will at least give you a fresh perspective. That's maybe half the battle right there.

8

Superstitions

Above all, we believe that naturalness is unnatural, that informality is unacceptable, and that individuality is unpardonable.

—TOTELarian Creed

To be nobody-but-yourself—in a world which is doing its best, night and day, to make you everybody else—means to fight the hardest battle which any human being can fight; and never stop fighting.

—E.E. Cummings

The first problem for all of us, men and women, is not to learn, but to unlearn.

—Gloria Steinem

This chapter concerns literary prudes. More specifically, it concerns the religion they make of Formal English, the superstitions they'd have us accept, and the serious moral implications of their whole ideology.

I confess I'm of mixed minds about how to treat people of this persuasion. Part of me wants to be gentle. I was once a literary prude myself—in fact, I still bear some of the marks—and I know they mean well. Another part of me wants to poke fun at their ludicrous rigidity and solemnity. Who cannot smile at someone ready to battle over a split infinitive?

Literary prudes, Donald Lloyd once observed, are the people who put triumphant exclamation marks in the margins of library books. They make themselves more readily identifiable, though, through their talk. Just to be sure we're thinking of the same people, I'll provide some samples of it: "But of course one must *never* split infinitives"; "Well, the

Rule says, you know, that contractions are unacceptable in serious prose";
"William, when are you going to learn that 'I' *must* be followed by 'shall,'
not 'will'?"; "Never say 'It's me,' dear. Say 'It is I.'"

These people arrived at their literary prudishness by various
means—some through a puristic concern for the language that gradually
stiffened into morbid scrupulosity; some through ignorance reinforced
by others' ignorance; some through a hunger for the security of dogma
and absolutes; and some, it would seem, merely through the snob appeal
of elitism. Upon arrival at their mental state, they were at once ushered
into a large congregation of True Believers whose faith is embalmed Formal English. Unaccountably, their faith has gone nameless. I will repair
that oversight right now and christen it "The One True English Language
Sect"—or "TOTELS," for short.

The history of this sect, its periodic holy causes such as the war
against *Webster III*,[1] its august leadership, its diverse membership—all
make for a fascinating story, but one too long for this little book. I will
merely focus on TOTELS' Articles of Faith, Creed, and Rules, for these
are more pertinent here, and I can dispose of them quickly.

First, the Articles of Faith. These provide TOTELS with its ideolog-
ical foundation, such as it is. But they also perform an invaluable function
once they are accepted: *They allow the believer to look at all contrary evidence with a tranquil heart.* In fact, as if by a miracle, they often let the
believer not even *see* any contrary evidence. The chief Articles, which I'm
taking the liberty to translate into plain English, are these:

Article I: The English Language is a system of Laws—not, as the new
Linguistic Heresy claims, just a system of human conventions for
communication.

Article II: Being a system of Laws, the Language was meant to be static,
not dynamic. Hence any changes in it are to be regarded as Corruptions.

Article III: Because of Articles I and II, Correct Usage depends upon our
honoring the Rules which our Elders have sagely inferred from the Laws
of the Language.

Following these Articles, and springing out of them, as it
were, are the TOTELarian Creed and Rules. The Creed, which the

---

[1]That is, *Webster's Third New International Dictionary,* which gained instant notoriety in
1961 for its editor's decision to abandon status labels like "incorrect" and "colloquial," main-
taining that a dictionary should describe how language is actually used instead of pronounc-
ing value judgments and trying to steer the language toward its own idea of "correctness."
For a full report on this bloody war, see the *Harbrace Guide to Dictionaries,* ed. Kenneth
Wilson et al. (New York: Harcourt, Brace, 1963).

devoutest members somehow know without ever having to read it, runs thus:

> *We believe in Rules, Authority, and The One True English Language.*
> *We believe in the sanctity of Formal English, which shall ever be revered*
>   *for its elaborate syntax, baroque sentences, ornate words, and stiff*
>   *expressions, all of which we pledge ourselves laboriously to employ.*
> *Above all, we believe that naturalness is unnatural, that informality is*
>   *unacceptable, and that individuality is unpardonable. Amen.*

The Rules, unfortunately, can't be reprinted so easily, since they're scattered among many Sacred Texts (which the world knows as old grammar books) and run into the hundreds. The seven Core Rules must suffice here. Everyone, I trust, remembers them, since they have been circulated far outside the faith and chanted with some regularity. They are, of course, the Seven Nevers:

1. Never begin a sentence with *But* or *And*.
2. Never use contractions.
3. Never refer to the reader as *you*.
4. Never use the first-person pronoun *I*.
5. Never end a sentence with a preposition.
6. Never split an infinitive.
7. Never write a paragraph containing only a single sentence.

There you have it in sketchy outline—the TOTELarian ideology, Articles of Faith, the Creed, and the Seven Nevers. Now, for the rest of the chapter, I plan to wrestle with the Nevers like an exorcist with unholy demons, hoping to free you from their hold forever.

If you can stand to see them again, read on.

1. "Never begin a sentence with *But* or *And*"

The many English teachers who still preach this superstition do so, I imagine, for three reasons: (1) they were taught it themselves at an impressionable age and have never thought to question its legitimacy; (2) they hope to discourage anything smacking of informality in student writing, perhaps because what informality they've seen has read like cafeteria chatter; (3) they can use this rule as a way to force students to move beyond simple sentences ("The plan is long overdue") to compound ones ("The plan is long overdue, but implementing it will be difficult").

The fact remains, though, that *But* and *And* are absolutely valid ways to begin a sentence. Not only valid ways, but *excellent* ways. And all seasoned writers know it. In fact, you'd be hard put today to find even a single book of award-winning nonfiction—or fiction either, for that matter—that *didn't* use plenty of these constructions. And were you to study the front page of, say, *The New York Times*, you'd find, every day, the same thing—maybe half a dozen of each, just on that one page alone. But, as I observed earlier, your true TOTELarians could look at all that contrary evidence with a tranquil heart—first, because they probably wouldn't even see it, thanks to the supreme naturalness of these little transitional words; and second, because even if they did, they wouldn't experience a logical disconnect. Why? Either because they would have it so well rationalized (e.g., *Well, that's a writer who's obviously been infected by the journalists*) or because they would have unconsciously taught themselves to compartmentalize such data—keep it out of their conscious thought process. That's the way to see it without seeing it.

But back to our two constructions. Just why are they so popular, at least outside the TOTELarian fold? I'd guess because they're simple, quick, and unobtrusive. Just look at the alternatives. For *but*, you have *however, on the other hand, nonetheless,* and *nevertheless*—all heavy-footed. The alternatives for *and* are similarly formal—words like *furthermore, in addition, indeed,* and *moreover*. And all of these alternatives are not only polysyllabic but require a comma, too. So if you're a writer who aims to give people a fast, smooth read, the choice of conjunctions is easy.

Let me show you how naturally they fit in. Since it's close at hand, let's take Bergen Evans's *Atlantic Monthly* article cited in the last chapter—a stirring defense of the then newly published *Webster III*. In that article, Professor Evans begins 29 sentences with *But* and, coincidentally, another 29 with *And*. By doing so, he manages to quicken the pace of his prose, smooth it out, and increase its conversational tone to where you feel like you're hearing the man speak. It's uncanny. It's also a beautiful example of the "General English" style. Here are two short paragraphs:

> The ultimate of "permissiveness," singled out by almost every critic for special scorn, was the inclusion in the Third International of *finalize*. It was this, more than any other one thing, that was given as the reason for sticking to the good old Second International—that "peerless authority on American English," as the *Times* called it. But if it was such an authority, why didn't they look into it? They would have found *finalize* if they had.

> And why shouldn't it be there? It exists. It's been recorded for two generations. Millions employ it every day. Two Presidents of the United States—men of widely differing cultural backgrounds—have used it in formal statements. And so has the Secretary-General of the United Nations [U Thant], a man of most unusual linguistic attainments. It isn't permitting the word but omitting it that would break faith with the reader.

I should caution you, though, to use the *and* or *but* sentence with some restraint. Just because it's legitimate doesn't mean it can't grow tiresome. Mr. Evans's 29 *ands* and 29 *buts* manage to avoid monotony by being sprinkled through ten close-knit pages.

2. "Never use contractions"

If you believe, with the TOTELarians, that "naturalness is unnatural, and informality is unacceptable," then no amount of reasoning will persuade you that contractions have a place in serious writing. You will even be able to close your eyes to all those instances where respected writers *do* use them in serious writing. (The two paragraphs just quoted from Bergen Evans's article contained four such instances. Note, too, the passages quoted earlier from John Updike, E. B. White, Pauline Kael, Anne Lamott, and James Michener.)

We could go 'round and 'round on the question of contractions, but ultimately it comes down to nothing more than our taste and values—that plus what we imagine our readers will accept. Perhaps this last point is the heart of it, even for TOTELarians. What writer—and particularly what fastidious writer—doesn't want to make peace with his or her readers? As I pointed out earlier, the fear of rejection is potent; each of us, I suspect, can identify with T. S. Eliot's Prufrock or Lennon and McCartney's Eleanor Rigby. If we imagine our readers to be rigid and forbidding, as our classroom experiences have conditioned many of us to do, and if we thus imagine they will approve of us only in a starched collar, we will usually wear that collar, however much we abhor it. It's the same in writing as in life: each is always imitating the other.

I think, though, that we might try paying our readers a compliment—by writing as if they preferred unaffected, unsolemn, conversational prose to the pretentious Formal variety. I think, too, that we might take a second look at the popular assumption that one can't—or shouldn't—be informal and serious at the same time. What is more agreeable than such a mixture? Robert Frost observed:

> The style is the man. Rather say the style is the way the man takes
> himself; and to be at all charming or even bearable, the way is almost
> rigidly prescribed. If it is with outer seriousness, it must be with inner
> humor. If it is with outer humor, it must be with inner seriousness.
> Neither one alone without the other under it will do.

To my mind, a writer who never uses contractions is akin to someone whose outer seriousness has no inner humor under it. But the other side of the coin is equally true: a writer who constantly uses them is like someone whose outer humor has no inner seriousness under it.

I would only repeat the admonition I offered in the last chapter: Contractions are best used in moderation. When your ear tells you that the rhythm of a sentence seems to require a contraction, go ahead and use it without apology. It's perfectly acceptable in a "General English" style. (In fact, it's hard to write in such a style *without* using occasional contractions.) But where a contraction is not required, it's best not to use one, for to do so is to risk overweighting your style with informality.

3. "Never refer to the reader as 'you'"

The alternatives, of course, are never to refer to him at all or else to refer to him as "the reader." The first alternative is frequently difficult and nearly always bad psychology, for it contributes to what critic Wayne Booth has termed the "pedant's stance." As he defines it, that stance

> consists of ignoring or underplaying the personal relationship of speaker and audience and depending entirely on statements about a subject—that is, the notion of a job to be done for a particular audience is left out. . . . The writer who assumes that it is enough merely to write an exposition of what he happens to know on the subject will produce the kind of essay that soils our scholarly journals, written not for readers but for bibliographies.

The second alternative is equally bad psychology because it's so utterly depersonalizing and stuffy. What reader wants to be addressed as "the reader"? It's akin to saying, in conversation, "I'm glad to hear the listener has recovered from her cold."

You can see that it's the old issue in another guise: Is naturalness unnatural, and is informality unacceptable? The first part of that question I trust answers itself; the second part of it is answered by daily experience. As Theodore Bernstein observed in his book on outmoded rules of English usage, *Miss Thistlebottom's Hobgoblins*, "Informality in all kinds of writing has been in the ascendancy in recent times and now the indefinite *you* is accepted and widely used." Mr. Bernstein ought to have known. He was not only *The New York Times*'s English-usage expert but also served in Paris as founding editor of the paper's international edition.

I only want to add to his remark the caution that while *you* is widely used, it can be overused. Just as some speakers wear out our ears with "you know" punctuating every sentence, so some writers push a close relationship upon us with the reiterated *you*. We instinctively pull back from such chumminess, regarding it as an unwanted bear hug. Moral: If you don't need to say *you*, don't. If you do need to, say it without embarrassment exactly as you would in conversation.

4. "Never use the first-person pronoun 'I'"

The alternatives recall those just described under Rule #3: Either you practice complete self-effacement and disappear from your prose, or else you attempt the closest thing to it, self-transcendence, in which case you elect to become either an objectification of yourself (*the present writer*) or something more than yourself (*we*). This rule, and the alternatives it allows, clearly assumes that the best expository prose is the most scrupulously impersonal. In theory, then, the best prose would come from a machine, which is precisely what many TOTELarians try to imitate. (Recall their Creed: ". . . and individuality is unpardonable.") Little wonder that their prose is so bloodless: all the life has been drained out of it.

But this is just the beginning of the rule's ludicrousness. Since what we write is presumably what we believe and feel, why pretend that it is scientifically detached Pure Thought, and that our words just dropped out of thin air onto paper? Moreover, the pretense itself is a piece of absurdity. It's akin to ducking behind a screen every time you say something in conversation so as to persuade your listeners that they are hearing merely some Voice, some disembodied Intelligence, speaking to them.

Common sense and honesty recommend simple forthrightness: We should feel free to acknowledge our convictions as *our* convictions. We need not be loud about it, of course—we don't wish to appear egocentric or too subjective in our viewpoints. And we needn't label every view as our own, for who else's will they be thought to be? But let us allow some of our personality, which means some of our "I," to come through in our style. Let us, in short, be ourselves.

All that being said, I'd still like to second the advice that Strunk and White offer in *The Elements of Style.* "Place yourself in the background," they say. Young writers especially need to hear that advice, because they'll often confuse a critical analysis with autobiography, and end up making themselves the co-subject of their essay. They'll write openers like this (I'm only slightly parodying here): "When I first read this work, I thought such-and-such. And I had a terrible time with it. But as I turned things over in my mind, it eventually dawned on me that. . . . And then I saw that. . . ." What reader wants a recital of the writer's reading process? And who cares about the problems that the writer had with it? Don't they go without saying?

I also admire screenwriter–director Nora Ephron's take on this issue. The following comes from her Preface to *Wallflower at the Orgy*, a collection of her wonderful magazine pieces:

Because I began as a newspaper reporter, it took me a long time to become comfortable using the first-person singular pronoun in my work. In the articles in this book I use it gingerly, often after considerable prodding from my editors. I was uncomfortable with it. The work I have done subsequently is considerably more personal and considerably more full of the first-person singular pronoun, but I still believe that the best approach to its use ought to be discomfort. Do you really need it? Does it add something special to the piece? Is what you think interesting enough to make the reader care? Are you saying something that no one has said? Above all, do you understand that you are not as important as what you're covering?

For closing advice, let me offer this: Reserve "I" for when you truly need it—either to emphasize that such-and-such is admittedly just a conjecture or personal prejudice, or to add some humanity to an otherwise dry account. The rest of the time, try to generalize objectively and more or less impersonally, as if you're pointing out what any intelligent person could see for himself. If your assertions are indeed intelligent and well supported, they won't need props like "it seems to me," "I think," "I feel," and "in my opinion."

5. "Never end a sentence with a preposition"

H. W. Fowler, the preeminent British authority on questions of usage, wrote a crushing rebuttal to this piece of nonsense in his acclaimed *Dictionary of Modern English Usage.* I will quote only his conclusions and leave you to read on your own the wealth of evidence he marshaled to support them:

> It is a cherished superstition that prepositions must, in spite of the incurable English instinct for putting them late . . . , be kept true to their name [preposition comes from a Latin word meaning "to place in front"] and placed before the word they govern. . . . Those who lay down the universal principle that final prepositions are "inelegant" are unconsciously trying to deprive the English language of a valuable idiomatic resource, which has been used freely by all our greatest writers except those whose instinct for English idiom has been overpowered by notions of correctness derived from Latin standards. The legitimacy of the prepositional ending in literary English must be uncompromisingly maintained; in respect of elegance or inelegance, every example must be judged not by any arbitrary rules, but on its own merits. . . .

Perhaps it was Sir Winston Churchill, though, even more than Fowler, who delivered what should have been the *coup de grâce* to this superstition. When the prime minister—a Nobel laureate in literature—found that an editor of his memoirs had had the cheek to "correct" one of his sentences ending in a preposition, he wrote back, "This is the kind of impertinence up with which I shall not put."

6. "Never split an infinitive"

I am reminded of a cartoon in *The New Yorker*. Satan is seated on his throne in Hell, silently glowering. Before him stands one of his lieutenants, obviously worried, asking uncertainly, "If everybody's doing it, is it still a sin?"

Splitting an infinitive (for example, saying "to fully cooperate" rather than "fully to cooperate" or "to cooperate fully") wasn't always deemed a sin, and it's not a recent phenomenon either. In fact, infinitives have been split repeatedly by reputable authors (Shakespeare among them) ever since the 14th century. But in the 18th and 19th centuries, a group of TOTELarian grammarians set about trying to "regularize" English grammar—that is, make it conform to quasi-laws—and among other things, they decreed that, as in Latin, infinitives should not be split by adverbs. The principle they invoked was that related words belong together. Since the infinitive form of a verb requires the preposition *to* plus the verb, these are logically related words—a unit of syntax, in other words.

All this, at first blush, seems rational enough. Unfortunately, not just grammarians use the language. People use it too, and people will do what they will do; and one thing most people instinctively will do is split infinitives. We have just heard Fowler speak of "the incurable English instinct" for putting prepositions at the end of sentences; here we have yet another instance of human intractability—or is it untutored wisdom again?

Most infinitive-splitters probably never think about it: they just do it. But if they tried to explain their practice, they'd likely advance three justifications. First, the split infinitive usually sounds better—that is, it has a more idiomatic rhythm to it, in part at least because we invariably hear infinitives split in common speech. Second, it allows the modifying adverb to be positioned where it will receive the most notice, which is directly ahead of the verb. (Example: "To really know her, you have to live with her." Third, since grammarians recommend that modifiers should come, if possible, next to the word they modify, the adverb has as much right to sit next to the verb as the preposition *to*—and perhaps more right, not only because it is the more weighty of the two words, but because it frequently changes the very sense of the verb. All three of these reasons strike me as commonsensical. There certainly must be something to them, for why else would so many people instinctively use the split construction?

As for my own practice, like most writers I go by ear and sense. When my ear tells me that a split construction sounds more natural, and when my sense assures me there's no ambiguity, I happily split the infinitive. If my ear tells me it's a toss-up, I don't split it because there's no pressing reason to. In general, though, I concur with the eminent grammarian George Curme, who argued in his book *Syntax*, "The split infinitive is an improvement of English expression." Any skeptic who takes the trouble to read Curme's massively documented, nine-page scholarly analysis of the issue will find it hard to dispute that conclusion.

7. "Never write a paragraph containing only a single sentence"

Generally this rule is sound. What makes it so offensive is the dogmatic "Never." Mr. Bernstein rightly says in *Miss Thistlebottom's Hobgoblins:* "One cannot be arbitrary about paragraphing. It is a means of grouping thoughts, but much more it is a visual device. Much depends on the subject, the typography, the purpose of what is being written, the readers to whom it is addressed, and the conditions under which they are likely to read it."

Take newspaper stories, for instance. The one-sentence paragraph is ideal for them. It simplifies the reporters' task of presenting their facts in descending importance; it enables a hurried reader to digest those facts quickly; it offsets the tedium created by narrow columns and small type; and so on.

Unfortunately, though, because we encounter the one-sentence paragraph most often in news stories, most of us are inclined to view it as a device best left to journalists. It's legitimate for them, we grant, but not quite respectable in so-called "serious" writing.

This view is prudish and misguided. Any number of reputable works prove it. One of them is Robert Selph Henry's *The Story of the Confederacy*, considered by many historians to rank among the indispensable studies of the American Civil War—a work, I might add, surely as distinguished for its elegant, vivid prose as for its brilliant scholarship. Mr. Henry, I note, uses 17 one-sentence paragraphs in the first two chapters alone. Indeed, he opens the book with two in quick succession:

> The Confederacy was a belated attempt to exercise the right of a state to withdraw from the United States of America.
> Because it was belated, because it opposed a mere right in the abstract to the concrete force of economics and the inevitable trend of history, because it was burdened with the defense of the anachronism of slavery, it failed.

Three situations in essay writing can occasion a one-sentence paragraph: (1) when you want to emphasize a crucial point that might otherwise be buried; (2) when you want to dramatize a transition from one stage in your argument to the next; and (3) when instinct tells you that your reader is tiring and would appreciate a mental rest.

The one-sentence paragraph is a great device. You can italicize with it, vary your pace with it, lighten your voice with it, signpost your argument with it. But it's potentially dangerous. Don't overdo your dramatics. And be sure your sentence is strong enough to withstand the extra attention it's bound to receive when set off by itself. Houseplants wilt in direct sun. Many sentences do as well.

Closing Thoughts

Just how entrenched are these superstitions? I began finding out in the 1970s. As a fledgling assistant professor then, and as new to Texas as I was to teaching, I was eager to learn just who and what I might be dealing with in the Lone Star State. So for three years running, at the start of each semester I would take a few minutes to informally ask my classes about their previous experience with English courses. Among other questions, I soon learned to slip in one about stylistic taboos. "Did you by any chance have any no-no's drilled into you in high school?" I'd ask innocently, then add with a smile, "I just want to know if we're all on the same page here," still giving them not a hint as to what that page might be. Well! No matter whether they were freshmen, seniors, or graduate students, I kept hearing the same seven no-no's—*and from nearly everyone in every class.* And nearly everyone still absolutely subscribed to them—in fact, they seemed scandalized when I announced my own position on them. They thought I was some Berkeley heretic who had broken ranks with the English Teachers' Union. It proved quite a demonstration of something that John Dewey, the pioneering educational theorist, wrote in his classic *Experience and Education* (1938): "He is lucky who does not find that in order to make progress, in order to go ahead intellectually, he does not have to unlearn much of what he learned in school."

Over time, though, I came to realize how easy it was for them to hold onto these notions. They had, after all, been taught them at an impressionable age—and by teachers seemingly packing lots of authority. Also, while their general reading, especially in college, gave them myriad examples of superb professional writers blithely ignoring these same "inviolable rules," they, like most readers, would unconsciously allow themselves to gloss over inconvenient evidence, so it was actually hard for them to put the taboos to a pragmatic test. But there was one other reason, perhaps even more compelling, for their clinging to them: The very *naturalness* of a style that breaks these taboos makes it unlikely for the taboo-breaking to draw any attention to itself. Everything feels right, smooth, and assured—which of course is exactly why professionals break the taboos so blithely. They want to achieve an *intelligently conversational* style. They want to sound *at ease*—with themselves, with their subject, and with their reader. And they know that we, too, want them to sound at ease with all three of those things.

So professional writers, unlike rank-and-file writers, give themselves permission to sound at ease on the page, making it seem as if writing were as simple and as natural as talking. In fact, *talkableness* is one of their prime criteria of a good style.

When you put their prose to the sternest test—when you try reading whole paragraphs of it aloud—you hear true, colloquial speech rhythms in it, with all the right pauses, elisions, and emphases in all the right places. Judge Jerome Frank was spot-on when he said: "The basic appeal of the language is to the ear. Good writing is speech heightened in tone and polished in form."

That is why I find myself urging students and editing clients alike, "**If you wouldn't say it, don't write it.**" Also, "**Don't write any sentence you can't speak easily.**"

Those two cautions, I submit, need to be burned into every writer's brain. Heeding them will make a world of difference in the readability of your prose.

9

Critical Analysis:
Jousting with Mencken

*If I am a writer today, it is because my betters tugged and
teased and bullied and seduced me into learning a craft,
when all I had to begin with, like so many hundreds of others, was a talent. So I did learn; I go on learning.*

—Brendan Gill, *Here at* The New Yorker

*Anybody who learns how to write learns how by doing it
very intensively and also by being a reader and sort of at-
tentive to styles.*

—Peter Goldman, former *Newsweek* senior editor

"If you could write lucidly, simply, euphoniously and yet with liveli-
ness," novelist Somerset Maugham once proclaimed, "you would
write perfectly: you would write like Voltaire."

Other scribes have made similarly high claims for H. L. Mencken
(1880–1956). Perfect he wasn't, God knows; some of his prejudices make
today's world cringe. But few writers have proved so consistently witty,
audacious, or trenchant.

Although he was a Renaissance man of American letters, winning
distinction as a journalist, critic, philologist, and editor, Mencken won
greatest note as a debunker and stylist extraordinaire. Indeed, some rank
him America's premier stylist of the 20th century. The wittiest, too. So
he's clearly worth our attention.

Let's try submitting a bit of his writing to a critical analysis.

For this occasion, I'm choosing "Literature and the Schoolma'm," a
short polemic merrily trashing both writing teachers and their students.
Mencken published it back in 1926 in a volume he aptly titled *Prejudices*,

Fifth Series. It was one of six volumes by that same main title that he cranked out between 1919 and 1927, each a collection of essays he had originally written for one of the two monthly literary journals he successively edited: *The Smart Set* and *The American Mercury.*

I love this sassy little pop-off, and for nearly three decades I made it a staple in my Advanced Expository Writing seminar, English 325M, at the University of Texas. In fact, I built the sixth week's writing assignment around it. That assignment, a free-wheeler, merely asked for "something at least tangentially related" to Mencken's essay—and it could take "any form you please." I was always curious to see what form it *would* take. I knew Mencken would initially make my students squirm. Here was a famous author telling them, with enormous confidence and panache, that in all likelihood their writing teacher was a fraud, that his little handbook on style deserved the heave-ho, that they themselves would always write mediocre stuff because, unlike real writers, they lacked the brains to think clearly, and that maybe they ought to resign themselves to becoming Ph.D.'s like their mentor and find a career writing textbook nonsense themselves.

So why was I assigning such a heretical essay? Lots of reasons. It was provocative. It was hilarious. It was fearless. It was intellectually challenging—a seductive mix of truths, half-truths, and fallacies. It was proof that *everyone* can use an editor. It was an object lesson in word power. It was also an object lesson in the perils of single-draft prose. On top of all that, I felt that Mencken's stylistic example—outlandish, irrepressible, risk-taking—plus his taunting might provoke some shyer students to really speak out for a change, to take their own writer's voice a little further, and to find fresh ways of making writing as much fun for themselves as it obviously had been for Mencken. So this was both a loosening-up assignment and a toughening-up one. And each writer had a chance to make it his or her own. What a week it would be!

Let's have a look at this notorious essay—a long, eager-but-wary look, the kind you give a dazzling new date who may spell big trouble ahead.

LITERATURE AND THE SCHOOLMA'M

*H. L. Mencken**

With precious few exceptions, all the books on style in English are by writers quite unable to write. The subject, indeed, seems to exercise a special and dreadful

---

*From PREJUDICES: FIFTH SERIES by H. L. Mencken, copyright 1926 by Alfred A. Knopf, a division of Random House, Inc. and renewed 1954 by H. L. Mencken. Used by permission of Alfred A. Knopf, a division of Random House, Inc.

fascination over schoolma'ms, bucolic college professors, and other such pseudo-literates. One never hears of treatises on it by George Moore or James Branch Cabell, but the pedagogues, male and female, are at it all the time. In a thousand texts they set forth their depressing ideas about it, and millions of suffering high-school pupils have to study what they say. Their central aim, of course, is to reduce the whole thing to a series of simple rules—the overmastering passion of their melancholy order, at all times and everywhere. They aspire to teach it as bridge whist, the American Legion flag-drill and double-entry bookkeeping are taught. They fail as ignominiously as that Athenian of legend who essayed to train a regiment of grasshoppers in the goose-step.

For the essence of a sound style is that it cannot be reduced to rules—that it is a living and breathing thing, with something of the devilish in it—that it fits its proprietor tightly and yet ever so loosely, as his skin fits him. It is, in fact, quite as securely an integral part of him as that skin is. It hardens as his arteries harden. It has Katzenjammer on the days succeeding his indiscretions. It is gaudy when he is young and gathers decorum when he grows old. On the day after he makes a mash on a new girl it glows and glitters. If he has fed well, it is mellow. If he has gastritis it is bitter. In brief, a style is always the outward and visible symbol of a man, and it cannot be anything else. To attempt to teach it is as silly as to set up courses in making love. The man who makes love out of a book is not making love at all; he is simply imitating someone else making love. God help him if, in love or literary composition, his preceptor be a pedagogue!

The schoolma'm theory that the writing of English may be taught is based upon a faulty inference from a sound observation. The sound observation is that the great majority of American high-school pupils, when they attempt to put their thoughts upon paper, produce only a mass of confused and puerile nonsense—that they express themselves so clumsily that it is often quite impossible to understand them at all. The faulty inference is to the effect that what ails them is a defective technical equipment—that they can be trained to write clearly as a dog may be trained to walk on its hind legs. This is all wrong. What ails them is not a defective technical equipment but a defective natural equipment. They write badly simply because they cannot think clearly. They cannot think clearly because they lack the brains. Trying to teach them is as hopeless as trying to teach a dog with only one hind leg. Any human being who can speak English understandably has all the materials necessary to write English clearly, and even beautifully. There is nothing mysterious about the written language; it is precisely the same, in essence, as the spoken language. If a man can think in English at all, he can find words enough to express his ideas. The fact is proved abundantly by the excellent writing that often comes from so-called ignorant men. It is proved anew by the even better writing that is done on higher levels by persons of great simplicity, for example, Abraham Lincoln. Such writing commonly arouses little enthusiasm among pedagogues. Its transparency excites their professional disdain, and they are offended by its use of homely words and phrases. They prefer something more ornate and complex—something, as they would probably put it, demanding more thought. But the thought they yearn for is the kind, alas, that they secrete themselves—the muddled, highfalutin, vapid thought that one finds in their own text-books.

I do not denounce them because they write so badly; I merely record the fact in a sad, scientific spirit. Even in such twilight regions of the intellect the style remains the man. What is in the head infallibly oozes out of the nub of the pen. If it is sparkling Burgundy the writing is full of life and charm. If it is mush the writing is mush too. The late Dr. Harding, twenty-ninth President of the Federal Union, was a highly self-conscious stylist. He practiced prose composition assiduously, and was regarded by the pedagogues of Marion, Ohio, and vicinity as a very talented fellow. But when he sent a message to Congress it was so muddled in style that even the late Henry Cabot Lodge, a professional literary man, could not understand it. Why? Simply because Dr. Harding's thoughts, on the high and grave subjects he discussed, were so muddled that he couldn't understand them himself. But on matters within his range of customary meditation he was clear and even charming, as all of us are. I once heard him deliver a brief address upon the ideals of the Elks. It was a topic close to his heart, and he had thought about it at length and con amore. The result was an excellent speech—clear, logical, forceful, and with a touch of wild, romantic beauty. His sentences hung together. He employed simple words, and put them together with skill. But when, at a public meeting in Washington, he essayed to deliver an oration on the subject of the late Dante Alighieri, he quickly became so obscure and absurd that even the Diplomatic Corps began to snicker. The cause was plain: he knew no more about Dante than a Tennessee county judge knows about the Institutes of Justinian. Trying to formulate ideas upon the topic, he could get together only a few disjected fragments and ghosts of ideas—here an ear, there a section of tibia, beyond a puff of soul substance or other gas. The resultant speech was thus enigmatical, cacophonous, and awful stuff. It sounded precisely like a lecture by a college professor on style.

A pedagogue, confronted by Dr. Harding in class, would have set him to the business of what is called improving his vocabulary—that is, to the business of making his writing even worse than it was. Dr. Harding, in point of fact, had all the vocabulary that he needed, and a great deal more. Any idea that he could formulate clearly he could convey clearly. Any idea that genuinely moved him he could invest with charm—which is to say, with what the pedagogues call style. I believe that this capacity is possessed by all literate persons above the age of fourteen. It is not acquired by studying text-books; it is acquired by learning how to think. Children even younger often show it. I have a niece, now eleven years old, who already has an excellent style. When she writes to me about things that interest her—in other words, about the things she is capable of thinking about—she puts her thoughts into clear, dignified and admirable English. Her vocabulary, so far, is unspoiled by schoolma'ms. She doesn't try to knock me out by bombarding me with hard words, and phrases filched from Addison. She is unaffected, and hence her writing is charming. But if she essayed to send me a communication on the subject, say, of Balkan politics or government ownership, her style would descend instantly to the level of that of Dr. Harding's state papers.

To sum up, style cannot go beyond the ideas which lie at the heart of it. If they are clear, it too will be clear. If they are held passionately, it will be eloquent. Trying to teach it to persons who cannot think, especially when the business is attempted by persons who also cannot think, is a great waste of time, and an immoral imposition upon the taxpayers of the nation. It would be far more logical to devote all the energy to teaching, not writing, but logic—and probably just as useless. For I doubt that the art of thinking can be taught at all—at any rate, by school-teachers. It is not acquired, but congenital. Some persons are born with it. Their ideas flow in straight channels; they are capable of lucid reasoning; when they say anything it is instantly understandable; when they write anything it is clear and persuasive. They constitute, I should say, about one-eighth of one per cent. of the human race. The rest of God's children are just as incapable of logical thought as they are incapable of jumping over the moon. Trying to teach them to think is as vain an enterprise as trying to teach a streptococcus the principles of Americanism. The only thing to do with them is to make Ph.D.'s of them, and set them to writing handbooks on style.

Well! As you can see, Mencken is an equal-opportunity satirist, convicting both writing teachers and their students (not to mention 99.88% of "the rest of God's children"). Because he doesn't allow either party to enjoy a sense of martyrdom at the other's expense, the reader must determine whether he is fair or unfair in his characterization of *both* groups, not just one. Happily for those of us wanting to strengthen our critical-thinking skills, this alone is a big assist, for it keeps us from succumbing to a comfortably simplistic Good Guys vs. Bad Guys mode of thinking. That alone is an excellent reason to spend time with Mencken.

If we hope to read him smartly, we must be prepared to think through his every assertion, which, Mencken being Mencken, means grappling with a new argument virtually every sentence. With each, we must ask: Does this claim, on its face, really ring true? Does he support it convincingly, or does he merely assert it and expect us to accept his say-so? (*I'm H. L. Mencken, so you'd better believe me.*) Does what he say here in paragraph three jibe with what he says over there in paragraph five? Does he define his terms wherever they really need defining, or does he expect words to mean whatever suits his convenience? For example, in his opening sentence he claims that most books on style "are by writers quite unable to write." What does he mean there by "write"? Surely he's not saying that these Ph.D.'s are clueless about grammar, spelling, sentence construction, etc. So what *is* he saying? Can we afford to give him a pass there? Can we say, "I accept glibness if it's witty enough"?

To alert my students to such issues, I provided them with various tips, cautions, and resources—body armor for a good joust.

For example, I gave them a short handout explaining the most common logical fallacies, for how could they be expected to spot what they didn't know existed, or describe what they lacked terms for?

I urged them to look up every exotic word in a good dictionary; also, to resist assuming that just because Mencken uses some words *they've* never heard before, they can hang him for first-degree pedantry. It may be more a comment on them than on him, and he also may have been using some of those biggies for comic or sonorous effect.

I urged them to read a bunch of other things by Mencken so as to get a surer sense of the man—his style, his brand of humor, his habitual grumps and preoccupations, his strengths and weaknesses.

I recommended they review George Orwell's short essay "Politics and the English Language," perhaps the most famous article on style ever written. Published in 1946, just two decades after "Schoolma'm," it shows us someone attempting what Mencken assures us is impossible, so it bears study.

I urged them to take some time to crystallize their *own* notions about the teaching (and learning) of writing. Since Mencken argues that neither style nor thinking can be taught, they might consider what, if anything, they'd learned in 325M the previous few weeks—from class discussions, from writing their papers, from reading the many readings, from editing their classmates' essays, and from wincing over all our marginal and interlinear edits. (In this seminar, everyone had to read, and carefully edit, copies of the whole class's weekly 4-page papers, plus of course writing their own. A student once joked that the "M" in 325M stood for "Masochism.") From all this brainsweat, had their style improved? Their editing? Their reading skills? Their thinking? If so, how?

I recommended that they remember that Mencken wrote this polemic back in 1926. Part of our task as fair-minded readers would surely be to weigh the relevance of that fact. For example, just how bad *were* most of the writing texts and English teachers of that period?

I urged them to treat "Schoolma'm" exactly as if it were just another classmate's 325M paper. Don't be awed, I told them; be genially skeptical. When testing Mencken's claims, consider counter-hypotheses. For example, he claims that American high-school kids produce "confused and puerile nonsense" because "they lack the brains." Assuming high-school prose really is that bad, could they come up with three or four better explanations, maybe some rooted in their own experience in comp classes? Similarly, he discounts "technical equipment." What does that term actually cover, and do they agree with him?

Finally, I told them:

As you scrutinize "Schoolma'm," you may discover that, for all its panache and cocksure polemics, it sacrifices accuracy for power. In fact, you may find it contains some familiar 325M-style logic—internal contradictions, non sequiturs, begged questions, etc. Mencken was only human, after all, and he probably fired off the piece in one draft, as he did most of his prose. At any rate, such glitches need noting, and weak arguments warrant careful rebuttal. But you should also weigh the argument as a whole, as we presumably want our own to be weighed. Syndicated columnist James Kilpatrick once wrote, "That was Mencken—extravagant, intrepid, full of wild humor and large hyperbole, but he has a way of passing from the sands of human affairs the nugget truth." Do you spot any nuggets in this essay, even if they're only half-truths?

So with that I turned them loose . . .

And what did I get in return? Let me open my files and treat you, first, to four of the many glorious openers I have stored there. In each case, the student had taken to heart yet another piece of advice I had offered: "Try penning an opener that gets right down to cases. Please, no stroll through the tulips. Just give us a simple, direct statement of your convictions—something like Mencken's own opening graf. Be brave like him. Jump right in." And so they did, and here's what their brave jumps looked like:

Can writing be taught? No, declares Mencken. Clear writing requires clear thinking. Clear thinking necessitates brains. Brains are inherited, not acquired. And only one-eighth of one percent of the human race inherits brains. But does clear writing require clear thinking? Clearly not. Ironically, Mencken's own essay is a paradigm of clarity but a cauldron of muddled ideas.

Without a doubt, he is the most infuriating writer ever to assault my thinking. He is arrogant, unfair, and closed-minded. He stretches the truth and invents "facts." He thoughtlessly dismisses his critics as too stupid to recognize his intellectual superiority. Worst of all, he manages to get away with all this. How does Mencken do it? For one thing, even when he's saying rubbish, he says it beautifully. His prose immediately engages—then charms—the reader because it is direct and simple, yet never boring. And he is never short on ideas. You may think that what he is saying is asinine, but you can't deny that he is saying something. One thing you'll never get from Mencken is empty drivel. But beyond this, Mencken can usually get away with excesses because he is usually right. That is, his main argument is usually right on target, even if some of his particulars are a little iffy. Seemingly he is never sidetracked, but sees right through the muck to the crucial issue, the heart of the matter, the bottom line. Who has ever used Hemingway's "built-in, shock-proof shit-detector" with more accuracy than Mencken?

When H. L. Mencken chose to include "Literature and the School-ma'm" in *Prejudices: Fifth Series*, at least he was honest. His beautifully written but irrational essay can best be described as an illogical exercise in intolerance. Not that Mencken would have clamored to deny this accusation. He once admitted: "I believe that a good phrase is better than a Great Truth," and "My prejudices are innumerable and often idiotic." But considering his purpose—convincing us that good writing and logic are inseparable, cannot be learned, and cannot be taught by inept schoolma'ms anyway—his own style, lack of reasoning, and writing background seriously weaken his thesis.

H. L. Mencken's "Literature and the Schoolma'm" is a hoot; I grin at his exaggerations, his crazy comparisons, his biting humor. From the first sentence to the last, the essay is a rollicking good read. But the old curmudgeon makes three statements that simply don't make sense. First, he claims that writing can't be taught. Second, he claims style is as much a part of a writer as his skin, and "to attempt to teach it is . . . silly." Third, he claims that people write poorly because they have no brains. All this is just nonsense. But his outlandish statements and my firm dissents are academic because what Mencken really wants to do here is to skewer dullards.

Wouldn't you enjoy following each of these charmers to their triumphant finale?

In a moment I want to share with you a complete short paper on "Schoolma'm"—a classmate's essay quite different in tone and emphases from the four abridged ones we've just sampled but no less fun, no less effective. I'll do this to show you that there are always *lots* of ways to skin the cat, and part of our perpetual challenge as writers is to find a way—more often, *create* a way—that exploits our own talents and individual interests.[1] Not everyone, for example, plans a career in law, as three of the four students just quoted did, so not everyone is going to jump at the

---

[1]Stephen Shadley, one of America's top interior designers, said it memorably: "You learn that there are a jillion different solutions to every problem." —*Architectural Digest*, Sept. 2001, p. 100.

chance to play litigator with Mencken and expose his every misstep as a logician. But as a former pre-law student myself, and now as a writer and editor—and, let's be honest, also as a pedagogue with his honor to defend!—I, too, would probably play the litigator if I were facing the same writing assignment. That's not to say that I wouldn't find plenty to praise in "Schoolma'm," but my chief focus would be on the major flaws, as I see them, in Mencken's argument.

Should you be curious, these are the key points I'd want to make:

1. Mencken fails to connect bad student writing with the very teaching he repeatedly lambastes. If, as he claims, the pedagogues really are pseudo-literate quacks, and if the "suffering" students are daily victims of their incompetence, isn't it safe to assume that poor student prose stems at least in part from poor teaching?

2. He fails to apply to students the very lessons he draws from his two case studies. Both Harding and his niece write ably on topics they're interested in and knowledgeable about; and both write ineptly on topics they're not interested in and know little about. That being so, why assume that students are any less human? Perhaps their writing assignments inspire apathy. Perhaps, too, those assignments often ask them to discuss subjects outside their "range of customary meditation."

3. He contends that the art of thinking is "not acquired, but congenital"; hence, it can't be taught. This argument overlooks several ways in which one can, in fact, learn to think more logically. Here are a few:

- Study varieties of bad thinking (non sequiturs, rash generalizations, begged questions, false analogies, etc.) so that you can then guard against them yourself.
- Learn that unsupported assertions are just claims. They don't constitute proof.
- Learn to link each sentence to the ones before and after it so that you achieve a clean narrative line.
- Accept the importance of having a thesis—more, a thesis that's unambiguously stated, ideally in just one sentence, and emphatically positioned—so both you and your reader will know the main point you're trying to argue.
- Learn the difference between a fact and an opinion, and between fair sampling and unfair sampling (i.e., convincing examples and unconvincing examples).
- Learn to anticipate and ward off your reader's probable confusions.

If writers can teach themselves such things, as many do, why can't they also learn them from able teachers?

4. He claims that style is as uncontrollable as one's mood; he also claims that style, being a reflection of one's mind and personality, can't be taught.

Actually, style is simply how one expresses oneself on paper—i.e., how one presents oneself and one's ideas. Daily experience proves that self-presentation can be controlled. It can also be taught. If a teacher impresses upon her students the importance of simplicity, directness, and honesty, their style will begin reflecting those values. If she teaches them to avoid wordiness, fuzziness, and dullness by tightening, sharpening, and brightening, their style will promptly appear more intelligent. If she encourages them to use occasional contractions, fragments, and first-person pronouns, their style will appear more conversational and natural. If she encourages them to become fanatical about their bridges between paragraphs, their style will appear more flowing. If she encourages them to use short, punchy diction rather than abstract biggies, their prose will appear more vibrant. And so on. Granted, our style does reflect our personality and settled habits of mind, but it can be radically modified in the ways just explained. Consider this comment by Mencken himself in his essay "The Poet and His Art":

> The early prose of Abraham Lincoln was remarkable only for its badness; it was rhetorical and bombastic, and full of supernumerary words. It took years and years of hard work for Abe to develop the simple and exquisite prose of his last half-decade.

5. He contends that "style cannot go beyond the ideas which lie at the heart of it." Generally true, yes. But Mencken's own style transcends the ideas in this piece. His style appears clear even though his ideas are contradictory; his style appears fresh even though his ideas, while provocatively stated, are often quite commonplace or naive (e.g., you can't teach writing; the style is the man; people who don't write clearly just lack the brains; passionately held ideas will invariably be expressed eloquently, etc.).

6. He contends that it's silly to teach lovemaking out of a book. Maybe he was born too soon. The many millions of people who have bought sex manuals like Alex Comfort's pioneering *The Joy of Sex* (1972) would roundly disagree, as would those who have taken a university course in Human Sexuality or who have made Dr. Ruth a household name. We aren't born with a knowledge of sexual anatomy, the varieties of sexual technique, the gender differences in sexual response, and so on, and what's really silly is to think that we are.

7. He fails to distinguish between "style" and "writing." The latter is in fact governed by many rules, and necessarily so. To write competently, one must know the conventions ("rules") of grammar, spelling, punctuation, and usage. If, for example, you're guilty of dangling participles and squinting modifiers and run-on sentences and misused idioms, you'll end up writing "confused and puerile nonsense" even if your ideas themselves are sound. English teachers are right, therefore, to teach such things; and when they fail to, writers discover they must learn them on their own, just as Mencken himself did. "Style," on the other hand, being the personality of one's prose, is far less susceptible to rules, but it can be significantly modified, as explained above. Also, such "rules" as Orwell provides are probably ones that Mencken himself would warmly endorse.

8. He fails to distinguish adequately between speech and writing. "There is nothing mysterious about the written language," he says; "it is precisely the same, in essence, as the spoken language." The words "precisely" and "in essence" contradict each other, but even more to the point is Mencken's oversight about the crucial differences between talking and writing. When talking, our audience is directly before us and, normally, continuously responsive, whereas when writing, our audience is imagined. That enormous disadvantage obliges us to (a) create the entire context of our thoughts with no outside help, (b) build in all the necessary cues to convey our intended tone and emphases, (c) think linearly and unambiguously, and (d) master the conventions of edited American English (correct grammar, punctuation, spelling, and so forth).

9. Mencken says of Harding, "He employed simple words, and put them together with skill." That last phrase implies craft. Can't craft be taught? If we can teach ourselves, can't we in turn teach others? Isn't editing a form of craft? Doesn't recursive editing make the difference between a lousy first draft and a polished final draft, and can't principles of editing be taught?

10. Finally, to bring it all home, I'd want to offer my rationale for putting the class, and myself, through such a tough assignment:

> One of our big challenges in life is to practice a healthy skepticism—to be always thinking, "Well, does that square with my common sense? With my own experience? With what other alleged authorities also say?" We can't consider ourselves truly "college-educated" until we've learned to think for ourselves and independently test every claim we're exposed to. This is what "critical thinking" is all about. Somehow, we have to practice two kinds of listening simultaneously: we must keep our minds open to new and challenging ideas, but we must also listen to those ideas critically, thoughtfully, knowing that some of them may turn out to be hogwash.

Let's now look at the complete essay I promised you. It's by Jolene Shirley, then a major in geology. Wanting to try a more imaginative approach, you'll see she creates a little story involving a writing teacher and a befuddled student. The point? To show how a capable teacher can bring along even the most seemingly hopeless writer. Jolene takes advantage of this scenario to introduce all manner of writing tips that she herself had acquired in 325M during the preceding five weeks, proving that she had paid close attention and could now be an evangelist for those same tips. I found myself stunned at how many of them she managed to work in—and effortlessly, too. Here's her delightful, encouraging essay. It makes for a terrific rebuttal to Mencken.

CAN WRITING BE TAUGHT?

Jolene Shirley

Can writing be taught? Yes. Does that mean all students will become Mencken-caliber stylists? No. Great style, as Mencken said, has "something of the devilish in it." That something can't be taught; it's talent. But grammar, spelling, a way of organizing your thoughts, the need for conciseness, clarity, and vividness—all these things can be taught.

Let's say you're a teacher. One of your students has just turned in a piece of "puerile nonsense." Do you write it off as bad genes? Stupidity? A hopeless case? Maybe you would if you were Mencken. But you're better than Mencken. You take the student aside and say, "This paper really needs some work."

The first problem with the paper is that it doesn't make sense; it contradicts itself. You can tell the author was unsure of what she wanted to say. You ask her some probing questions: What you said here in your opening sentence, is this what you really believe? Or do you really believe what you said here, in graf four? You tell the student that she needs to think about the subject more, do a little more research. Maybe try making an outline. You tell her that every sentence should support her thesis. And that she really does need to *have* a thesis.

She goes home, kicks back with a Shiner, and thinks some more about what she really wanted to say. She does some more research. She ruminates. She pinpoints exactly what she wants to say.

A thesis is born.

She writes different supporting ideas on slips of paper and mixes and matches them into some coherent order. She writes it all out in a second draft.

This draft is better, but it has a long way to go. It now makes sense, but it is wordy and vague. You tell her to get to the point more quickly, to remember that the reader is busy and wants to get the goods and get them now. You tell the student to get rid of her verb phrases, put things in active voice, avoid being redundant.

She goes home. She murders her darlings. (She did it in Word with the delete button.) She tightens her sentences, challenges every adjective and adverb, makes sure they don't make her prose seem busy. She also makes sure she uses -*ion* nouns only as a last resort. All other things being equal, she uses shorter words instead of longer words. She checks for redundancies. She gets rid of everything superfluous. She begins to develop her own internal editor, one that perks up every time it reads a verb phrase. "Is there a simpler way to say that?" it demands. "Could I use fewer words to express that idea?" She comes back to you with a paper so streamlined it wouldn't cause an eddy in a wind tunnel.

Now you get down to the more nitpicky stuff. You explain the difference between "effect" and "affect." You tell her the difference between "its" and "it's." You tell her to run the paper through the spell checker—again. You teach her how to make parenthetical documentation correctly. You explain the myriad possible misuses of "only." You teach her about semicolons and colons: when to use what and where. You tell her the comma rules, especially the one about separating the two parts of a compound sentence. You give her a short lecture on why she'd be smart to use the serial comma. You explain, "The closing punctuation, whenever it's a period or a comma, always goes *inside* the quotation marks."

She goes home and sets to combing through her paper for spelling, punctuation, and usage errors.

The third draft is much better. But the style remains blah. Merely adequate. In soft focus. You send her home again with instructions to study each word, make each one as specific as possible. You tell her to add more details, give more examples. And the paragraphs—they're all the same length. The eye gets bored looking at the print. You tell her to try an occasional one-sentence graf. You tell her to put in some anecdotes, some quotes, some analogies. Use dashes more freely. Maybe a sentence fragment . . .

She takes the North Riverside bus home to her cozy one-bedroom apartment, trudges up the 13 stairs to her triple-bolted, pastel-painted steel door, and hunkers down to her ancient laptop. She takes out all the vague phrases and replaces them with detailed examples. She uses precise words. Now, instead of saying, "She got in the car," she says, "She slid into the cherry red Camaro her Daddy bought her." And her brother wasn't just riding in the back, "He was folded up in the back seat like a put-away lawn chair."

After all this trial and error, the paper is finally presentable. It's tight, it's bright, it's sharp. By her teacher's having pointed out all these tricks of the trade, the student now has the blueprint and the tools she needs to build good prose. So, yes, writing *can* be taught. And the next time she writes a paper, she will be able to follow this blueprint to build another good paper. Even better, each time she writes, her internal editor will get more and more proficient and her style will likewise improve in kind.

10

Dramatizing Your Ideas

My first newspaper city editor gave me a piece of advice that I have always remembered: "When you write a page of copy, kid," he said, "take it out of your typewriter and read it over. If any part of it bores you, then God only knows it's going to bore the reader."

—Tommy Thompson, author of *Blood and Money*

Being, like all those who have worked in Hollywood, somewhat of a connoisseur of the damp fart, I place Mr. [Edmund] Wilson high on the list. His careful and pedestrian and sometimes rather intelligent book reviews misguide one into thinking there is something in his head besides mucilage. There isn't.

—Raymond Chandler, author of *Farewell, My Lovely* and *The Big Sleep*

If you survived that high-school initiation rite known as the "Five-Paragraph Theme," you probably learned to view form rather mechanically, as a rigid organizing structure into which you dutifully slotted your ideas.

But for pros and accomplished amateurs alike, form is happily a good deal more creative. They've learned to think of it as *artful presentation*. Thus understood, it actually can involve just about everything on the page: punctuation, layout, word choice, phrasing, sentence structure, paragraphing, plotline—even the content itself, which can be significantly reshaped in myriad ways, one being by tough-love cutting. (Pros call it "murdering your darlings.") All these elements, it turns out, carry rhetorical potential. That is, they can help create desired effects in the reader. And what is the chief such effect? For me, and probably for you as well, it's *pleasure*. No one voluntarily reads for long without pleasure. But no one writes for long without it, either. So achieving artful presentation proves as important to writers as to readers.

One pro who thought a lot about artful presentation was Barbara Tuchman, two-time winner of the Pulitzer Prize for General Nonfiction and, until her death in 1989, the country's premier popular historian.

Her book *Practicing History* opens with an amusing account of how, years before, she'd botched her maiden attempt at history writing—her undergraduate honors thesis at Radcliffe. "The experience was terrible," she recalls, "because I could not make the piece sound, or rather read, the way I wanted it to. The writing fell so far short of the ideas. . . . I finished it, dissatisfied. So was the department: 'Style undistinguished,' it noted."

Translation: You bored us.

But being a plucky 20-year-old, she refused to quit writing. Instead, she boldly chose journalism as a career, thinking it would give her useful training. It did. Eventually feeling more secure as a writer, she bade farewell to journalism and resumed "practicing history" in earnest.

Six bestsellers and umpteen honors later, she explained in *Practicing History* what she learned and how she learned it. Two excerpts must suffice here. Each time she says "history," I suggest you substitute your own discipline and you'll instantly see the relevance:

- To write history so as to enthrall the reader and make the subject as captivating and exciting to him as it is to me has been my goal since that initial failure with my thesis. A prerequisite . . . is to be enthralled one's self and to feel a compulsion to communicate the magic. Communicate to whom? We arrive now at the reader, a person whom I keep constantly in mind. Catherine Drinker Bowen has said that she writes her books with a sign pinned up over her desk asking, "Will the reader turn the page?"

- The writer of history, I believe, has a number of duties *vis-à-vis* the reader, if he wants to keep him reading. The first is to distill. He must do the preliminary work for the reader, assemble the information, make sense of it, select the essential, discard the irrelevant—above all, discard the irrelevant—and put the rest together so that it forms a developing dramatic narrative.

You can see, then, her major epiphany: *Be kind to your readers.* They need all the help they can get—to get interested, to stay interested, to follow the arguments, to grant their validity. In truth, they'll not only need it, they'll insist on it. If she bores or confuses them, even for a paragraph, especially at the beginning, they'll ditch her without ceremony. All this she intends to accept soberly, as a fact of life. But while chilling, it also poses a seductive challenge to her ego and to her growing skill as a writer. No longer will she let herself be a mere chronicler, writing chiefly for herself. She will become a *dramatist of ideas*. She will aspire to somehow make each thought feel fresh and arresting. She will try to stage her key points for maximum drama, lest they get lost in the welter of detail. And she will work to orchestrate their sequence so seamlessly that the reader feels swept along.[1]

At chapter's end, I'll share with you a short student essay that does all that. But to get you properly primed, let me first flesh out this notion of "artful presentation" and offer some tips for you to try out in your future writing.

Artful presentation boils down to three things.

1. Attractive Formatting

At the purely visual level, it involves *attractive formatting*, or eye-appeal. Dr. Johnson, the great 18th-century critic, once famously declared that "all pleasure consists in variety." If true, it will pay us to vary what we can most readily vary—our word length, sentence length, and paragraph length. And not just a little, but a lot.

This would seem easy, but if you're one of those people stuck in the Five-Paragraph Theme mindset, it's a bear. You spent several years learning to produce the approved paragraph, with its main point and three supporting examples, so naturally you'll feel uneasy now delivering anything less. It will neither look nor feel "correct," which was doubtless the chief criterion of success in at least one of your former classrooms. But you're not there any longer, and you surely want to feel emancipated from all that, so I urge you to begin monitoring the paragraphing practice of professional writers. Also their sentence length. Also their word length. Not only watch what they do, especially with respect to variety, but, equally important, *monitor how their stylistic choices make you feel*. I think you can assume that if something gives you pleasure, doing the same thing will give your own readers pleasure, too.

You might start right here—say, with the opening seven paragraphs of the present chapter—since they let you sample the practice of both Tuchman and Trimble. I don't pretend to be in her league, but I try to practice her habits, so at least in the stylistic areas you'll now be assessing, maybe she and I aren't so different.

Note that three of the first seven paragraphs consist of *just a single sentence*. Good or bad?

---

[1]And that's exactly how one Amazon.com customer felt when reading Tuchman's *The Guns of August*, which recounts the outbreak of World War I. "Ordinarily I can only read about 75 pages at a time before I start to lose interest and need a break," the customer wrote. "This book I began one morning and didn't put it down until I finished it. Tuchman kept my interest throughout, and at times, though I knew the outcome, I found myself sitting at the edge of my chair wondering what would happen next. Even some of the best novels do not have this kind of power."

Now check out the sentence length. Perhaps hunt first for the shortest sentences. Taking them in order of appearance, one turns out to be 6 words long; another, 7; another, 4; another, also 4; and another—my goodness, just 2! Good or bad?

What about the average words per sentence? By my calculations, it's 14, with the two longest sentences running 33 and 38 words respectively. Good or bad?

And now the average word length. Honestly, I'm too tired to count syllables for you, so let me quote Ms. Tuchman on this subject and tell you that I mostly agree with her:

> In my opinion, short words are always preferable to long ones; the fewer the syllables the better, and monosyllables, beautiful and pure like "bread" and "sun" and "grass," are the best of all.

Where do I disagree? With her word "always," which feels glib. (And I bet she'd now retract it if she could.) Like you, I can think of lots of words that are both longish and fun—"higgledy-piggledy," "balderdash," "curmudgeon," and "persnickety," to cite just a few—and I would surely want to save room for them in my own prose. On occasion, they might be not just delightful but indeed the very best word—best for accuracy, tone, rhythm, variety, *impact*. (Drama!) As a general rule, though, she's right: the fewer the syllables, the better.[2] Why? It makes for a smoother, clearer, more conversational style—and a perfect foil for whatever longer words you might want to sprinkle in. Over the years I've learned to revere simplicity and economy of means; I've also learned to hate needless complexity. Which is why I'm always pushing myself—and now you—to shorten and simplify.[3] I had to smile recently when reading Malcolm Gladwell's tribute to his mother in

---

[2]Vincent Bugliosi, the famed Los Angeles prosecutor and author of *Helter Skelter*, agrees, noting that "Lincoln's Gettysburg Address consisted of only ten sentences. Of his 271 words, 202 of them were just one syllable. But these historic words went through five drafts and were the result of two weeks' thought and preparation. . . ." —*Outrage* (NY: Norton, 1996), p. 151. And H. W. Fowler, England's preeminent writing authority, also agreed, saying "it is a general truth that the short words are not only handier to use, but more powerful in effect; extra syllables reduce, not increase, vigour." —*A Dictionary of Modern English Usage* (Oxford, 1926), p. 333.

[3]Judge Richard Posner, who rates Benjamin Cardozo one of the four most eloquent judges in the history of the United States Supreme Court, has compared 60 of Cardozo's opinions—all in the New York Court of Appeals—against an equal number of opinions by his colleagues. Posner's conclusion? "Cardozo's sentences are shorter, making for a crisper, more dramatic style than that of his colleagues." As for Cardozo's Supreme Court opinions, "The best of them are memorable for the drama and clarity of their statements of fact, the brevity and verve of their legal discussion, the sparkle of their epigrams, the panache with which precedents are marshaled and dispatched, the idiosyncratic but effective departures from standard English prose style." —*Cardozo: A Study in Reputation* (Chicago: University of Chicago Press, 1990), pp. 135, 127.

the Acknowledgements page of his 2008 bestseller *Outliers: The Story of Success*. She apparently had done some pushing, too. Says Gladwell, "My mother, for her part, taught me how to express myself; she taught me that there is beauty in saying something clearly and simply."

So here's my tip: In the next essay you write, challenge yourself to work in both a *one-sentence paragraph* and a *two-word sentence*. For a gold medal, toss in a one-word sentence, too.[4] Then see how your prose reads. See if you like its rhythm and look. I predict you will. This is one way writers learn to emancipate themselves from silly taboos and to create their own voice on paper. Few things are more important in the writing game.

Another suggestion: In your next major essay—say, an essay that's four pages or longer—try *segmenting* it. That is, break it into big chunks, each several related paragraphs long. (Two such chunks per essay is fine, but three is normally much better, especially with longer essays, since it looks more thought-out.) The easiest way to do this is by using what editors call "white space." Wherever your exposition wants to make a big turn, simply double or triple your normal line spacing between chunks, thus visually marking that shift. The advantages? The chief one is that it breaks up the monotony of a long, undifferentiated trail of text, just as a new book chapter will. Marching along, readers view that white space up ahead as both a nice intermediate goal to reach and a welcome rest stop. And you, meanwhile, are spared having to concoct an elaborate transition there, since the shift speaks for itself. Everybody wins.

Another way to achieve those same results is by inserting *subheads*— short, boldfaced phrases that announce, like a headline, the topic of the section they're introducing. Pros normally position them either centered (as in this book) or flush-left, beneath a cushion of white space. Besides all the advantages offered by just plain white space, they have two additional ones: they enable a reader to glean the subtopics of your argument on the fly, when she's just skimming, and they simplify her locating a particular section should she ever want to revisit it.

There's lots more one could say about attractive formatting, as anyone knows who's familiar with Jan V. White's classic *Editing by Design* (3rd ed., 2003), the bible of many designers, art directors, and editors. I urge you to check it out. But before leaving the subject myself, I really

---

[4]Is it grammatically legal? Sure. America's top grammar-and-usage expert, Bryan Garner, supports the practice, covering the issue with typical erudition in an entry called "Incomplete Sentences" in his *Garner's Modern American Usage*, 3rd ed. (Oxford U.P., 2009), 455–457. If you don't yet own this extraordinarily useful book, you should. David Foster Wallace called it a work of genius, and I agree. For details, see Wallace's fascinating *Harper's* book review (April 2001), reprinted as "Authority and American Usage" in his *Consider the Lobster and Other Essays* (New York: Back Bay Books /Little, Brown, 2006), 67–127.

ought to take a moment to explain the proper formatting of *lists*, since they're ubiquitous these days, thanks in part to PowerPoint, and since their formatting has some wrinkles that leave many people confused.

Most younger writers, I've found, and most lawyers, too, think it's not kosher to indent lists, at least in so-called formal writing, so they run any listed items right in their body text, using just commas or semicolons to organize the jumble. Pros call this mistake "burying the information." They might also call it "making life hard for the reader." If the listed items really are important, and if each of them deserves the individual attention that the list is implying, they need to be *displayed*, not buried. Putting lots of white space around them does that job beautifully. It's just another way to dramatize your ideas, isn't it? And it can be extremely effective.

Let me walk you through the proper formatting.

Whenever you indent a list, you have two choices. One choice is called *enumeration*. Here, you use *numbers* (sometimes set in parentheses, sometimes not—it's all taste) and either of the following styles of punctuation, with your lead-in sentence ending in a colon, as here:

1. Item one.		1. item one;
2. Item two.	or	2. item two; and
3. Item three.		3. item three.

I prefer using this style, especially the version on the left, whenever my lead-in speaks of a *particular number* of items (e.g., "The top ten things to see in Santa Fe are: . . ."). Why? Because if I don't also display a number next to each item, some readers may wonder how come. After all, I had primed them to count along with me. Also, if I later need to refer to an item in the list, I can do so simply by citing its number—e.g., "As we saw in case #3, the legislature. . . ."

But say you need simply to *list* points, which is far more common. And say you don't mention the specific number but instead use some nonspecific adjective like "several" (e.g., "This year's model boasts several improvements: . . ."). In that case, use *bullets*. They imply no rank order, dispense with the clutter of numbers and parentheses, display your points with even greater white space, and offer visual variety.

Below are two equally reputable ways of formatting with bullets. As before, I myself prefer the leftmost version. I like that it eliminates the need for "and" in the next-to-last item; also, that it gives more prominence to each item via the capped first letter and the no-nonsense period. But in any case, please note that both lead-ins end in a *colon*, thereby syntactically anchoring the list to the lead-in. Also, in the leftmost example, note that each bulleted item, *even though a fragment*, is allowed to begin with a capital letter and end with a period. (This convention is now almost universally accepted.) Finally, note that the listed items are kept *syntactically parallel*; otherwise, readers could stumble as they moved from point to point. Look how smoothly and efficiently these lists read:

We expect several benefits:	We expect several benefits:
• New customers.	• new customers;
• Expansion of our business overseas.	• expansion of our business overseas;
• More efficient use of our warehouses.	• more efficient use of our warehouses; and
• Fewer staff members on overtime.	• fewer staff members on overtime.

And what a nice break in the text they provide, too!

One last point here. A key principle in aesthetics is this: *Any change in a pattern will draw the eye*. Look, for example, at these lines of type and see where your eye immediately alights:

●●●●●●c●●●●●●●●●●●●●●●●●●●●●●●●●●●

xxxxxxxxxxxxxxxxxxxxxxxxxxxxxxxxxXxxxxxxx

bbbbbbbbb   bbbbbbbbb   bb   bbbbbbbbbbbbb

The moral for us writers is this: Anytime you want to throw extra emphasis on something—a word, a sentence, a paragraph, a section—make it different from its surroundings. You'll also create more variety in the bargain.

2. Interesting Phrasing

At the sentence level, meanwhile, artful presentation involves *interesting phrasing*—casting each sentence so that it compels our readers' attention and renews their interest.

Here we have many resources to tap, especially if we're blessed with at least modest creativity. Some of them are purely stylistic, learned by observing how more advanced writers put their words together. (Hence the truism, "You can't write better than you can read.") Others involve companionable personae, or narrative "voices," channeled for their engaging effect. I can't begin to catalogue all these resources, but a few of the more effective ones, at least to me, are wit, succinctness, frankness, off-beat diction, irony, quick shifts in tempo, sprightliness, fresh metaphors, spot-on analogies,[5] and droll hyperbole.

---

[5]Anne Fadiman, in her charming little book about books and book-lovers, *Ex Libris: Confessions of a Common Reader*, quotes her brother Kim, a fellow bibliophile, explaining why his bedside table currently supports three spread-eagled volumes: "They are ready in an instant to let me pick them up. To use an electronics analogy, closing a book on a bookmark is like pressing the Stop button, whereas when you leave the book facedown, you've only pressed Pause."

Take that last one, droll hyperbole. The essayist Joseph Epstein, in a delicious piece on high school reunions, once quipped that an old classmate of his now looked to be "a woman with more eye shadow than a raccoon."

A seasoned writer like Epstein will work hard for such a phrase, partly because he wants to give himself something fun to read (he is, after all, his own first reader), but equally important because it buys him attention for his next sentence. There, of course, he'll confront the same challenge all over again, but that's writing, isn't it?

In effect, we writers, amateurs and professionals alike, get the honor of Center Court, and if we aim to keep playing there, we'd best play each shot intently, as if it were match point. After all, besides our own pride, we have onlookers to satisfy—our readers. And we know they can't possibly foresee what wonderful shots (phrases) may lie ahead, whether on the next page or even in the next sentence. All they have to go on are the shots they've already seen, plus the current one. And the current one is invariably where they decide whether to stick around. So, from their viewpoint, each shot amounts to match point, and we need to play it accordingly.

Most students are slow to grasp this because, unlike professionals, they routinely write for a captive audience—a teacher paid to read their every word. Maybe we teachers ought to occasionally imitate a friend of mine, Bill Broyles, founding editor of *Texas Monthly* and, later, editor in chief of *Newsweek*. When editing manuscripts for *Texas Monthly*, he'd draw a heavy blue line across the page at the first point where his attention wandered, then immediately return the MS to its author for rewriting. "If I drift off there," he explained to my students, "our readers are apt to also. They'll page right ahead to the next article. So the writer's got a problem there—a big one—and he needs to address it before we can proceed."

The problem will sometimes stem from what Tuchman would call a failure to "discard the irrelevant." At other times it stems from a patch of humdrum, underthought ideas—though maybe that's more of the same failure, since so much of writing consists of refining, refining . . . which also means discarding, discarding . . . James Dickey, winner of a National Book Award for poetry (*Buckdancer's Choice*) and author of the best-selling novel *Deliverance*, knew all about refining, it seems. He once confessed:

> It takes an awful lot of time for me to write anything. I have endless drafts, one after another; I try out 50, 75, or a hundred variations on a single line sometimes. I work on the process of refining low-grade ore. I get maybe a couple of nuggets of gold out of 50 tons of dirt.

But perhaps most often the problem stems from an excess of what I call "MA phrasing." ("MA" is my shorthand for "merely adequate," a kind way of saying "inadequate.") My students, when editing each other's papers, would quickly see the prevalence of that problem and, adopting my abbreviation, would pepper many a page with "MA" alerts; then, time permitting, they'd often thoughtfully propose clever rephrasings, either interlinearly or in the margins. Few things will more quickly teach a writer the importance of fresh phrasing than seeing all those MAs, especially when they're accompanied by witty recastings that take the very same idea and make it sing. And when the writer starts pouncing on MAs himself and creating his own rephrasings, he begins to finally get Robert Frost's great one-liner: "All the fun's in how you say a thing."

Another of my quirky editing symbols that these students found handy was "MO," for "missed opportunity." I'd use it to flag any place where the writer missed a great chance to make things more interesting for us (and himself), especially if he sounded like he had slipped into term-paper mode—you know, abstract statement after abstract statement, without an ounce of personality or charm. Maybe he'd missed a natural place for an anecdote. Or some dialogue. Or an analogy. Or a list. Or a personal example. Or a witticism. Or a description. Or a structural surprise . . . So they'd all start doing what professional writers routinely do: instead of just waiting for opportunities to use these devices, they'd look for ways to *create* those opportunities.

3. Dramatic Plotting

We come, finally, to the macro level. Here, artful presentation involves what I call *dramatic plotting*.

Let's say, for illustration, that you're writing an essay. An important question is how you view that project.

If you view it primarily as an essay, which seems logical enough, beware. Why? Because the conventional essay format, which you've had pounded into you since junior high, is dead. It's static, formulaic, boring—in a word, undramatic. (Which is why you instinctively hated learning it.) You may have good ideas, and they may be coherently organized, but the form itself is still dead. *Readers want variety; they want ideas dramatized.* They don't want just to read about ideas, they want to *experience* them. They want to feel that those ideas really matter somehow—that it's not just a cerebral exercise. They want suspense, excitement. And they want an easy way to keep everything clear in their heads as they move through a piece.

The more conscious you become of your own responses as a reader, the more you'll grant all this.

The solution?

The solution—and here's where expository writing becomes really fun—is to give readers the sense of hearing a *story*. You'll recall Jolene Shirley ingeniously did exactly that in her reply to Mencken, back in the previous chapter. Her essay *is* a story—and a most memorable one.[6] More often, though, even if we can't turn our entire exposition into a story, we can inject *story elements*, as, for example, my recounting of Ms. Tuchman's Radcliffe debacle at the start of this chapter. Anecdotes like that one—*especially when they contain dialogue, either real or imagined*—are intrinsically engaging, and veteran writers will work in as many as possible, knowing that they function just like illustrations in a book.

But whatever our approach, the key here is to consciously contrive what Ms. Tuchman calls a *"developing dramatic narrative."* At its simplest, this is a "story" that does three things:

1. immediately hooks the readers' curiosity with some intriguing problem, issue, or question—something intrinsically dramatic enough for them to care about it;
2. goes on to develop aspects of the problem, thereby sustaining the dramatic tension; and
3. finally resolves the problem, thereby achieving closure.

If you manage to do these three things, your readers will have plenty of incentive to keep forging ahead. And that's the #1 object of writing: getting readers to turn the page.

It all rests, then, on your skill at "plotting"—your skill at keeping readers actively tuned in.

From now on, I suggest you think a lot about plotting. Start by thinking about it at the sentence level. As we saw only a minute ago, your individual sentences need to be freshly phrased and varied so as to pull your readers in and pass them eagerly along. Phrasing is thus a form of plotting, isn't it? You also need to think about plotting when dealing with paragraphs and whole pages. There, you want to remember to creatively vary your paragraph length, look for places to insert white-space breaks or subheads, and be hyperconscious of your overall story line—the narrative thread holding everything together. Learn to see that story line through your *reader's* eyes, not just your own. Is it coherent? Is it "clean"

---

[6]Two of the most perennially popular sentences in English are each just four words long: "Tell me a story" and "Once upon a time." Stories would seem to be one of humanity's most potent sources of pleasure. All writers, not just fiction writers, need to be mindful of this. Anytime we can weave in a pertinent anecdote (a little story) and tell it well, we're doing everyone a favor.

(uncluttered)? Is it reasonably dramatic? And does it stage your key points in such a way that they get the notice they deserve?

No, it's not easy. Simply absorbing these concepts can be hard. Putting them into practice is harder still, though it eventually turns writing into a far more creative, and enjoyable, experience than ever before, since you get to think more like an entertainer than just an idea-pusher, and you start to enjoy a sense of *collaboration* with your readers. Ah, you finally realize, they're not your enemy after all! They're your *audience*, eager to enjoy you at your best—and to inspire you to *be* your best. Eager to be surprised by you. Eager to laugh at your humor. Eager to identify with you, learn from you, get inspired by you . . . Granted, you have to bring that much more to the table, but you're bringing it for yourself as well. You're your own audience, too, aren't you? So why not make it fun?[7]

Let me leave you with two handy questions to guide you—questions you should ask yourself with every sentence you write. They distill most of what I've been telling you here.

The first question is, *"If I were the reader here, would this excite me or bore me?"* ("This" can refer to whatever you're looking at—a sentence, phrase, idea, opening paragraph, etc.) It's a useful question to ask because it compels you to read your prose through a stranger's eyes—which is precisely how it *will* be read, of course. You can't expect a stranger to find any more excitement there than you would if you were in their shoes, right? So it's pointless to kid yourself, and this question will prevent that.

The second question is, *"How can I dramatize this point more vividly?"* As I've suggested, there are many ways to heighten the impact of your ideas. Mainly, aside from cooking up story elements and playing creatively with your formatting and essay architecture (paragraph size, sentence length, etc.), you just need to tinker with the phrasing. I myself will normally cast a sentence four or five ways in my head before actually typing it out. But that's just the start, for I'll go on rethinking it each time I later reread the paragraph, always challenging myself to improve it. Can I cut some words to quicken its pace? Can I find a way here to smuggle in some wit? Can I devise an example to make the point seem less woolly? Can I freshen the diction? Oh, the questions are endless—and happily so, for each is a fresh challenge to one's creativity, wit, and inge-

---

[7]And surely no one had more fun with his writing than Mencken. Remember his line, in "Literature and the Schoolma'm," about the pedagogues who "fail as ignominiously as that Athenian of legend who essayed to train a regiment of grasshoppers in the goose-step"? There was no such legend. Mencken made it up, probably guffawing and slapping his knee as he did so—not only laughing at his own wit but also laughing at all those pedagogues who, like me, would go off in futile search of that same crazy Athenian, only to discover, again like me, that Mencken was just pulling their leg.

nuity. Maybe I should set this point off in its own ducky little paragraph lest the reader fly over it. Maybe I should turn it into a question so that it challenges him to react. Maybe I should try boiling it down to a punchy one-word sentence . . .

Tinkering, always tinkering. That's the heart and soul of writing for me. And once I'm really into it, I always remember Gloria Steinem's wonderful remark: "Writing is the only thing that, when I do it, I don't feel I should be doing something else instead."

Now for the student essay I promised you. Its author, Amy Jetel, then an English major in my Advanced Expository Writing seminar, had waited tables in two wildly popular Austin restaurants—first at Macaroni Grill, then at Chuy's, a Tex-Mex mecca—for over three years. Because she was self-supporting, most of that was full-time employment, during which she squeezed in UT courses on the side. When she wrote this essay in 1999, she had just scaled back to waiting tables part-time because of the demands of my course. "Friendly Persuasion," the theme for that week's writing assignment, offered her a chance to teach her classmates what the real life of a server is all about. Here is her essay—one of the most instructive ones I read all semester. It forever changed how I viewed waiters and their customers.

THE PRICE OF SERVICE

Amy Jetel

Imagine you're a waiter, and a big-top (a party of 7 or more) just sat down in your section. While you're trying to get their drink order, someone at the next table is tugging at your apron because their enchiladas are cold. Another table is waiting for you to get the staff together to sing "Happy Birthday"; the people in the next booth are staring at you while loudly slurping down the last of their drinks; another party has empty plates sitting in front of them; you still have to get 3 margaritas, 2 Bud Lights, 6 waters, 2 Cokes, and 2 teas for your big-top; the restaurant is out of ice; someone forgot to make more tea; the Coke syrup just ran out; and you really, really have to go to the bathroom. That's what we servers call being "in the weeds."

Now imagine going through all of that and not getting paid.

Servers who value their jobs wouldn't dream of asking customers why they left a lousy tip, or no tip at all. We can only speculate. Maybe they didn't expect their bill to be so high, and can't fathom paying much more. Perhaps some people start their gratuity meter at 15% and look for any reason to knock off percentage points throughout the meal. But most likely, those who regularly tip 10% or less are just uninformed about the service industry.

Let me share some basic facts that every restaurant patron should know.

Fact: Tips are not "extra" income—waiters rely on them

In Texas, servers make $2.13 an hour. At the end of each shift, we claim how much money in tips we made—this is our taxable income. The government then taxes us out of our hourly wage. Since $2.13 an hour doesn't go very far after taxes—paychecks under a dollar are a common occurrence—a waiter's livelihood rides on the generosity of his or her customers. Our only source of income is tips.

Fact: Waiters don't keep your entire tip

People dine out so they don't have to cook, clean up after themselves, or even get up to refill their drinks. A restaurant is where you pay someone to do all of this for you. And the standard price of the waiter's service is at least 15% of your bill. Restaurants pay waiters an unlivable wage as an incentive for them to work harder and sell more. Counting on that 15% gratuity—the bigger the bill, the bigger the tip—a waitress will push bar drinks, appetizers, and desserts, making more money for the restaurant and, with luck, for herself.

But if you tip less because you think your server is getting too much help (someone else brought chips to your table or refilled your glass), you should know that she's paying those people to help her. This is called "tipping out." For example, at my restaurant, we have to tip out 4% of our sales. So if your bill was $100, and you gave your waitress $15, she gets to keep $11. If you left 10%, or $10, she would keep $6. If you got so inebriated that you forgot to leave a tip, she would lose $4. Our customers aren't required to pay us for our service, but we still have to pay the bussers and the bar—tip or no tip.

Fact: Waiting tables requires profound patience

One night, I waited on a woman who asked for silverware as soon as she sat down. Since I was in the weeds at the time, I considered this a low-priority request—after all, she hadn't even ordered. When I returned to my section, loaded down with tea pitchers, food, and extra plates for my four other tables, she hissed, "I asked you for silverware!" I smiled and told her I would get it right away, but this didn't satisfy her. She jabbed at the heavens with open palms and snapped, "I have to wipe my hands!" Seeing the urgency of the situation, I promptly returned with her silverware—which, at my restaurant, isn't wrapped in a napkin.

The Silverware Lady has plenty of company. She shares a special place in all waiters' hearts with a host of other personalities: like Queenie, who answers the question, "Hi, how are you?" with, "Diet Coke and a bowl of queso"; or like Mute Woman, who gestures her requests with the subtle shaking of a chip-basket or empty glass; or like Mr. Condescension, who tries to make even the most self-assured waiter feel responsible for a kitchen mistake, a dirty fork, a cold nacho. With our income in the hands of these characters, we must smile, comply, and resist the urge to demand respect.

So why do we do it? Well, work is never boring and access to food is a plus. But for college students, as most servers are, it's the only way to work less than 25 hours a week and still make rent. The aching feet and back, late hours, and hectic work can all be worthwhile when someone shows their appreciation, not by telling you what a great job you did, but by leaving a fat 20%. It's what waiters live for.

I recently asked Amy, now a successful Austin attorney—in fact, a name partner in her law firm—to take us behind the scenes of "The Price of Service." What had prompted her to write the piece? What had she hoped to accomplish with it? Why had she written it in the form that she did? Here is the pertinent part of her emailed reply to me:

> After waiting tables for over 3 years, I was fed up with people's lack of empathy for others, their desire to get something for nothing, and their view that waiters are, by definition, less intelligent and less worthy human beings than they. Although the essay is primarily about tipping, my hope was to also give readers insight into the world of waiters so that they could have a little compassion.

> So I guess you could say that my mood when writing the essay was irritated, my state of being, jaded. And it felt really, really good to write it—very cathartic!

> I felt it absolutely necessary to add drama to the paper if I were to successfully foster a sense of compassion in my readers. I wanted them to actually feel a little stressed out by my opening scene of being in the weeds; I wanted them to personally dislike the Silverware Lady, Queenie, and Mr. Condescension. I also figured that nobody would personally identify with the "bad customer" caricatures (even if they were, in fact, bad customers!); and seeing themselves as the "good customers," perhaps they'd strive to be even better. After all, who wants to be called some nasty nickname behind their back by a disgruntled waiter? :)

Here are some of the many elements in her essay that helped Amy dramatize these ideas and that left us, her classmates and me, feeling exceptionally well taught—one mark of a great essay:

- The direct invitation, couched in the second-person "you" ("Imagine you're a waiter"), to enter her world and briefly experience her work night. That night would start when "a big-top (a party of 7 or more) sat down in your section," which begins inducing our identifying with her and preparing us to empathize with other servers, too. This opener epitomizes "drawing the reader in."
- The many concrete details that actualize the scene (a song title, exact numbers and brands of beverages, and, my favorites, "tugging at your apron" and "staring at you").
- The 92-word stretched sentence in the opening graf ("Another table is waiting for you . . .") that dramatizes, with clause after clause after clause, what a chaotic, exhausting, impossible environment we're now asked to imagine ourselves working in—and at below minimum wage, no less.
- The 21-word sentence about "Servers who value their jobs . . ." that is immediately lightened by the next one, a crisp 4-word sentence ("We can only speculate") whose shortness gains it extra emphasis for transitioning into the three conjectures that follow.
- The fascinating lessons in Server Lingo ("big-top," "in the weeds," "tipping out") that also further accredit the author, who knows the score and who is generous with her knowledge.
- The eye-opening facts that prove as disturbing as they are informative ("In Texas, servers make $2.13 an hour"; "Our only source of income is tips"; "Waiters don't keep your entire tip"; etc.).
- The two one-sentence paragraphs, one of which packs a mule kick ("Now imagine going through all of that and not getting paid") while the other neatly lays out what's ahead for us and simultaneously piques our curiosity ("Let me share with you some basic facts that every restaurant patron should know").
- The comic anecdote about the hissing Silverware Lady ("One night . . ."), which allows both Amy and the reader to have more fun with the essay, an essay that might otherwise feel preachy—precisely what she did *not* want.
- The snatches of dialogue—not much, but enough to put us there and hear some very spoiled patrons talking ("I asked you for silverware!"; "I have to wipe my hands!"; "Diet Coke and a bowl of queso"), plus Amy's cordial "Hi, how are you?"
- The patrons who, behaving like stereotypes, really earn their pejorative nicknames ("The Silverware Lady," "Queenie," "Mute Woman," "Mr. Condescension").
- The 76-word sentence in which Amy brings together, as if at one table, "a host of other personalities" that "share a special place in all waiters' hearts."
- The effortless bridging throughout.
- The short, inevitable question ("So why do we do it?") opening the final graf that has exactly the right, conclusive sound and that prepares us for her thoroughly sensible answer.

- The fluid, conversational style—16 contractions, all of them ever so easy on the ear, plus simple but very effective conjunctions used as transitional words ("And," "But," "So").
- The clever formatting of the three "Fact" statements, which are not only boldfaced but, for even greater impact, centered on the page, thereby reinforcing the essay's already strong structure and ensuring that her key points don't get lost.
- The assumption, straightforwardly presented, that actually drives this essay ("But most likely, those who regularly tip 10% or less are just uninformed about the service industry").
- The pleasingly direct statement of the author's plan for us ("Let me share some basic facts that every restaurant patron should know").
- The comfortable sentence length, averaging just 19 words—an average that would have dropped to 16 without the two stretched sentences (92 and 76 words). But who would have wished those two magnificent sentences any shorter?

It's a great little essay. With it, Amy changed my life. What higher praise can a reader give an author?

11

Revising

Interviewer: *How much rewriting do you do?*

Hemingway: *It depends. I rewrote the ending of* Farewell to Arms, *the last page of it, thirty-nine times before I was satisfied.*

Interviewer: *Was there some technical problem there? What was it that had stumped you?*

Hemingway: *Getting the words right.*

—*Paris Review* INTERVIEW

12

Proofreading

Don't expect your reader to accept a piece of writing that you wouldn't accept yourself.

—Donald H. Ross

Years ago, back when I was a graduate student at Berkeley, I had the extraordinary good fortune of taking a seminar with Professor Maynard Mack, then on semester's leave from Yale.

To my classmates and me, it felt like taking a class with Einstein, for Professor Mack was, by all counts, the most distinguished English scholar in the world. President of the Modern Language Association, chairman of Yale's English Department, preeminent authority on Shakespeare, the last word on Pope and Homer as well, general editor of Norton's acclaimed *World Masterpieces* series, author of the most frequently reprinted article ever penned on *Hamlet*—the honors ran on and on. An authentic genius, this man. Also a singularly gracious, unpretentious individual.

Anyway, for this Pope seminar, which proved a real doozie—of the 20 students who started, only 7 of us finished—we had to write a major research report every other week and, occasionally, read it to the group. The only cautionary instructions Professor Mack had given us were some terse words appended to his first assignment. They were enough to stop the heart:

P.S. Put it in apple-pie order, as if submitting it to a learned journal.

One day, some weeks into the term, a classmate was delivering his report when Professor Mack, who normally listened in silence, softly interrupted.

"Excuse me, Mr. Rierson," he said. "Is that last quotation correct?"

"I believe so, sir," Rierson replied, blushing.

"But you're not sure?" Mack's voice carried only the barest edge. We felt the room chill.

"I'm almost positive it is, sir."

"Would you kindly double-check it for us?"

"Yes, sir," said Rierson, who immediately began thumbing through his volume of Pope for the passage in question. Having found it, he began silently comparing his transcription of it against the text while the rest of us held our breath.

Suddenly Rierson blushed scarlet. "Uh, I made a small mistake," he said. "The word 'fearsome' should have been 'fulsome.'"

"Everything else correct?" Professor Mack asked, the mild question hinting of further disasters.

Rierson's eyes darted back to the text and he resumed checking. More blushes. "There are two other errors, sir," he confessed, looking like the unhappiest person on the planet.

"Please tell us what they are," Professor Mack said. Whereupon Rierson proceeded to explain them, his voice cracking in embarrassment and growing so low that we had to strain to hear him.

When he had finished, Professor Mack looked him dead in the eye and said: "Mr. Rierson, the most important thing a writer has going for him is his credibility. Transcribing quotations correctly is the most mechanical of tasks, requiring minimal intelligence." Pause. Then Mack's voice, normally ever so civil, began crescendoing as he resumed: "If a writer can't be trusted with so mechanical a task, what then, Mr. Rierson, *can* he be trusted with?" Long pause. Then: "From here on, Mr. Rierson, I want you to double-check—*triple*-check, if necessary—everything you quote. Let us have no more careless errors."

That little incident taught me more of lasting value than many entire courses. Among its great lessons was the meaning of *professionalism*.

Odds & Ends

13

Punctuation

Punctuation, to most people, is a set of arbitrary and rather silly rules you find in printers' style books and in the back pages of school grammars. Few people realize that it is the most important single device for making things easier to read.

— Rudolf Flesch

In conversation you can use timing, a look, inflection, pauses. But on the page, all you have are commas, dashes, the amount of syllables in a word. When I write, I read everything out loud to get the right rhythm.

— Fran Lebowitz

Semicolons

The average college student isn't ready for semicolons. She hasn't discerned any need for them, nor is she eager to. They look forbiddingly exotic—about as tempting as a plate of snails. The literary gourmets can have them; she'll stick with her comma and period—though, if truth be known, she isn't too comfortable even with these. Confessed one sophomore, a veteran of the trenches: "The first semester of Freshman English I used to write only short sentences so I wouldn't have to put commas in."

Experience brings a change of attitude, though—especially if that experience includes extensive reading. Eventually you feel ready to handle longer, more complex sentences; you're newly concerned with tightening up your slack phrasing; you've found delight in balancing off ideas against one another; you're hungry for ways to add elegance to your style; and with your new confidence, you've developed an interest in doing things with the language beyond what the more routine punctuation marks allow. That's when you start discovering the many resources of the semicolon.

Let's start with how semicolons work. Basically, they're like the automatic coupling device on railroad cars: they let you join two or three or even more related sentences so as to form a single, complex thought—something we do in conversation all the time with half-pauses. They're a sign that says to the reader, "Take a rest here to gather in the preceding clause, but then keep right on going—this thought isn't finished yet."

Since the sentences you're joining are closely related, you don't have to insert *and* or *but* or any other connective between them, though you may if you want to; all you really need is the semicolon. It's that simple. And you won't have any trouble if you just remember one caveat: *Don't try to join anything less than complete sentences with it.* Here's my easy test:

> **If you can replace your semicolon with a period, you're OK. If not, try a comma or a dash.**

About the only exception is when you're using semicolons like super-commas to separate a series of lengthy items—especially when one or more of those items uses a comma itself, as in the second paragraph of this very chapter.

Let's look at some examples. Suppose you had these two sentences:

A beauty is a woman you notice. A charmer is one who notices you.

Now, these short sentences would profit from being linked, especially if surrounded by many others just like them. Kept separate, they read choppily; and what they're expressing is really a single thought—the difference between a beauty and a charmer. One way to link them—the most popular way—is with a comma followed by a conjunction (a joining word) like *and, but*, or *while*:

A beauty is a woman you notice, while a charmer is one who notices you.

But you can also link them with a semicolon:

A beauty is a woman you notice; a charmer is one who notices you.
    —Adlai Stevenson

Note how much crisper this last version is than the earlier ones. The first version is weak because it spreads the witty contrast over two sentences. The second version is weak because it's doing all our thinking for us: the *while* feels too explicit, plus it's one word too many—a glaring fault in clauses that are otherwise so spare. The final version rectifies all these problems. It's unified, uncluttered, balanced, elegant. This is what it means to do things with the language beyond what the more routine punctuation marks allow.

As you become familiar with the semicolon, you'll find it offers several benefits.

First is variety. The comma-plus-conjunction formula, the most popular way of joining sentences, grows tiresome after a while—as tiresome as a succession of simple sentences ending in periods. An occasional change in the formula not only gives readers something different to look at (variety for the eye) but also changes the rhythm and pace of your sentences (variety for the mind's ear).

Second is compression. The semicolon is efficient: it lets you eliminate most of those conjunctions or prepositions that are required with a comma—words like *whereas, because, for, or, but, while, and*. Each time you condense a thought, you increase its power of effect. It's like distilling whiskey: you're extracting the concentrate, the pure essence of the thought. In this next example, try mentally replacing the semicolon with a comma plus the word *for*. You'll find that the sentence now reads exactly one word too long:

> Many American lawyers would disagree; they have long prided themselves
> as generalists, able to perform any legal task.
>   —*Newsweek*

Third is tighter contrasts. As the Adlai Stevenson example showed, the semicolon is ideal for linking contrasting ideas that are parallel in structure. At such times it acts like the fulcrum of a seesaw, balancing the ideas off against one another. The effect—neat, concise, epigrammatic—is that of a couplet, like this beauty by Alexander Pope:

> True ease in writing comes from art, not chance,
> As those move easiest who have learned to dance.

Fourth is unity. The semicolon permits a smooth, quick, coherent grouping of ideas into one tidy bundle. Let me show you. In the paragraph below, Mark Twain cites four reasons for his once being unaware that there was anything wrong with slavery. Had he not linked them, the effect would have been choppy; yet had he linked them with commas and conjunctions, the effect would have been chaotic. Using semicolons and roughly parallel structure, he pulls them together into one coherent sentence:

> In my school-boy days I had no aversion to slavery. I was not aware that there was anything wrong about it. No one arraigned it in my hearing; the local papers said nothing against it; the local pulpit taught us that God approved it, that it was a holy thing, and that the doubter need only look in the Bible if he wished to settle his mind—and then the texts were read aloud to us to make the matter sure; if the slaves had an aversion, they were wise and said nothing. In Hannibal we seldom saw a slave misused; on the farm, never.[1]
> —Mark Twain

Now that you know the benefits of semicolons, let's look at four occasions where they prove especially useful. There are others, to be sure, but these are the chief ones:

1. When you have two or more sentences that you want to present as parts of a single thought:

> Training is everything. The peach was once a bitter almond; cauliflower is nothing but cabbage with a college education.
> —Mark Twain

2. When a sentence is so long, or so complex, that the reader needs a rest stop along the way:

> With all the world to choose from, [creative writers] invariably select subjects closest to their inner feelings; and when they choose subjects seemingly alien to them they invariably alter them to correspond to their personal condition, even though what emerges may seem, to the uninitiated, remote and unrelated.
> —Leon Edel

3. When you have two or more related sentences that are parallel in structure and thus invite pairing to emphasize either their contrast or their likeness:

> Some [football critics] would create a sliding scale making long kicks worth more points than short ones; others would return the ball to the line

---

[1]While that last semicolon seems to violate the rule about never joining anything less than complete sentences, it really doesn't. The words *on the farm, never* are an elliptical construction, with the comma correctly used to mark the omission. As readers, we translate those words to mean "on the farm we never saw a slave misused"—a syntactically complete clause.

of scrimmage instead of the defenders' 20-yard line after missed kicks, making it riskier to attempt long ones.
—Pete Axthelm

As in all off-year elections, many of this year's scattered races were decided on purely local issues. In Detroit, for example, the voters cast their ballots along racial lines to elect the city's first black mayor; in New York, the local Democratic organization overwhelmed three lackluster rivals to pull off Controller Abraham Beame's mayoral victory.
—*The New York Times*

4. When you want to separate items within a series, especially when commas occur within one or more members of the series. Also when you want to separate items into classes, as in the first of these examples:

Among its 35 or so working members are Ivan Allen Jr., the former mayor of Atlanta, and William Baker, the president of Bell Labs; Mary Wells Lawrence, of her own advertising agency, and Clare Boothe Luce; Daniel Patrick Moynihan, now ambassador to India, and Sol Linowitz, former ambassador to the Organization of American States.
—*Newsweek*

Of course, essential to any good history or memoir is the venerable triad of rules: to respect the facts enough to keep burrowing for them, especially when they confound your preconceptions; to care enough about your subject to express judgments clearly, vigorously and if necessary, in a way that may antagonize; and withal, to exercise restraint on yourself so that what you call history or memoir is not an emanation of your own prejudices and self-interests but a work which makes an honest and sustained effort to deserve that fine old adjective, fair.
—Eric F. Goldman

The recordings, she said, were full of "funny things"—the President plunking his feet on the desk, where the bug was, with an impact "like a bomb"; fragments of talk drowned out by rattling china, by a marching band blaring outside, by Mr. Nixon inexplicably whistling during meetings; hopeless scrambles when four people talked at once "and you couldn't get one voice."
—*Newsweek*

One last point. Occasionally you'll hear that semicolons make the tone of a person's writing heavier, more formal. This is nonsense. The misconception arises because semicolons tend to congregate in academic writing, which is often ponderous—not because of the semicolons but because of plain bad writing: pretentious jargon; galumphing sentences and

paragraphs; excessive abstractness; impersonality; passive verbs; humor-
lessness;[2] and so on. The charge, then, amounts to guilt by association.

If you need proof that semicolons can mix agreeably with a readable
style, go to the nonfiction of Mark Twain, one of America's most readable
stylists. You'll find maybe half a dozen semicolons per page. Or go to the
writings of George Bernard Shaw, one of England's wittiest stylists. You'll
find the same thing. Better still, since it's close at hand, open any copy of
Newsweek. As my examples show, the pages of that magazine are sprinkled
with semicolons, yet I've never heard *Newsweek* called heavy or formal.

It all comes down to who's using them, and how—plus how often.
Like anything else, semicolons can be used to excess. They can begin
calling attention to themselves, can begin looking gimmicky, can even
overcompress a writer's ideas on occasion. But when they're used moderately, and when we're taking pains to write for our readers rather than to
impress them, semicolons can seem downright elegant.

Commas

Most people have trouble with commas. Where do you put them
in? When can you leave them out? If you demand a definitive answer,
lock yourself in a padded cell with one of the thick handbooks. If you'll
settle for something incomplete but useful, read on.

My first tip, applicable to most situations, is this:

> **Use a comma when there's a light pause AND a drop
> in pitch.**

Test any sentence this way: Read it aloud, in your best radio voice,
as if to a national audience. If you find that you pause somewhere to make
things intelligible, and *if you hear the pitch of your voice drop there too*,
insert a comma. If still in doubt, have a friend read the sentence aloud.
The pauses—and drops in pitch—should quickly announce themselves.

Don't be cowed by commas. Don't think you have to master 85 rules
(though even professional writers—*especially* professional writers—will
periodically consult them). Correct comma usage is mostly a matter of
ear and common sense. In fact, in most cases the rules simply codify what

---

[2]"There's got to be wit. And that's very, very much left out of a lot of this labored stuff. It
doesn't sparkle at all." ⌐Robert Frost

common sense recommends. Which is why one of the country's top style authorities, *Words into Type*, can say, without threat of contradiction, "the primary purpose of the comma is to *prevent misreading*" (italics added). Even this business of being guided by your ear really boils down to common sense. Your "ear" tells you to pause in a given place because your good sense, if it's awake, tells you that a pause there—a moment of separation—is needed. *Without one, the parts of your sentence would bump into each other, and you'd risk a misread.*

Let's test that. Pretend this next sentence is your own, and recite it aloud in your very best radio voice:

Taking the long subway ride home to Queens Tom reviewed his hectic day.

Where did you lightly pause? After "Queens," right? *And the pitch of your voice dropped there too, didn't it?* You instinctively wanted to warn us against thinking there's a place called "Queens Tom." And you may also have wanted us to know where that introductory "Taking" clause ended and where the main clause began. You might not have been thinking in those precise terms, but you probably sensed that there were structural elements, or chunks of text, that you needed to keep separate.

So it is with most of the sentences you'll write. The clauses, too. Wherever elements may bump into each other and cause a misread, or at the very least a moment's confusion, you'll need to "set them off," as editors say, which means separate them. And when you do, you'll simultaneously be helping your reader grasp how the parts relate.

Let me show you how all of that applies to one of the bedrock comma rules—the rule for compound sentences. A "compound sentence," you may recall, is made by connecting two smaller ones. Sometimes, as in this very sentence, the connector is a semicolon; more typically it's a little conjunction like *and* or *but*. OK, ready for the rule? It's one of the few that I ask my students to burn into their brains—in fact, to chant to me on command. This is really, really important:

> **Separate the parts of a compound sentence with a comma before the conjunction.**

The key thing here is the *comma*. Writers will often leave it out—and when they do, readers invariably get stuck in momentary confusion. Try some actual examples that I myself have tripped over. Please read each of these sentences aloud—again, in your finest radio voice—so you'll hear as well as see how the elements collide:

> Because of the late hour he expected to find no one there but Larry, who had a project due the next morning, was still at his desk.

> The Bible can teach you to love God and Dostoevsky can teach you to write great novels.

> Bob went to the ranch hoping to see Rebecca and David, thinking Kate would be there, too, arrived an hour later.

> She seems to be focused on money and Victor's indecisiveness about getting a new career guarantees she won't see more money from him anytime soon.

> The U.S. currently participates in agreements with more than 85 countries and as many as 20% of our domestic research programs have some international component.

> But this was a decision made by the former editor and the current editor said that he disagreed with his decision that Spellcheck undermines the responsibility of copy editors.

> His involvement in the confrontation displays Sammy's emerging autonomy and his decision to quit his job liberates him from the subordinate position he fills there.

> The question of who is a "responsible person" under §6672 is interpreted as a mixed question of law and fact and certain facts will almost invariably prove dispositive of a finding of responsibility.

> But Bill had been given scarcely a month to invent a new house and the plans Jim bid on, though nice-looking, were sketchy.

Time and again, the missing comma plays us for a sucker, doesn't it? It dupes us into thinking that the subject of the second clause is actually the grammatical object of something in the first clause—either the verb or a preposition. That's why observing this rule is so important.

Let's look at another basic rule and see whether, at bottom, it isn't just common sense as well. Read it twice, please:

> **Transitional words** like *however, therefore, then, consequently, besides, indeed, likewise, otherwise,* and *nevertheless* are set off by a comma on both sides—or by a semicolon and comma if they fall between complete clauses.

Now read aloud my example sentence below, and listen for where you both *pause* and *drop your pitch*. If you know how to read music, imagine that your words are notes and that your voice pitch is the staff:

You'll agree however that Wagner's music is better than it sounds.

Your pitch took a dip after *agree*, didn't it? And why? Because you needed to interrupt yourself to slip in the transitional word *however*. But once on the last syllable of *however*, your pitch started rising again to indicate that the interruption was over, right?

Many people would unthinkingly punctuate that same sentence like this:

You'll agree however, that Wagner's music is better than it sounds.

Can you spot the problem there? That's analogous to:

You'll agree however) that Wagner's music is better than it sounds.

However interrupts the flow of the sentence, so it's clearly parenthetical, which means it must be set off on *both* sides. One comma simply won't do the job, just as one parenthesis wouldn't. It's common sense. Here's the same sentence correctly punctuated:

You'll agree, however, that Wagner's music is better than it sounds.

Let's try one more sentence that uses *however* and see in what ways it might be different. Read it aloud, please:

She is old enough to see her parents' faults however she is not old enough to forgive them.

Once again you have to pause at *however*, right? But now you face the challenge of deciding which half of the sentence that transitional word really modifies—and the further challenge of showing it unambiguously to the reader. Many people would punctuate the sentence like this:

She is old enough to see her parents' faults, however, she is not old enough to forgive them.

But that fails to tell us which side *however* goes with. Parsing the sentence, we see that the transition belongs with the second half. In fact, what we have really amounts to two complete sentences, each with a subject and a predicate:

> She is old enough to see her parents' faults. However, she is not old enough to forgive them.

We can leave them like that, sure. But we can also use our semicolon and bring the two halves back together again, elegantly and grammatically:

> She is old enough to see her parents' faults; however, she is not old enough to forgive them.

One more basic rule, please. This one has to do with something called "direct address." You'll confront direct address the rest of your writing life, I guarantee, so you need to get it straight. Let's first clarify our terms. Talking *about* somebody is indirect address ("I knew Holly back in Berkeley"), whereas talking *to* somebody is direct address ("Hey there, Holly, how're you doing?").

Now here's our rule:

When you address a person directly by name, set off the name with commas to prevent a miscue.

In each of the pairs below, the first sentence is what the writer actually wrote; the second sentence shows what he or she thought was conveyed. Note how much rides on a little comma:

> I hear Charlie.
> I hear, Charlie.

> Most Scots are either one or the other. But you are both my friends.
> Most Scots are either one or the other. But you are both, my friends.

> Remember Nancy.
> Remember, Nancy.

> See that Howard, not a bother at all.
> See that, Howard? Not a bother at all.

> Corey isn't that screwed up?
> Corey, isn't that screwed up?

Our rule applies even when you call the person by a substitute name such as "sir," "coach," "ma'am," "Sis," "Dad," or "my dear." Read these examples aloud and listen for the drops in pitch:

> You know, ma'am, that flight is canceled.
>
> Yes, sir, I promise.
>
> Sit still for me, buddy.
>
> OK, Mom, I'll be there shortly.
>
> What's up, y'all?

The sole exception is when you have two words working in tandem:

> Hey Bobby, got a spare jersey?

To determine if that's the case, see if you drop your pitch. If you do, add a comma. But if, as in "Hey Bobby," the pitch actually *rises* with the name, kill the comma. Compare:

> Hey Bobby, got a spare jersey?
>
> Hey, man, got any spare change?

OK, just two last important remarks about commas. The first concerns the "serial comma"—the comma sometimes assigned to help set off the last item in a series.

Should you write "apples, peaches and pears" or should you write "apples, peaches, and pears"? Believe it or not, among professional writers, few style questions are more contentious. Journalists, especially newswriters, reject that comma before *and*, insisting that it's usually superfluous and wastes space. Most usage experts and editors, meanwhile, defend it ardently. I'll side with the defenders here. Why? Because a final comma eliminates any ambiguity that would oblige a rereading of the sentence. There's no ambiguity, of course, with so simple a series as "apples, peaches and pears," particularly when it's detached from context; but the more complex the series and its context, the more inevitable the ambiguity. The beauty of the serial comma is that it instantly signals our arrival at the last item. Without it, we might not be able to determine what the writer means—or might even be seduced into a misreading. Look at this teaser:

> The motley prisoners in that cell included an unemployed actor, a murderer, a junkie, a man obsessed with flying saucers, an ex-cop with a craving for doughnuts and assorted females—all of them coexisting in surprising harmony.

Are the "assorted females" among the prisoners, or are they only on the mind of the ex-cop? We'll never know.

An equally pragmatic reason for using it is this: Most careful writers outside the journalistic guild, having learned its value, routinely use it and expect others to as well. When they find it absent, they become huffy. Wary, too. (*What else doesn't this writer know about clear writing?*) It's not that they're elitists; they simply resent having to worry about the momentary confusions they anticipate just ahead—and not only from missing serial commas, but from other miscues as well. They've learned to view the serial comma as a writer's credibility test. So be prudent. Insert that comma as a matter of course.

And finally a word about "comma splices." Most of us have heard the term, but few recall what it means. A comma splice is a punctuation fault that occurs when we use just a comma to connect ("splice") two independent clauses—in effect, two sentences:

> Bob wanted to leave early, he had a date that night.

A mistake like this will often occur when we know the relation between two thoughts but forget to show it to our reader. Repairing the error is easy. We can (a) slip in an explanatory conjunction (like *because* or *for*) right after the comma. Or we can (b) replace the comma with a semicolon. Or we can (c) break the two clauses into separate sentences. Or (d) we can simply recast. Here are the four possibilities:

> a. Bob wanted to leave early, for he had a date that night.
> b. Bob wanted to leave early; he had a date that night.
> c. Bob wanted to leave early. He had a date that night.
> d. Since he had a date that night, Bob wanted to leave early.

Parentheses

Parentheses give us a way of muscling in a clarification or an aside that we can't fit in grammatically, or that we don't want to bother trying to, or that we want to de-emphasize because the information is incidental:

> That second trip to Italy (the one in '95) cost me a lost heart, but I'm not complaining.

Note that we can usually accomplish the same goal with two other separators—a pair of commas or a pair of dashes:

> That second trip to Italy, the one in '95, cost me a lost heart, but I'm not complaining.

That second trip to Italy—the one in '95—cost me a lost heart, but I'm not complaining.

So we have a choice here that lets us vary our punctuation. But of all the separators, parentheses should be used most sparingly. They're physically intrusive and soon become eyesores. Equally bad, they stop the forward march of our prose, and can leave the reader feeling whispered at. They like to *breed*, too. So use them uncomfortably, and keep them brief. If you don't, they're apt to overwhelm their context, like this:

Sir Harvey's most recent book (it was originally published in 1994 in Great Britain under the title *All You Ever Wanted to Know About Me But Were Afraid to Inquire*) sank without a bubble.

Here's an often misunderstood rule concerning parentheses:

A parenthetical insert is part of the *preceding* clause. So if that clause needs a final comma, put it *after* the closing parenthesis.

Let me illustrate that rule, showing you first the right way to apply it, then the wrong way. In my example below, our *"preceding* clause"—the one preceding the parenthesis—is "finally agreeing." That clause will need to end in a comma. Note where the comma finally ends up:

"OK, we're settled on *All in the Family* as the title," the network executive replied, finally agreeing (though half in spite of himself), "but I really do draw the line on calling the guy Oedipus. I think we can come up with a more American name than that."

And now the wrong way. Again, keep your eye on that comma:

"OK, we're settled on *All in the Family* as the title," the network executive replied, finally agreeing, (though half in spite of himself) "but I really do draw the line on calling the guy Oedipus. I think we can come up with a more American name than that."

Do you see how the parenthetical insert now seems to be hanging out there in grammatical limbo? That's why we have this little rule. Now let's boil it down and make it even simpler to remember:

Never put a comma right before a parenthesis. Always wait until *after*.

We need to couple two other useful rules with that one. The first deals with exclamation points and question marks before a parenthesis:

> **Question marks and exclamation points can go before an opening parenthesis if they end a quotation there. Otherwise, they go after the closing parenthesis.**

Some examples (with the parentheses indicating hypothetical page citations):

"Was that Billy who called?" (119), she asked.

"Oh, come on, bite!" (221), the fisherman yelled, exasperated.

Did the fisherman actually yell, "Oh, come on, bite!" (221)?

The other rule specifies what you do when the preceding clause wants to end in a period, not a comma. Here's the rule, with two examples built in:

> **If you want a parenthetical remark to stand as a separate sentence, capitalize the first letter and put the period *inside* the closing parenthesis. (This sentence is an example.) But if you want the remark to remain with the preceding clause, put the period *outside* your closing parenthesis (like this).**

Dashes

Let's first review a point I touched on a minute ago. The dash, comma, and parenthesis are sister marks belonging to the family of Separators. Each of them sets off parenthetical matter. The comma handles all the routine chores, as in this example:

But George, who hadn't had lessons, was as graceful as a drunk Schnauzer.

The parenthesis takes over when some incidental information—say, a quick explanation—wants to be slipped into the sentence as a low-voiced aside, or when it isn't grammatically part of the sentence and must be walled off, like this:

That letter (a copy is enclosed) explains the School Board's position.

The dash, meanwhile, the most dramatic and spirited of the three, boldly steps in when the parenthetical matter wants to be set off for emphasis, or when there's to be a sudden break in the flow of the sentence.

Actually, the dash is so versatile and so eager to work that it occasionally moonlights as a colon ("We got the quickest—a border collie"), as a trailing-off thought ("If I could only—"), as a censor ("Oh, d—!"), as an interruption in dialogue ("Jerry, you just said—." "No, honey, you misheard me"), and other such things. Unfortunately, young writers pick up on this trait and work it silly, asking it to double as a comma, a semicolon, a parenthesis, a period, *ad scandalam*. This is why it's tagged as a mark of Easy Virtue by many staid writers, especially lawyers, who rarely let it near their prose. Such an overreaction is a pity, because when the dash errs, it's a victim, not a culprit, and nothing can quite replace it. In fact, of all the punctuation marks, it's the most indispensable for brightening our prose.

Here are five things that the dash can do particularly well:

1. Mark an interruption or break in thought:

> Life without romance—well, you might as well be in prison or a slug under the earth.
> —Charlie Chaplin

> To be middle-aged is to be—well, *what* is it? It is to have hope without expectation, courage without strength, desire without the fire.
> —H. L. Mencken

2. Serve as a conversational colon or light bridge:

> Furthermore, recent discoveries in the physiology of the brain suggest that there may be two different kinds of intelligence—analytic, conceptual, verbal intelligence, located in the left hemisphere of the brain, and intuitive, artistic intelligence in the right hemisphere.
> —*Newsweek*

> That's the worst of facts—they do cramp a fellow's style.
> —C. S. Lewis

Deadly, deflating accuracy is Sheed's game—the art of the neatly nipped hope.

⌐ Melvin Maddocks

Sorry for the exclamation mark—I know how much you loathe the overpunctuation of under-thought frivolity.

⌐ Gale Hickman

3. Isolate a concluding phrase for emphasis or comic effect:

The Dow Jones industrial average plummeted nearly 52 points in a week—the worst break in years.

⌐ *Time*

For three days, Rose Mary Woods, 55, sat tense and bristly before an openly skeptical Judge John J. Sirica and testified that she may have erased at least some of the eighteen minutes missing from one of Mr. Nixon's secret Watergate tapes—all, of course, by "a terrible mistake."

⌐ *Newsweek*

Fashion is illusion, shimmer, magic, mirage—and money: $62.3 billion a year.

⌐ Shana Alexander

Fame creates its own standards. A guy who twitches his lips is just another guy with a lip twitch—unless he's Humphrey Bogart.

⌐ Sammy Davis, Jr.

I could never learn to like her—except on a raft at sea with no other provisions in sight.

⌐ Mark Twain

4. Insert a parenthetical explanation, qualification, or amplification:

Easter weekend arrived, and our cherry trees—about thirty of them—blossomed in unison.

⌐ Peter Mayle

Many of the wars fought by man—I am tempted to say most—have been fought over such abstractions. The more I puzzle over the great wars of history the more I am inclined to the view that the causes attributed to them—territory, markets, resources, the defense or perpetuation of great principles—were not the cause at all but rather explanations or excuses for certain unfathomable drives of human nature.

⌐ J. William Fulbright

IQ tests—and the academic establishment built upon the assumptions about the supreme value of conceptual intelligence—do not measure right-brain intelligence, much less such other vital performance factors as emotional understanding and patience.
    — *Newsweek*

5. Mark a gathering-up of several ideas, often a series of subjects:

> The art of the surprise witness, the withering cross-examination, the sudden objection phrased in arcane formulas—all seem to bespeak a profession based on elaborate training and requiring consummate skill.
>   — *Time*

What these examples show, I think, is how beautifully the dash animates a sentence. (How apt its name! One of its meanings is "animation in style and action," as in the phrase "He cut a dashing figure.") Journalists have long recognized this; it explains why we encounter the mark so frequently in newsmagazines, whose staff writers must somehow make week-old stories newly interesting—which is to say, *dramatic*. For this purpose the dash is almost essential. It's intrinsically graphic and dramatic.

There are four additional reasons, though, why journalists rely on the dash. Since they're pertinent to general writing as well, you ought to know them:

1. A long column of type can look heavy unless it's relieved by occasional dashes to lighten it up and offer variety for the eye.
2. When only commas are used to set off modifying phrases, the commas can pile up and clog the flow. The dash helps to relieve the congestion, not to mention the monotony.
3. Dashes serve as a substitute for italics to call attention to a key word or phrase. They dramatize it by setting it off at a distance and leading the eye right up to it. As a result, readers can't run over it mentally the way they could if a mere comma were setting it off.
4. Dashes make a good substitute for colons, too. Whereas the colon can look staid, the dash looks light, quick, and conversational. It seems virtually to move on the page.

A few last cautions and explanations, and then we're done . . .

First, learn to distinguish between the *single* dash (which sets off something at a sentence end) and the *double* dash (a *pair* of dashes used for wedging in some parenthetical matter). The two marks are identical except that the double dash, like parentheses, comes in a set. I point this out to caution you against using both kinds of dashes in the same sentence. You'll simply confuse your reader, and your prose will look like chopped carrots. The example below illustrates the confusion. Here, the first two dashes are a double dash (for inserting) while the third is a single dash (for setting off):

> Just as Rebecca wearily printed out her paper—it had taken her nearly two weeks of writing—she learned that she had missed Rupert's deadline—by an hour.

Actually, it's a good idea to rest the dash for three or more sentences after each use. If you overuse it, it will lose its effect; in fact, it will begin looking gimmicky, and your readers may wonder whether you know how to write without it.

Second, watch out for misusing the double dash. Here's my simple fingertip test:

> **Cover all the words inside your double dashes. If what remains is coherent and grammatical, you're home free.**

Try that test now:

> Our purple martins arrived today—a sight we'd been anticipating all winter—I couldn't be happier.

It flunks the test, doesn't it? What remains is a run-on sentence:

> Our purple martins arrived today I couldn't be happier.

But the repair is easy. Just add a conjunction (*and*) right after the second dash:

> Our purple martins arrived today—a sight we'd been anticipating all winter—and I couldn't be happier.

Third, don't use a comma after a dash, even if the syntax seems to want it. The dash works alone and will silently absorb the work of the comma. (This is a 20th-century simplification. Earlier prose often used the dash and comma in tandem.) Let me show you how it works. Take any old sentence:

> I'd heard Vancouver was gorgeous, but nothing prepared me for *this*!

Now let's add a double-dash construction right in the middle:

> I'd heard Vancouver was gorgeous—all the travel books gush over it—but nothing prepared me for *this*!

Do you see how that second dash does double duty? Technically, there ought to be a comma there as well, marking the delayed end of the first independent clause, but the dash takes over that job while setting off its own clause.

Fourth, note that the dash is printed in books and magazines as one long line. And perhaps 95% of the time now it's also printed "attached," to use a copyeditors' term. That means the mark is jammed right up against the surrounding text; there's no space before or after it. Some writers, though, still prefer an "open" look. I'll show you the two styles:

> When text is attached—as this phrase is—you have no spaces.

> When text isn't attached — and you'll note this phrase isn't — you do have spaces.

It doesn't matter which style you use so long as you're consistent. I myself prefer the attached style because it's the house style for most publishers and it saves space, but I concede that the unattached style looks more expansive.

Fifth, be alert to an increasingly common mistake: using the hyphen as if it were a dash. Here's how that mistake looks:

> When the little hyphen is mistakenly used for a dash - as is the case here - it looks weird.

You'll never make that mistake yourself once you learn the interesting differences between a hyphen, an en dash, and an em dash—a family of horizontal lines. Let me take you on a little typographical tour.

The *hyphen*, a wee thing, is the shortest of the family. It's used for small jobs, like making compounds (*self-interest*), setting off any prefixes that might otherwise create ambiguity (*pre-engineered*), and showing syllable breaks in words (*hy-phen-a-tion*).

A bit longer is the *en dash*. It's called that because it's nearly the width of the letter "N" in whatever typeface you're using. Sad to report, it's normally mistyped as a hyphen because most writers have never heard of it. But if it's ever set in print by a typesetter, or typed on a computer by someone who knows her business, the en dash comes out almost twice as long as a hyphen. It's used to express the words *to* or *through*:

1998–1999	Matthew 3:5–6
April–May 2010	Chicago–New York flight
pages 28–32	8:00 a.m.–5:00 p.m.

To alert the typesetter, copy editors who work with a pen or pencil will specify an en dash by writing the numeral "1" over the hyphen and an "N" right under it. The result looks like a fraction. (This notational system is handy to know when you're editing other people's prose.) If, like me, you work on a Mac with Microsoft Word, you can easily create an en dash yourself by hitting the Option and hyphen keys simultaneously. If you use a PC, try hitting "Ctrl" + the minus sign on your numeric keypad.

Still longer—about twice the length of an en dash—is the "1-em dash" (or, more simply, the "em dash"), so called because it's approximately the width of the letter "M." This is the most common dash—the very one I just used right there. In fact, it's so common that even many pros will call it by its colloquial name ("a dash") rather than by its technical name ("an em dash") unless there's a chance of confusion. On typewriters, which have no separate key for a dash, it's conventionally typed as two consecutive hyphens, with no space before or after them. On a Mac with Word, you make it by typing Option-Shift-hyphen. And on a PC, equipped with Windows, you hit these three keys simultaneously: Alt + Ctrl + the minus sign on your numeric keypad. Copy editors specify an em dash by writing a "1" over an "M." I guarantee, once you start creating true em dashes on your computer, you'll never go back to the double hyphen, which looks primitive in comparison.

The remaining dashes are the "2-em dash" (twice the width of an "em") and the "3-em dash" (triple the width of an "em"). The 2-em is used to indicate missing letters ("His source was Col. B——"), while the 3-em (roughly the equivalent of six consecutive hyphens) is used in bibliographies to replace the name of an author if he or she has just been cited in the preceding entry. Both dashes are specified by using the same notational system as explained earlier: a numeral over an "M."

Colons

As we saw earlier, the semicolon is used to join related thoughts while still preserving some separation between them—like this:

> The first half of life consists of the capacity to enjoy life without the chance;
> the last half consists of the chance without the capacity.
> —Mark Twain

The colon also joins related thoughts. But it's used only when the first thought acts as a prelude to the second. If your first clause waits to be *explained*, or *particularized*, or in some way *completed*, then you should drop in a colon and proceed to give us what you've primed us to hear. In the example below, the second clause gives us all three things simultaneously:

> Girls have an unfair advantage over men: if they can't get what they want by playing smart, they can get it by playing dumb.
> —Yul Brynner

> **A good tip: The colon is roughly equivalent to *that is* or *namely*.**

But sometimes a writer, risking redundancy, will want to spell that out, using either of those phrases in conjunction with the colon:

> Nothing else is so likely to teach us what at this moment we most need to learn: namely, that more things can be actually *said* than we seem to believe and that so far as prose at least is concerned the best is that whose texture is firmly denotative and which can, as statement, stand firm on its own legs.
> —Joseph Wood Krutch

In such cases as this, the colon really isn't necessary; a comma before and after *namely* would be equally grammatical. The sentence is a long one, though, and Mr. Krutch apparently decided that his readers would welcome more of a break than the first comma would have provided. I think he was right. It's an awkward sentence.

The basic use of the colon, then, is to signify *that is* or *namely*.

> **But when the colon introduces a list or series, its meaning changes to *the following* or *as follows*.**

Here again a writer can spell it out, using the phrase itself as well as the colon, or simply let the colon do its job alone—like this:

> The best methods of combatting organized crime are:
> 1. Telling the criminals you are not at home.
> 2. Calling the police whenever an unusual number of men from the Sicilian Laundry Company begin singing in your foyer.
> 3. Wiretapping.
>   —Woody Allen

Some authorities would wince here, seeing that colon right after a verb. The abrupt break between the verb and its object hurts their eye, or ear, or both. They prefer seeing a colon come only after a complete statement (e.g., "The best methods of combatting organized crime are these:") or after the words *as follows* or *the following* (e.g., "The best methods of combating organized crime are the following:"). You'll have to choose for yourself here. I do it both ways myself.

Below are some miscellaneous examples. They will teach you the use of the colon much more quickly and painlessly than a set of abstract rules will. Please observe that in most of the examples, the colon functions as a slightly more formal version of the dash. It readies the mind for the completion of the thought begun in the initial clause:

> Examining love is like examining a stocking: if you hold it up to the light and stretch it to search for snags, any snags there are may well run and ruin the stocking.
> —Jo Coudert

> We need an alternative which is as challenging, emotionally exciting, and dramatic as war—and we have one now: rebuilding the cities, making war on our old prejudices (this war is in man's skull), and defeating poverty.
> —John W. Gardner

> As an originator, powered by extraordinary energy of mind, Freud was capable of great forward bounds, so that he habitually extrapolated a whole system from a single item: saw the ocean in a drop of water, perceived a law of human behavior in a dropped handkerchief.
> —Barbara Tuchman

> Fields' very appearance evoked shouts of laughter from an audience: the manorial air that was so obviously false, the too benign smile, the larcenous eye.
> —Corey Ford

> I make a sharp distinction between two kinds of concentration: one is immediate and complete, the other is plodding and only completed by stages.
> —Stephen Spender

> The vision behind this book is simple and horrifying: it is the vision of the humanely educated Nazi.
> —Eliot Fremont-Smith

Here are a few other points you should know:

1. The colon is used to introduce a quotation when the quote is longer than a single sentence or when it illustrates the point just made in your lead-in clause. (I'll discuss this at the start of the next chapter, "Quoting.")

2. If the clause that follows your colon is a complete sentence, its first word may be capitalized or not, depending on the emphasis you desire.

> Starbucks got it right: Find a good location, and customers will find you.
> Starbucks got it right: find a good location, and customers will find you.

I myself normally cap it, figuring the reader has a right to know that a full clause is coming. (The more we anticipate our readers' needs—and the better we cue our readers as to what's ahead—the more easily we can be read at a fast clip.)

3. To avoid confusion, don't use more than one colon per sentence. For the same reason, try not to let a semicolon follow a colon—unless, of course, you have items in a series that need semicolons.

Hyphens

Let's focus now on a perennial trouble spot for writers, the compound modifier. A compound modifier (a.k.a "unit modifier" or "phrasal adjective") is *a phrase that's temporarily functioning as an adjective.* Sometimes it's short—just two or three words. Sometimes it's twice that long, or even longer. By itself, the phrase will rarely call for hyphens, but put it in front of a noun and suddenly they're essential. Why? To show that the phrase is now functioning as a *unit.* And why is that important? Because it can prevent confusion—anything from a momentary "Huh?" to total bafflement. It can also prevent what pros call "howlers"—i.e., gaffes that make a writer look silly.

Let's start with some short, real-life compound modifiers. In the left column, I've left them unhyphenated, just as I first met them. In the right column, I've written them correctly, to accustom your eye to good style:

Wrong	Right
iced over lake	iced-over lake
ear jarring sounds	ear-jarring sounds
tear stained page	tear-stained page
multiple choice tests	multiple-choice tests
last ditch stand	last-ditch stand
one track mind	one-track mind
dead end job	dead-end job
22 year old woman	22-year-old woman
small town boy	small-town boy

Now some longer ones, where things get rougher still:

stickler for the rules attitude	stickler-for-the-rules attitude
one day at a time plan	one-day-at-a-time plan
fast food chain operation	fast-food-chain operation
do it yourself mentality	do-it-yourself mentality
trial and error analysis	trial-and-error analysis
three steps to success model	three-steps-to-success model

Imagine yourself reading along and suddenly coming upon each of the items in the left column. What happens? Well, with no cue that you're embarking on a compound modifier, you press merrily on, only to arrive at a juxtaposition of words that makes no sense whatsoever: "over lake," "ditch stand," "track mind," "rules attitude," etc. What do you do? You stop, double back a few words, check to see if you've overlooked something, decide you haven't, and then parse the whole phrase for some latent meaning. *Oh!* you eventually say, grimly, *I get it now.*

But sometimes you don't. Consider these puzzlers. Can you say with perfect confidence what the writer meant?

long dead fish	rare book store
light red shirt	first floor plan

When one of my students confessed to having had "little hands on writing experience," was she making a statement about her small hands or was she confessing how little actual writing experience she'd had? When the army ordered "20 foot long rods of plutonium," did it actually want "20-foot-long rods of plutonium" (i.e., rods that were 20 feet long, but no telling how many) or "20 foot-long rods of plutonium" (i.e., 20 rods, each a foot long)? When the Texas state senator made some "last minute objections" to a bill, were these objections offered at the last minute, or were they some pretty tiny objections on top of ones he or others had already made?

Well, you get the point.

So start schooling yourself to watch for where good writers hyphenate. (As writers, we learn most of what we know just by watching pros, don't we?) And I also suggest that you start worrying about where your own phrasing might need hyphens. Try my simple two-part test:

Hyphenate your modifiers if you can't

1. **reverse their order**

or

2. **remove one of them**

without damaging the sense.

Say you had this phrase: "a hot, muggy night." Can you reverse the order of those modifiers without damaging the sense? Sure: "a muggy, hot night." And can you remove any of them without damaging the sense? Sure: "a hot night" or "a muggy night." True, you'd lose some information, but you wouldn't really damage the sense. So no hyphens are needed.

But consider this phrase: "a three base hit." Can you reverse the order? No: "a base three hit" makes no sense, at least to a baseball audience. And can you remove any of the modifiers without damaging the sense? Once again, no: "a three hit" is meaningless, whereas "a base hit," though it makes sense, utterly damages the intended meaning. Ergo, give it a hyphen.

My two-part test, though surprisingly comprehensive, given the crazy world of hyphens, carries two exceptions. They're worth remembering because they occur repeatedly:

1. Don't hyphenate compound modifiers starting with an *-ly* adverb. (Examples:"widely known speaker"; "firmly held opinions"; "sharply reduced prices.") Why? Because the hyphen is now redundant. An *-ly* adverb *has* to modify the next word, so it's automatically compounding.
2. Don't hyphenate when a compound modifier *follows* its noun ("artists are well known" versus "well-known artists"; "the pages were tear stained" vs. "the tear-stained pages"). Why? I honestly don't know. Convention, probably. I don't like the convention, but I heed it.

Two last points. First, whenever *self* acts as a prefix (and that happens a lot), it takes a hyphen. Examples:

self-confidence	self-esteem	self-made
self-denial	self-taught	self-preservation

Second, "suspension" hyphens are used whenever the parts of compound words get separated. Examples:

The high- and low-season rates differ by as much as $80 a day.
In second- and third-down situations, Murphy prefers a pass-option play.

Exclamation Points

Famed *New Yorker* editor William Maxwell used to advise writers, with a smile, that every writer has a lifetime ration of three exclamation points. Elmore Leonard, the best-selling crime-fiction guru (*Get Shorty, Out of Sight, Split Images*, etc.), is willing to cut us more slack—but not much. "Keep your exclamation points under control," he warns. "You are allowed no more than two or three per 100,000 words of prose."

Even allowing for some hyperbole there, I'm afraid I can't be quite so pure myself, being unwilling rein in all my playfulness and joy just to satisfy the god of dry wit. Deadpan can take a writer—and a person—only so far, I think. Or at least only so far in a direction I'm willing to go. Jim Holt, in a 2009 essay for *The New York Times Book Review* entitled "H. W. Fowler, the King of English," made a telling observation that applies here. Although it certainly pays us, he said, to know our *p*'s and *q*'s with respect to proper grammar and usage, there's a downside we need to beware: "Heightened self-consciousness about usage is the enemy of vigor."

And so it is with heightened self-consciousness about exclamation points. That, too, will increase our sense of inhibition by increasing our fear of looking foolish, so we'll likely shut down at least a part of our true self to avoid tongue-clucking from the more sober set.

Who wants to lose his vigor or playfulness? But who wants to look silly, either?

I think each of us needs to find a balance here. Using exclamation points effectively—more or less sparingly but not guiltily—is quite the challenge. But let me explain something you do need to know. Exclamation points—"screamers" in newspaper parlance—are generally ill-advised for four reasons:

1. Since they're cheapened by writers given to cuteness, exaggeration, and melodramatic effects, they have a bad odor among serious readers.
2. Many people prefer understated humor to the trumpeted, self-approving variety.
3. If the witticism is genuinely funny, it won't need an "Applause" sign. And if it's unfunny, what reader won't resent being coerced to applaud it?
4. Sophisticated writers know that omitting the exclamation point is a form of self-protection. If the witticism is deft, they'll be admired for the dryness of their wit. But if the witticism misfires, there's no proof of their having even intended a joke.

The exclamation point *must* be used, however, after true exclamations or commands: "Whew!" "Go!" "How lovely!"

14

Quoting

The first question in a manuscript reader's mind is: does the writer know his business? Little errors . . . raise a doubt.

—Gorham Munson

Punctuation Introducing Quotations

Use a *comma* whenever your quote[1] is short and you're introducing it with a phrase like "she said" or "he replied" or "[So-and-so] observed":

Twain observed, "Only presidents, editors, and people with tapeworms have the right to use the editorial 'we.' "

But use a *colon* in any of these other three situations: (1) when you've made a statement and are now supplying a quote to illustrate or prove it; (2) when your quote exceeds one sentence; or (3) when you're indenting the quote because it's hefty.

Here is that first case—a statement, grammatically complete, that awaits a quote to illustrate or prove it. The colon announces that the example is at hand:

Twain's pose as a connoisseur of good breeding allowed him to speak solemnly of the ridiculous: "Miss C. B. had her fine nose elegantly

---

[1]For some readers, using *quote* as a noun is one of those "little errors [that] raise a doubt." In 1978, a formidable 85% of *The American Heritage Dictionary*'s Usage Panel rejected *quote* as a substitute for *quotation* in writing, ruling it "unacceptable." It's too casual, they apparently felt, too colloquial. I'll side with the enlightened minority here—and with George Orwell ("Never use a long word where a short one will do")—though I'll occasionally use *quotation* where it won't overtax the sentence. *Quote* is simple and direct, and it certainly predominates in spoken English, so why stand on ceremony? Why opt for needless complexity?

enameled, and the easy grace with which she blew it from time to time marked her as a cultivated and accomplished woman of the world; its exquisitely modulated tone excited the admiration of all who had the happiness to hear it."

And here is the second case—a quote exceeding one sentence. Note how the colon, stepping in for the comma, quietly cues us to expect something longer:

> James Thurber remarked: "Word has somehow got around that the split infinitive is always wrong. This is of a piece with the outworn notion that it is always wrong to strike a lady."

The third case involves a bulky quote that's indented—what editors call a "block quotation" or "extract." The beauty of block quotes is that they let us see, up front, exactly how much awaits us. Typically, as in my Carver extract just ahead, block quotes follow a complete statement ending in a colon. But it's not uncommon to see them woven seamlessly into the lead-in, as in my second example, from Robertson Davies, which begins in mid-sentence. Here the lead-ins are my own, devised just for this occasion, while the quotes are real ones from Carver and Davies:

> Raymond Carver, a contemporary master of the American short story, seemed to have loved the process of writing as much as the product. And that love of process was reinforced by his perfectionism, plus his refusal to quit on a weak early draft. He was, he confessed, an incessant reviser:
>
>> I've done as many as twenty or thirty drafts of a story. Never less than ten or twelve drafts. It's instructive, and heartening both, to look at the early drafts of great writers. I'm thinking of the photographs of galleys belonging to Tolstoy, to name one writer who loved to revise. I mean, I don't know if he loved it or not, but he did a great deal of it. He was always revising, right down to the time of page proofs. He went through and rewrote *War and Peace* eight times and was still making corrections in the galleys. Things like this should hearten every writer whose first drafts are dreadful, like mine are.

The late Robertson Davies, Canada's most distinguished male novelist, took a similar delight in the process. When asked how the work of writing is actually done, at least for him, he confessed that it is

> in part an exploration of drudgery, of daily application, of heaping up the pile of finished pages as the beaver builds his dam. But if you are really a writer, you probably like that drudgery better than anything else you could possibly be doing. It is during those hours of drudgery that you are most in touch with what is of greatest value in yourself.

You are creating something, and therefore you are to some extent an artist; you are doing it by means of the technique you have painstakingly acquired, and perhaps mastered, and therefore you are a craftsman, and there is a special delight in plying one's craft.

So, you see, we can often dispense with introductory punctuation altogether. In fact, it's commonplace when we're quoting a phrase or clause. Learn to integrate it right into the mainstream of your own sentence. *No introductory punctuation is needed unless the syntax of your sentence requires it.* Example:

> Mencken said that *Comrades* "will lie embalmed in my memory as a composition unearthly and unique—as a novel without a single redeeming merit."

Be especially careful to dispense with introductory punctuation if your lead-in ends in *that*:

> *Wrong:*   Updike said that, "Writing and rewriting are a constant search for what it is one is saying."
> *Right:*   Updike said that "Writing and rewriting are a constant search for what it is one is saying."

Punctuation at the End of Quotations

Most stylistic conventions make sense. We may have to think about them a bit, but eventually their logic emerges. A few conventions, though, seem downright perverse. One of them is the basic rule governing punctuation at the end of quotes:

> **Commas and periods always go INSIDE closing quotation marks, even if the comma or period wasn't part of the original quotation.**

This is plainly counterintuitive. If the comma or period wasn't part of the quotation, why on earth make it look like it was? Well, in Great Britain they don't; everything you see published there has the comma or period outside the marks. But in the U.S., for some reason, long-standing convention dictates the odd rule we operate by. You cannot pick up a book, magazine, or newspaper in this country that doesn't put those marks inside. So we must learn to live with it—either that or we risk coming across as unschooled.

Fortunately, the corollary to this rule returns us to the world of reason:

> **Colons and semicolons go OUTSIDE closing quotation marks. And so do exclamation points and question marks—if they weren't part of the quotation.**

Remembering these rules is hard, even though, as I said, nearly everything we read gives us daily illustrations of them. But here are more examples. If you stare at them long enough, what looks wrong may eventually look right:

> Did I write "rain"? I meant "reign." No, no, not "rein," and certainly not "rain."

> Oscar Wilde remarked, "Truth is never pure, and rarely simple"; half-truths, however, suffer neither inconvenience, so have always proved more popular.

> What does he mean by "a spy in the enemy's country"?

Frequently we'll see people, confused about these rules, striking what they hope is a happy compromise—or, failing that, something they hope readers will chalk up to an overhasty pen. The "solution" involves placing the comma or period directly *under* the closing quotation mark. Resourceful, yes, but it's like observing a yellow light by stopping midway through the intersection.

Miscellaneous Small Points

When you're referring to a specific word or phrase, you need to isolate it from the surrounding text by setting it off, either with quotation marks or italics. Do the same with words that you're using in a special sense (e.g., technically, humorously, ironically):

> A more recent instance of euphemism was our calling the war in Vietnam a "conflict."

> "Puritanism," as defined by H. L. Mencken, is "the haunting fear that someone, somewhere, may be happy."

Many people apparently think that *imply* and *infer* are synonyms.

Does anyone around here know how to spell "comraderie"?[2]

Is this what they call "collateral damage"?

A helpful tip offered by Ken Macrorie in his excellent book *Telling Writing* is this: "More often than not, the words *say, call, refer to as* are followed by quoted words." One might add to that list *the word* and *the words*. Macrorie's own sentence illustrates the point.

For extra emphasis, or when several words are being cited, forget quotation marks and go with underlining or italics instead, as Macrorie himself just did. Those two formatting tools, by the way, are considered typographically equivalent. In fact, back in the days of typewriters, the way you indicated italicized text was by underlining it.

One further point, which probably ought to be set in bold caps: If you ever use a cliché, never—repeat, *never*—put it in quotation marks, like this:

Andy was a "chip off the old block."

Why the stringent prohibition? Two reasons: (1) quotation marks only compound your offense by highlighting the trite expression; and (2) they're bound to irritate readers because, implicitly, you're claiming that you really know better. If so, why use the cliché at all?

Indented Quotations

Block quotes are traditionally typed single-spaced (MLA style asks for double-spacing, which seems prodigal) and indented moderately (10 spaces, says MLA) from the left margin. The right margin, too, if you wish. All this enhances their appeal because it lets us gauge the length of the quote at a glance, so we needn't fret about overlooking a distant closing quotation mark and thus confusing quoted text with the writer's own.

Most professionals will indent prose quotes that exceed four lines. Verse quotes, on the other hand, normally get indented when they exceed two lines, since no one enjoys reading lots of lines of verse bumping into each other; also, most poems rely heavily on their form, so it needs to be displayed. Make sure that in both cases you *omit* quotation marks, since indenting is their equivalent and thus makes them redundant.

Block quotes, as explained earlier, normally get introduced with a *colon*. But sometimes you can marry the quote with your own lead-in so

---

[2] Try "camaraderie." This is one word you have to know how to spell before you can even look it up in your dictionary.

as to eliminate introductory punctuation altogether. The effect is pleasingly fluid:

> The problem, Senator Fulbright pointed out, is that
>
>> power tends to confuse itself with virtue, and a great nation is pecu-
>> liarly susceptible to the idea that its power is a sign of God's favor,
>> conferring upon it a special responsibility for other nations—to
>> make them richer and happier and wiser, to remake them, that is, in
>> its own shining image.

Now to the mistakes. Inexperienced writers commonly make three
big ones with block quotes.

Mistake #1 is to introduce their quote with a lead-in ending in a period instead of a colon. You can see, with a little thought, why it's crucial
to use the colon. Ending your lead-in with a period leaves the quote
hanging below it, unattached, in limbo. Your hapless reader will wonder,
"Is the quote meant to illustrate the comment *before* it or *after* it?" A
colon answers that very question.

Mistake #2 is to sandwich their big quote smack in the middle of
their own sentence:

> In 1922, while observing the behavior of hens and ducks, the Norwegian
> Schjelderup-Ebbe noticed a distinct "pecking order" among them:
>
>> In any small flock of hens there soon develops a rather firmly fixed
>> hierarchy, in which the top hen normally has the right to peck all
>> the others without being pecked in return: and each of the others
>> occupies a place subordinate to hers, usually in a linear series with
>> respect to one another down to the lowest bird, which all may peck
>> without fear of retaliation.
>
> and ever since that time anthropologists have applied the term to the hier-
> archy of dominance observed among humans as well.

This practice is bad for two reasons. First, it almost always compels a
rereading of the entire sentence, quote and all, since by the time we get
to the end, we've forgotten how the thing began. And second, the practice is usually ungrammatical since most quotes end in a period, which
stops the writer's own sentence right there.

Mistake #3 may be the commonest blunder of all. It involves leading
into the quote ultramechanically (e.g., "McMurtry wrote:"), saving all the
commentary—if in fact any is even given—until afterward. Here again, we'll
often have to reread the long quote just to confirm what the writer later
claims about it. But, honestly, we might not even read it at all, especially if

it's lengthy. We might take one look at that dense block of text and say, "Nah, I'm not messing with that." Skilled writers understand this—the often massive resistance that readers have to block quotes. And so they use them sparingly, worriedly. They do one other thing, too: *they take pains to sell their oh-so-precious quote in their intro*, giving us a real incentive to plunge in. Equally important, they preview the quote just enough to make us feel at home with that big hunk of text. We now have a *context* for it, including the writer's slant on the quote. That slant can be developed later, of course, but we need at least a bit of it up front to read the whole thing through the eyes of the writer. This illustrates a point I made way back in Chapter 1, when I defined writing as "the art of creating desired effects."

Below is a block quote from Larry McMurtry, the popular author of *Lonesome Dove*. Here he's taking a wry look at how his fellow Texans, always a breed apart, practice their frontier individualism on the state's roadways:

> Washington drivers must, to a degree, drive cooperatively: otherwise they would never get home. Texas drivers, on the other hand, are complete solipsists: their awareness of other cars is infrequent and patternless, though generally they seem to assume that other cars are on the road either to outrun them or attack them. Of pedestrians they simply take no note. They do not run them down for sport, as drivers do in Mexico City, but it would certainly be fair to say that their attitude toward pedestrians lacks a sense of remorse. Were one to have to characterize Texans solely on the basis of their driving, one would have to say that as a people they entirely lack the communal view. Their driving is manic, isolated, discourteous, and frequently dangerous; the humanistic realization that we are all, figuratively speaking, on the same freeway is not a realization that has yet struck home in the Lone Star state. The highways seem to be where frontier individualism is making its last-ditch stand.

If you devoured that long quote, and if you were able to make sure sense of it even from the opening lines, I did my job right. But so did McMurtry.

Orphan Quotes

An "orphan" is writers' slang for a quote lacking explicit attribution. To journalists, especially, it's a cardinal taboo, and rightly so. Say, for example, you had written:

> One congressman was openly scornful. "Anyone who believes him now is a fool." And Nixon's credibility stood in further peril still from. . . .

Here, it's only *implicit* who made that remark. We shouldn't have to guess, should we? Nor should we have to guess whether the quote is meant to illustrate what precedes it or what follows it. Let's look at four ways to fix that passage:

> "Anyone who believes him now," said one congressman, "is a fool." And Nixon's credibility. . . .

> One congressman was openly scornful: "Anyone who believes him now is a fool." And Nixon's credibility. . . .

> Scoffed one congressman, "Anyone who believes him now is a fool." And Nixon's credibility. . . .

> "Anyone who believes him now is a fool," said one congressman. And Nixon's credibility. . . .

Note that the second example, with its colon, syntactically ties the quote to its source, thus eliminating ambiguity. Otherwise, as in the other examples, you need to provide a speech tag—even if you also supply a footnoted reference—so as to spare your reader even momentary puzzlement.

By the way, don't confuse an "orphan quote" with a "blind quote," which is another, less serious, taboo among journalists and other nonfiction writers. A "blind quote" (which those example sentences also illustrate) is a quote that's attributed to some vague, conspicuously unnamed source such as "a congressman" or "a senior White House official." Blind quotes are sometimes needed to protect a source, but orphans are ALWAYS a no-no.

Dialogue

As you'll notice when studying prize-winning nonfiction, artful expository prose offers many occasions for working in dialogue. In fact, such occasions seem nearly unavoidable.

Often, for example, a writer will have to *transcribe* an actual taped conversation. (Far trickier than it might seem! The punctuation challenges alone can give even an expert the fits.) On other occasions the dialogue will have to be *recalled*, as when a writer, in a memoir, shares his recollection of various conversations. And sometimes the dialogue will have to be *imagined*. For example, the writer might give us what he understands a person was thinking or feeling at a given moment. There, the huge challenge is to represent the person's thoughts in his or her own idiom—a challenge that fiction writers face daily, of course.

Let me, then, offer you a starter kit for dialogue writing. Nothing fancy here, just basics:

1. If you aim to create truly realistic speech rhythms, you first have to give yourself permission to flout standard written English. Dialogue follows its own rules. And here's Rule #1: *"Authenticity before all else."* So make free use of the following:

- Sentence fragments (or "frags," as professionals term them).
- Short paragraphs—even one-word grafs. (More writers' jargon.)
- Colloquialisms and bits of verbal slumming (*gonna, wouldya* or *wouldja, dunno,* etc.).
- Contractions, including offbeat ones heard regularly in conversation ("Mel, why'm I making more than you?"; "What'd she see?").
- Monosyllabic words (e.g., *but* instead of *however*).
- Repeated words or phrases. (Most speakers get in verbal ruts.)
- Interruptions.

  > *Bob:* "But if you—"
  > *Sue:* "Forget it. I'm out of here."

  Note that the dash stands alone. No period needed.
- Internal interruptions ("Who's to say? Maybe—hey, could she have seen you at Danny's?").
- Internal pauses ("Everything's fine . . . well, relatively.").
- Trailing-off thoughts ("If the computer crashes . . . No, let's not even think about it"). Note that you use just three spaced dots to end such a sentence—and you insert a space before the first of them. (Were it an ellipsis at the end of a quotation, on the other hand, you'd need four spaced periods, not three.)
- Questions like "Why?" and "Really?" (You can hardly use too many. People talk in questions.)

2. Avoid semicolons—nobody talks in semicolons. Avoid long grafs for the same reason.

3. Avoid nonsense like "'Aw, you're not that old,' she *grinned*" and "'I am too,' he *grimaced*." Better to use extra words than risk an illogicality. The rule seems to be that if your verb normally describes both a facial expression *and* a way of talking (like "sneer"), it's OK. Some verbs, like "laugh," are close calls ("'I am too,' he *laughed*.") When in doubt, try these options:

> "I am too," he said, laughing. [or] He laughed. "I am too."

4. Let your reader supply 90% of the exclamation points and italics.

5. In direct address, set off the person's name with a comma, *even if that comma/pause is slurred over in normal speech*. Here's one place

where you can't ignore the niceties of standard written English. (You might review my tips on direct address in the section on "Commas.")

   6. Root around in this lexicon of hard-to-spell, semiverbal vernacular—grunts and noises that dictionaries fancily call "interjections":

> "Mm-hmm" (a mumbled assent)
> "Hm-hmm" (a mumbled denial)
> "Uh-huh" (affirmative)
> "Uh-unh" (negative)
> "Uh" (groping for words; followed by comma or three dots)
> "Huh?" (as in "Say that again?")
> "huh?" (when terminating a sentence, it means "Right?")
> "Hmm?" (grown-ups' version of "Say that again?")
> "Uh-oh" (sudden alarm)
> "Yeah" (to express assent)
> "Yea" (to cheer or encourage, as in "Yea, team")
> "OK" (*The AP Stylebook* prefers this spelling to "okay" & "O.K." So do I—it's cleaner.)

   7. Work in some daringly elliptical constructions and comma splices that mirror how people really talk. Want courage? Study these sentences culled from different pages of dialogue by novelist–screenwriter Elmore Leonard:

> "He got in a elevator, went upstairs."
>
> "It say who they were?"
>
> "So what now? Go home, maybe sleep some."
>
> "The store, they sell stuff like that?"

Leonard, maybe the cleverest dialogue-writer in America, made the cover of *Newsweek* back in 1985. If you like crime fiction and can handle raunchy low-lifes speaking authentic street talk and doing truly nasty things to each other, try Leonard—a brilliant technician and an A+ storyteller. Definitely not for the queasy, though. An equally talented technician, and unquestionably my all-time favorite writer of detective fiction, is Michael Connelly. Want real dialogue? Effortlessly natural place descriptions? Lifelike human beings? Awesome plotting? Connelly's your man.

   I'd also recommend you find yourself a copy of Studs Terkel's engrossing nonfiction bestseller *Working*, subtitled *People Talk About What They Do All Day and How They Feel About What They Do* (Ballantine paperback, 1974). For this book, Terkel tape-recorded in-depth interviews with over 130 colorful individuals, covering the widest imaginable range of careers and sensibilities. If you want to study how real people really talk (well, only lightly edited, anyway), and if you also want what amounts to a superb career manual, this is the book for you.

And let me also recommend an equally engrossing book—Michael Crichton's memoir *Travels* (Ballantine paperback, 1988), which I've heard him call his own favorite of his many bestsellers. Besides being fabulously entertaining, it's a virtual textbook on how to write great dialogue—how to punctuate it, pace it, interweave it with exposition, and vary it. Even if you don't read Crichton's fiction, you need to check out this book.

Punctuating Run-on Quotations of Poetry

To conserve space, verse quotations of two lines or less should be run in, in quotation marks, as part of your text. But be sure to use a *slash* (/)—also known as a *virgule*—to indicate the end of one line and the beginning of the next. (The slash should always have a space before and after it.) Also, begin each new line with a capital letter unless the poet has done otherwise. Example:

> In characterizing Belinda, Alexander Pope pays his supreme tribute to the power of beauty: "If to her share some Female Errors fall, / Look on her Face, and you'll forget 'em all" (*The Rape of the Lock*, II.17–18).

Note the lead-in there. Didn't you want to read on to learn Pope's "supreme tribute to the power of beauty"? Seductive lead-ins are as important for short quotes as for block ones.

References for Quotations

For the convenience of readers, you should specify the page reference (or line reference, if the lines are numbered) for each quotation.

One way to do that is with a footnote. The initial footnote to a book or article typically specifies all of the following: author, title, city of publication, publisher, date of publication, and page number of the quotation:

[1]Northrop Frye, *Anatomy of Criticism: Four Essays* (Princeton, N.J.: Princeton Univ. Press, 1957), p. 31.

Subsequent references to that source typically specify just the author's name and page number. Example: "Frye 32." (For answers to any questions you may have about other aspects of footnoting protocol, consult either the *MLA Style Manual* or, if you write in the sciences, the *Publication Manual of the American Psychological Association*, which spells out APA form. I'd also recommend *The Chicago Manual of Style*, 16th ed., from the University of Chicago Press.)

In recent years, however, what with the flood of arcane scholarly works, more and more writers have come to see footnotes as odious, especially in academic prose. When long, they're distracting to the reader; they're a nuisance to type; they smack of unreadable research papers; they waste space. As a result, footnotes are now being used more as a last resort than as a matter of course. In their place, writers have learned to use "parenthetical references"—i.e., *brief references supplied in parentheses immediately following their quotations*. This is now the preferred form, especially whenever most of the quotations are drawn from the same work.

This simplified form has itself undergone further simplification. More and more writers are now putting *merely the number* of the page or line in parentheses, provided the number is unambiguous. For example, instead of writing "(p. 192)," you'd simply write "(192)." If confusion is likely, though, you should either (a) explain in a footnote to your first quotation that page (or line) references will hereafter be given parenthetically in the text, after which you may go ahead and use just the numbers in parentheses, or (b) use these abbreviations: *p.* for *page* and *l.* for *line*. (The plural forms are *pp.* and *ll.*)

If you're quoting from multiple authors and multiple works, you can distinguish them by making sure that each parenthetical citation carries both the last name of the author and the page number of the cite, with only a single space, not a comma, separating them—e.g., "(Davis 27)." But if you're quoting just one author repeatedly and consecutively, the page number alone will suffice—at least until you quote, and need to cite, a different author, at which point you need to use last names again.

If you're citing more than one work by an author, and if the context doesn't make clear which work it is, add a shortened title reference to the cite—e.g., "(Callard, *Movies* 103)."

At the end of your essay, you'll then need to provide a list of all the works you've quoted. This list, which is labeled "Works Cited," follows the standard form for bibliographies. Given the many different kinds of sources, and the highly specific formatting procedures approved for each, I'll send you to a standard authority, like the *MLA Style Manual*, for the details.

The procedure for references to plays bears special explanation. When citing a line reference to a Shakespeare play, you have a choice of parenthetical references: (II.ii.553), (II.2.553), or (2.2.553). Note that the last number in each case refers to the line, not the page. Shakespeare's plays, remember, were written in blank verse, so all the lines are numbered, just as for any long poem. Incidentally, when referring to a particular Act of a play, capitalize *Act* to distinguish the word from *act* and use capital roman numerals. Example: Act II. The word *scene* is not capitalized since there's no threat of ambiguity. If you quote from a non-Shakespearean play, it's usually sufficient to cite just the Act and page number. Example: (III, 88).

Punctuating Parenthetical References

The three related rules here are these:

> **Rule #1:** A parenthetical reference *completes* the clause containing your quote, so your final punctuation of that clause should *follow* the reference, not precede it.
>
> **Rule #2:** As for any comma or period that originally appeared at the end of your quote, simply cut it—it's now functionless and would create double-punctuation.
>
> **Rule #3:** But if your quote ends in a question mark or exclamation point, keep that punctuation so your quote will read intelligibly.

If you study the following example, you'll see how simple all this really is. Focus, please, on the parenthetical references. Notice that there's no punctuation at the end of the two quotes—that punctuation got silently dropped. But also notice that we have punctuation *after* the closing parentheses, since that's where the two clauses actually end:

When King Henry describes how, by being seldom seen, he managed to keep his presence "like a robe pontifical, / Ne'er seen but wonder'd at" (3.2.56–57), we hear telling echoes of Prince Hal's earlier words, "Being wanted, he may be more wonder'd at" (1.2.207).

This next example shows a quote ending in an exclamation point. We retain that mark so the quotation will make sense, but we also have to supply additional punctuation after the parenthetical reference to end the clause:

"Oh what a rogue and peasant slave am I!" (2.2.553), Hamlet exclaims.

References for indented quotations have their own, even simpler, procedure. First, end the block quote with whatever punctuation applies. Then, set the whole parenthetical reference *outside* that punctuation mark:

> But literary criticism, for Mencken, was a fine art, not a science. And why? Because, to his staunchly unsentimental mind, criticism is finally "no more than prejudice made plausible" (62). He summed up his attitude thus:
>
> > If the critic, retiring to his cell to concoct his treatise upon a book or play or what-not, produces a piece of writing that shows sound structure, and brilliant color, and the flash of new and persuasive ideas, and civilized manners, and the charm of an uncommon personality in free function, then he has given something to the world that is worth having, and sufficiently justified his existence. (102)

Ellipses

Ellipsis points—three *spaced* periods (. . .), a.k.a. "dots"—are used to show readers where you've omitted some text in a quotation. The omission itself is called an "ellipsis" (pl., "ellipses").

If you're quoting a mere clause or phrase, the dots aren't needed, for the fragment is self-evident. But if ever you think a failure to flag an omission might somehow mislead the reader or misrepresent the original, you should by all means insert the dots. Do try to use them sparingly, though, for they can become distracting when peppered about. The curious reader may be left wondering what lies behind all those intriguing dots and thus have half his attention diverted.

Normally, you can—and should—dispense with the dots whenever your ellipsis occurs at the start of a quotation. Simply create an introductory clause that flows smoothly into that quotation, taking care that the two parts are syntactically continuous. *The initial letter of the quotation, being in lowercase, will be enough to show us that the quote is truncated.* You'll know you've done it right if you can mentally delete the quotation marks and be left with a perfectly grammatical sentence—like this:

> Jacques Barzun summed up the importance of clarity with his remark that "a written exercise is designed to be read; it is not supposed to be a challenge to clairvoyance."

Let me now walk you through some common situations you're apt to face and show you how to handle them:

1. If you end one of your sentences with a quotation ending in an ellipsis, you must supply, in addition to the three dots, an appropriate

final punctuation mark, typically a period. The ellipsis, while written as three spaced periods, doesn't itself function as a period. Example:

> Mme. Geoffrin remarked of her grandmother, "She spoke so pleasantly about things she did not know, that no one wished she knew more of them. . . ."

In the original, a comma followed that last word, *them*. You're allowed to silently delete that comma (or any other punctuation mark that might be there) since the ellipsis indicates an omission anyway. Observe, too, that whenever you need to show that you're omitting the last part of a quoted sentence, you must insert a space after the last word, then add *four* spaced dots, the fourth one being your true period. Here is a sentence containing an ellipsis both in the middle and at the end. Note the difference:

> The professor replied, with a smile, "Writing is a difficult art . . . because it involves thinking logically and interestingly, two operations that are unnatural to our minds—well, at least to my own. . . ."

2. Now let's suppose you're quoting from a longish passage, only parts of which are useful to you. Let's say that after quoting its splendid beginning, you want to skip over an unimportant middle chunk of it before resuming your quotation. And let's say, further, that the quoted sentence that happens to precede your planned ellipsis (the chunk you're cutting) is a *complete* sentence, not a truncated one. In that situation, you'll still use four dots at the end of that sentence, but now you'll bump the first dot, here functioning as your true period, *right up against the last word of that quote*, showing that the sentence really did terminate there; and then, after adding a single space, you'll add three more spaced dots to indicate your ellipsis. This detail of the bumped dot, though minuscule, lets us know exactly where your ellipsis actually starts—*after a complete sentence.* And it also shows you to be scrupulous about your quoting. It's yet another way that writers have of quietly demonstrating their professionalism.

In the following example, we have three ellipses, each illustrating one of the common situations just discussed. The first ellipsis, found at the opening quotation mark, isn't explicitly flagged, but the lowercased "if" tells readers that the beginning of the quote has been dropped, so three dots there would be redundant. Happily, then, we can dispense with them. The second ellipsis, after "make-up," retains Bradbury's own comma for ease of reading, though we could have silently dropped it if the syntax hadn't required it. The third ellipsis, after "gusto," has a period bumped right up against that word, telling readers that Bradbury's sentence actually ended there and that the omission starts only after that point:

> Ray Bradbury, the old science-fiction master, won himself many new fans with his collection of essays entitled *Zen in the Art of Writing*. In one of those essays, he famously remarked that "if I were asked to name the most important items in a writer's make-up, . . . I could only warn him to look to his zest, see to his gusto. . . . If you are writing without zest, without gusto, without love, you are only half a writer."

3. If, in quoting a passage of verse, you wish to omit one or more whole lines, simply type an entire line of consecutive, moderately spaced periods, as wide as the poem itself, to indicate a substantial omission. Your parenthetical reference at the end of the quote will enable readers to determine the extent of the omission: they can simply subtract the number of lines you've actually quoted from the total of the lines you've given in the parentheses. Say, for example, your indented quote from a poem looks like this: you've quoted lines 20–21, then skipped some lines (which you've signaled with a single line of spaced periods), then quoted lines 28–29. Your citation will read "(20–29)." But since you'd have quoted only four lines, the reader will know that you had to have omitted six lines in the middle there.

4. If you ever need to express *a thought that is trailing off*, something we see in dialogue all the time, use just three spaced periods instead of the customary four at the end of the sentence, and skip a space before that first period:

> "Well, whatever . . ."

5. For how to handle any other issues with ellipses that I haven't covered here, I recommend you consult *The Chicago Manual of Style*, 16th ed. It's authoritative and wonderfully complete.

Editorial Insertions (Square Brackets)

This is another form of tampering with quotations. When you want to insert some brief note or clarification into a quote, don't make the common mistake of putting it in parentheses, for how will we know the insert is yours rather than the author's own? Instead, use *brackets*, like this:

> George Eliot says of Dorothea, "she felt that she enjoyed it [horseback-riding] in a pagan sensuous way, and always looked forward to renouncing it" (*Middlemarch*, I.i).

15

Abbreviations

The most essential gift for a good writer is a built-in, shockproof, shit detector.

—Ernest Hemingway

Here are some common abbreviations, most of them used chiefly in footnotes, where conserving space is vital. Don't use them too freely in your body text—you'll look either pedantic or lazy, plus you'll risk confusing anyone unfamiliar with the apparatus of academic writing. The Latin abbreviations in this list are followed by the complete word or phrase from which they're derived. In times past, writers italicized Latin abbreviations. Current practice favors no italics.

- **c.,** *circa,* about, approximately. It's used with dates: "He was born c. 1820." *Circa* is occasionally also abbreviated "ca."
- **cf.,** *confer,* compare. Use "cf." only when you wish readers to compare one thing with another. Example: "Cf. Monet's sketch of the same cathedral." Many novice writers mistakenly use "cf." when they mean "see" as in "See pp. 8–10 for a full discussion of this point."
- **chap.,** chapter.
- **cont.,** continued.
- **ed.,** edited by; edition; editor. The plural is "eds."
- **e.g.,** *exempli gratia,* for example. Use commas before and after it, just as you would if you were writing "for example," or else a dash before it and a comma after it: "Conrad uses this device in some of his short stories—e.g., 'The Secret Sharer.'"
- **et al.,** *et alia,* and others: "This essay was later anthologized in *Criticism,* ed. Mark Schorer et al." Since "et" is a complete Latin word, don't put a period after it—a common mistake.
- **etc.,** *et cetera,* and so forth. Often, people will write "and etc." or "etc., etc." Both are redundancies. "Etc." is preceded by a comma.

- **f.,** and the following page or line. The plural is "ff." "Her notebooks quoted on p. 23 f. and p. 60 ff. address the same issues." Observe that a space follows each "p." as well as each numeral. In the interest of exactness, it's best to avoid this lazy abbreviation; instead, try to specify the final number as well as the first: "Her notebooks quoted on pp. 23–24 and pp. 60–66 address the same issues."
- **ibid.,** *ibidem,* in the same place. "Ibid." is used in footnotes to specify the same title as the one cited in the preceding note. If the page reference as well as the title remains identical, "ibid." alone is sufficient. If the page reference differs, you must specify it. Example: "²Ibid., p. 42."
- **i.e.,** *id est,* that is. As with "e.g.," this abbreviation is set off by commas fore and aft, or, in some cases, by a dash and a comma: "The titles of books, however, must be underlined, i.e., set in italics."
- **l.,** line. The plural is "ll." Since this abbreviation can easily be confused with the Arabic numeral 1, avoid it. You'll spare your reader sentences like "A less complete statement of Eliot's theme appears in ll. 11–13."
- **l.c.,** lowercase.
- **MS,** manuscript. The plural is "MSS." A period after "MS" is optional, but current usage dispenses with it.
- **N.B.,** *nota bene,* note well. Example: "N.B.: this characterization was deleted in the original transcript."
- **op. cit.,** *opere citato,* in the work cited. "Op. cit." is sometimes used in footnoting to eliminate the need for repeatedly writing out a long title. If you've already cited a work—say, Eugene O'Neill's *Long Day's Journey into Night*—you may now substitute "op. cit." for the title and give the new page reference: "⁸O'Neill, op. cit., p. 40." A much clearer procedure, though, is to provide a shortened form of the title instead of "op. cit.": "⁸O'Neill, *Long Day's Journey,* p. 40."
- **p.,** page. The plural is "pp." But be sure to put a space after the period—"p. 21"—just as you would after the word you're abbreviating here: "page 21."
- **pub.,** published by.
- **sic,** thus, so. If you're quoting something that contains an error—say, a misspelling, factual inaccuracy, grammatical lapse, or nonsensical expression—and you don't want it misattributed to you the transcriber, embed a "[sic]" in square brackets right after it. It tells us, "This is just how I found it." *Sic* normally takes italics, and the square brackets flag it as an editorial interpolation. Example: "Bridgeport is the largest city in Conneticut [*sic*]."
- **viz.,** *videlicet,* namely. Set it off by commas fore and aft.
- **vol.,** volume. The plural is "vols."
- **vs.,** *versus,* against, versus. But in court decisions, it's written "v." and italicized, as are the names of the two parties: "*Remy v. Thompkins.*"

16

Tips on Usage

*Good writers are those who keep the language efficient.
That is to say, keep it accurate, keep it clear.*

—Ezra Pound

*Let us do these things not to satisfy "rules" or to gratify
the whims of a pedagogue, but rather to express ourselves clearly, precisely, logically, and directly—and to
cultivate the habits of mind that produce that kind of
expression.*

—Theodore Bernstein

accommodate   Regularly misspelled "accomodate." This word gets my
  vote as the most frequently misspelled word in American English.
  Just remember: two c's *and* two m's. Two o's as well!

affect–effect   Few word pairs can rival these terrors for the headaches
  they breed. Bad enough that they sound alike, but each word also
  has both a noun and a verb form. And one of the verbs, *affect*, even
  has two different definitions itself. Worse still, it uses the other
  word, *effect*, in one of them. And when *affect* works as a noun, it
  has an entirely new pronunciation ("AFF-ect")! No wonder everybody's confused.

Let's sort out the principal meanings here:

> *affect* (verb) = to influence, have an effect on ("That movie deeply
>   affected me")
> *affect* (verb) = to feign ("She affected indifference, but I know she
>   cared")

affect (noun) = emotional reaction ("The patient showed no affect")

effect (noun) = an influence or impact ("California had a big effect on me")

effect (verb) = to bring about ("To effect any change here, we'll need Superman")

Dr. Mary Knatterud, an editor friend and research associate in the Surgery Department of the University of Minnesota, offers a sentence she once devised for a colleague to clarify four of the five meanings: "The effect of the patient's affect was profound: it deeply affected her mother and effected a change in their relationship."

all right   *All right* is right; *alright* is wrong. So many people don't know *alright* is wrong, though, that eventually it will be accepted as Standard English. And it should be. It's quicker than *all right* and says the same thing. Nothing would be lost except surplusage. (Shortened forms that resemble it, and that no longer raise alarm, are *already*, *altogether*, and *although*.) Meanwhile, however, I suggest you stick with *all right*. It will spare you being labeled a poor speller.

a lot   It's written as two words, not one. Many people, though, would prefer that you not write it at all, at least in serious prose. They view it as "colloquial"—i.e., too informal. But one of my own favorite usage experts, Theodore Bernstein, in his invaluable *The Careful Writer*, notes how much more relaxed even most serious writing has become these days. He thinks the term "colloquial" has outlived its usefulness; it's too restrictive, he says, even misleading. He proposes redefining expressions like "a lot" as "*casual*, in the sense of relaxed, easy, familiar," and defends their frequent appropriateness. If not a green light, he says, give these "casualisms" (as he calls them) an orange light. I agree with him. It's interesting how the chatty looseness of *a lot*, for example, seems to vanish in certain contexts: it will be such a good fit that you won't even notice it, and if by chance you did, it would defy criticism. Flip back to the Updike passage near the end of Chapter 6 and you'll see what I mean. The typical alternatives—*many* and *much*—simply wouldn't work there. Conclusion: Let your ear and good sense be your guide. And take time to think through every good writer's inevitable question: *Who do I want to sound like?* Quentin Crisp put it eloquently. "Style is being yourself," he said, "but on purpose."

and/or   To many readers, this is an ugly coinage associated with income-tax prose. Its sole virtue is convenience. Without it one would have to say "X or Y, or both"—itself something of an unwieldy monstrosity, in my opinion. Use it sparingly, if at all. And always ask yourself if *or* alone won't suffice.

assure–ensure–insure   All three words mean "to make certain or safe." Use *assure* with persons, *ensure* with things, and *insure* when talking about money and guarantees (e.g., life insurance): "I assured Mary that our spending the extra $20 to insure the package would ensure its safe delivery."

between–among   When speaking of just two persons or things, use *between*; of three or more, use *among*. But if a tight relationship is implied, use *between* regardless of the number: "The quarrel between Mike, Jim, and Larry still rages"; "The flights between London, Geneva, and Berlin have been canceled."

cannot   *Cannot* trumps *can not.*

consensus   The word means "collective opinion" or "general agreement." Since it already includes the idea of opinion, the phrase *consensus of opinion* is redundant. So, too, *the general consensus.* Simply say, for example, "The consensus is that the bill will pass the Senate."

criterion–criteria   You can have but one *criterion.* But you can have two or more *criteria.* Moral: Don't use *criteria* when you're speaking of just one thing. Some allied words, all Latin derivatives:

datum–data   phenomenon–phenomena
medium–media   stratum–strata
memorandum–memoranda

different from–different than   Since one thing differs *from* another, say *different from* except where it creates a cumbersome or wordy clause after it, in which case *different than* is not only acceptable but preferable ("The temptations there are different for adults than for kids").

disinterested–uninterested   If you are *disinterested*, you are unbiased or impartial. If you are *uninterested*, you aren't interested. The difference is so radical that it's worth making a point of remembering which word says which.

effect–affect   See the entry for *affect–effect.*

equally   Use it alone ("Hugh and Stu are equally talented"). Don't tack on the redundant *as* ("Hugh and Stu are equally as talented").

factor   Doesn't it have a lovely scientific ring to it? Maybe that's why it appears with such depressing frequency in college writing. We ought to put a 10-year moratorium on this word. We could get along perfectly well with *component*, *ingredient*, or *element*.

famous–notorious   If people are widely known and acclaimed, they're *famous*. But if they're widely known because they are disreputable, they're *notorious* (infamous).

first–firstly   In enumerating several items, say *first*, not *firstly*. The reasons: *first* is as genuine an adverb as *firstly*, is a simpler form, and is easier on the ear. The same applies to *second, third, fourth*, etc. Occasionally you may decide that the numerals themselves are preferable to the words, as in this serious joke from Twain: "To be a writer, one must observe three rules: (1) write, (2) write, and (3) write." Note that the numerals are enclosed on *both* sides by parentheses. (Why do people so often want to use just one parenthesis?) Note, too, that a comma plus *and* precedes the final numeral. (The serial comma, remember?) When the enumerated items are each quite lengthy, substitute semicolons for the commas to enhance readability.

imply–infer   If someone, such as an author, has *implied* something, she has hinted it or intimated it instead of saying it outright; if someone else, such as a reader, gets the hint, he has *inferred* it—that is, deduced the veiled point. It's analogous to the difference between giving and receiving.

irregardless   If you use the word, you mean *regardless*. Technically we can't call *irregardless* a nonword, for there it is, but it deserves to be a nonword since the suffix *less* makes the prefix *ir-* plainly redundant. In any case, it's "nonstandard."

its–it's   Here's another pair of commonly confused words. *It's* is the contraction of *it is*, whereas *its* is the possessive form of *it*. That's counterintuitive, of course. Normally, possession is indicated by the apostrophe. In this case, though, *its* belongs to a special class of words called "possessive pronouns" (*its, hers, theirs, yours, ours*) that, by some fluke of custom, dispenses with the apostrophe. You need to know that the correct spelling of these two words is, to many readers, one of the bedrock credibility tests for writers.

lay–lie   The verb *lay* means "to put or set down," as in "I'll lay the baby in her crib" or "Please lay the book on the table." Basically, then, *lay* means "to place," which is a good memory tip, since *lay* and *place* share the same vowel sound. The past tense of *lay* is *laid*, as in "I laid it there only yesterday." Note that *lay*, in all its forms, *always takes a direct object*, even when it uses its alternate meanings, such as "to arrange" ("I'll lay the table for dinner") or "to produce and deposit" ("Our hen laid three eggs last week"). *Lay* is declined like this: *lay, laid, laid, laying*.

Lie, on the other hand, *never* takes a direct object. *Lie* means "to recline"—note the near rhyme—as in "Let's lie down for a bit." Here are examples of its other tenses: "They lay down" (past); "They had just lain down when the phone rang" (past perfect); "They were just lying down when the phone rang" (past progressive).

like–as   If no verb follows your comparison, use *like*. But if a verb follows it, use *as*. Compare: "Molly giggles like her sister" versus "Molly's a gem, as I knew she would be." Note, however, that when *like* means *as if*, a verb may follow it: "Write like you're actually talking to that friend."

loathe–loath   You may *loathe* a bad habit, yet still be *loath* (unwilling) to give it up.

loose–lose   If a button is *loose*, you're apt to *lose* it.

neither   See that it's followed by *nor*, not *or*. Example: "Neither Bill nor his father ate the turnips with relish." Use *or* only with *either*. And let the number of the verb following a *neither . . . nor* construction agree with the noun closest to it. Both of these sentences are correct:

> Neither Jack nor Susan was happy about it.
> Neither Jack nor his roommates were happy about it.

none   Is it singular or plural? Well, it can be either. If it's followed by a singular noun, it's construed as singular; if by a plural noun, it's construed as plural. Thus:

> None of the work was done.
> None of the guests were here when we arrived.

If no noun follows it, simply decide whether you're talking about more than one and pick your verb accordingly. If you want to emphasize the fact of singleness, substitute *no one* or *not one*: "Not one of his shots was good."

only   Here's my nominee for the most commonly misplaced modifier in American English. Be sure to put it *immediately adjacent* to the word it actually modifies. Compare:

> Sam only plays golf on weekends.
> Sam plays golf only on weekends.

The first version implies that Sam does nothing each weekend but play golf—he doesn't mow the lawn, take the family out, come home to eat, nothing. The second version implies that the only time Sam plays golf is on weekends.

oral–verbal   If it's spoken, it's *oral* (e.g., "oral contract"); if it's in words, it's *verbal* (e.g., "verbal contract"). An oral reply is always verbal (unless it's wordless), but a verbal reply isn't always oral. (And do you see how parentheses breed?)

¶   Although it seems illogical, the proofreader's symbol for a new paragraph is ¶, not a "P" with an extra leg.

precede   *Precede* ("to come before") is, next to *accommodate*, perhaps the most commonly misspelled word in college prose. It apparently gets confused with *proceed* and comes out misspelled as *preceed*.

principal–principle   If you're referring to a rule or basic truth, say *principle*. This word functions only as a noun. Its sound-alike, *principal*, denotes "chief" and can be used as either a noun or an adjective: e.g., "the principal of the school," "the principal witness."

reason is because   Redundant. *Because* means "for the reason that." Say one or the other, not both. The following sentences are equally correct:

> He double-parked because he was rushed.
> The reason he double-parked is that he was rushed.

revert–regress   Both mean "go back." Thus the expressions "revert back" and "regress back" are redundancies. Simply say, for example, "He reverted to his old ways."

shall–will   When your grandparents were in school, they were taught the vital difference in usage between these two words. But they forgot that difference along with nearly everybody else—apparently it was not so vital after all—and now the words are interchangeable. *Shall*, though, sounds slightly fussier and more bookish to the average ear, so if you're aiming at a conversational style, use *will* instead. The exception would be a first-person interrogative: "Shall we dance?" "Shall I pick her up at the station or will you?"

so   Many people believe that *so* is an intensifier synonymous with *very* ("This coffee is so hot"). It isn't, however, at least not in grown-up prose. Note that when you write a sentence like my example, readers will unconsciously—and properly—expect a *that* clause to follow: "This coffee is so hot that I can't drink it."

supposed to   In conversation it's hard to hear that final *d*, but it's there—or should be—since it's the past participle of the verb *suppose*. Thus, say "I was supposed to leave today," not "I was suppose to leave today."

there is–there are   Both are empty phrases and should be used sparingly. Eliminating them by recasting usually results in sentences that are more vivid, concrete, and direct. There are many exceptions, though, and this is one of them.

though   When you end a sentence with *though*, set it off with a comma: "That was not the first time, though." The word functions just like *however* there. Curiously, many writers who wouldn't dream of not setting off *however* treat *though* as if it weren't parenthetic. They'll write it this way: "That was not the first time though." Try reading that aloud. Don't you hear the big drop in pitch as you arrive at *though*? That's your proof that the word is parenthetic—and thus needs setting off.

throughout   Includes the idea of "entire," whereas *through* does not. Say either "Throughout the story . . ." or "Through the entire story. . . ."

thus   *Thus* is an adverb. Many people, not knowing better, think they must attach to it the regular adverbial suffix *-ly* to use it as an adverb. *Thusly*, however, is an illiteracy. It's ugly, too.

unique   If a thing is *unique*, it's the only one of its kind. The condition is an absolute one, like perfection. Thus you can't logically talk about *unique* in terms of degree. You can't say, for example, "rather unique" or "the most unique" or "very unique." A thing is either unique or it's not unique, just as a woman is either pregnant or she's not pregnant. When writers misuse *unique*, they usually mean "uncommon," "unusual," or "rare." "A rather unique invitation," for example, should read "a rather unusual invitation."

used to   As with *supposed to*, we're dealing with a silent *d* again—the past participle of the verb *use* ("to be accustomed to"). Say "I used to work there," not "I use to work there."

whether   Use it alone. Don't tack on the redundancy *or not* as in the sentence, "He doesn't know whether or not to go." The *or not* is necessary only when you mean to convey the idea of *regardless of whether*. Example: "We're going biking today whether it rains or not."

> *I would be most content if my children grew up to be the kind of people who think decorating consists mostly of building enough bookshelves.*
>
> —Anna Quindlen

The entries above represent just a handful of the many usage questions that arise in our writing lives. For help with all those other ones, consider buying at least two of the following reference texts, which you'll find both authoritative and indispensable:

- Theodore Bernstein, *The Careful Writer: A Modern Guide to English Usage* (New York: Atheneum, 1965)
- H. W. Fowler, *A Dictionary of Modern English Usage: The Classic First Edition*, ed. David Crystal (New York: Oxford U.P., 2009)
- Bryan Garner, *Garner's Modern American Usage*, 3rd ed. (New York: Oxford U.P., 2009)
- Merriam-Webster, *Merriam-Webster's Dictionary of English Usage* (Springfield, MA: Merriam-Webster, Inc., 1994)
- Marjorie Skillin, ed., *Words into Type*, 3rd ed. (Englewood Cliffs: Prentice-Hall, 1974)
- Andrea Sutliffe, ed., *The New York Public Library Writer's Guide to Style and Usage* (New York: HarperCollins, 1994)
- University of Chicago Press, *The Chicago Manual of Style*, 16th ed. (Chicago: University of Chicago Press, 2010)

One other book I want to plug here, though with a strong qualification, is Strunk and White's classic, *The Elements of Style*. At just 105 pages, it can't pretend to be comprehensive, and it's often dated, over-prescriptive, and misinformed, yet its succinctness and general utility have made it a bible to legions of writers. They affectionately refer to it as "Strunk & White," and they've helped make it perhaps the most popular style manual in history. But it turns out to be far more flawed than most readers would imagine. In April 2009, on the 50th anniversary of the book's publication, *The Chronicle of Higher Education* published a scathing reassessment of it by Professor Geoffrey Pullum, Head of Linguistics and English Language at the University of Edinburgh and co-author of *The Cambridge Grammar of the English Language* (Cambridge U.P., 2002). Pullum's boldly explicit essay, entitled "50 Years of Stupid Grammar Advice," makes for a riveting read. It's freely available online,[1] and I would recommend it to anyone inclined to deify Struck & White. You won't want to throw out your copy of their manual, but you will want to read it more critically—and you'll be a better writer for doing so.

---

[1] http://chronicle.com/article/50-Years-of-Stupid-Grammar/25497

17

Epilogue

*A writer's problem does not change. He himself changes
and the world he lives in changes but his problem remains
the same. It is always how to write truly and having found
what is true, to project it in such a way that it becomes
part of the experience of the person who reads it.*

—Ernest Hemingway

*A writer provides his reader with a role model of both
the courage to experience without dimming or repress-
ing this or that facet of self and the courage to share this
experiencing with others.*

—Sidney Jourard

Some time ago I ran across a cartoon depicting a scene aboard a com-
mercial airliner. As the startled passengers look on, the whole flight
crew, outfitted in parachutes, strolls down the aisle towards the rear es-
cape hatch. Leading them out is the pilot, his hands nonchalantly tucked
in his pockets and a casual whistle on his guiltily upturned face.

I confess I see myself in that pilot. Here I am, cravenly parachuting
out of harm's way on the wings of a final paragraph, and there you are,
abandoned to your own devices just when the trip has started getting
bumpy. I hope, though, that this book, brief as it is, has given you new insight into how skilled writers think, plus the itch to go out and write like
them yourself. Writing well is hard work, but it can be *pleasant* hard work
if we view it for what it really is—a challenge to our creativity, an opportunity to know our own mind, and a chance to share our thoughts and
feelings with others. That's certainly what this book has meant for me.

Thanks for listening.

Sources

Note: Because I started collecting these quotations for personal use only, long before the book itself was conceived, I occasionally neglected to record any source beyond the author's name. I've managed to track down most of the fugitive quotations, but a few regrettably remain at large. Unattributed examples are my own.

page vii Gloria Steinem, quoted in *Writers on Writing*, ed. Jon Winokur (Philadelphia: Running Press, 1986), 13.

2 Ernest Hemingway, "Advice to a Young Man," *Playboy*, XI (January 1964), 153.

2 F. L. Lucas, *Style* (London: Cassell, 1955), 76.

8 W. Somerset Maugham, *The Summing Up* (Garden City, NY: Doubleday, 1938), 30–31.

8 George M. Trevelyan, *Clio, a Muse and Other Essays Literary and Pedestrian* (London: Longmans, Green, 1913), 34.

8 James A. Michener, quoted in A. Grove Day, *James A. Michener* (New York: Twayne, 1964), 135.

9 E. B. White, quoted in Donald M. Murray, *A Writer Teaches Writing* (Boston: Houghton Mifflin, 1968), 245.

11 George Bernard Shaw, in *Ellen Terry and Bernard Shaw: A Correspondence*, ed. Christopher St. John (New York: The Fountain Press, 1931), 113.

12 Walter W. "Red" Smith, quoted in John Brady, *The Craft of Interviewing* (New York: Vintage, 1977), 202. This witticism is also sometimes attributed to the journalist Gene Fowler (1890–1960).

12 Matt MacDonald, my former 325M student at the University of Texas and now a creative director at JWT, in an email to me.

14 Pauline Kael, *Deeper into Movies* (Boston: Little, Brown, 1973), 316–17. Reprinted in Kael, *For Keeps: Thirty Years at the Movies* (New York: Dutton, 1994), 392.

175

15   Russell Page, *The Education of a Gardener* (London: Atheneum, 1962), 45–46.

16   E. M. Forster, *Aspects of the Novel* (New York: Harcourt, Brace, 1927; reprinted 1954), 152, quoting a character in André Gide's novel *Les Faux Monnayeurs*.

16   E. L. Doctorow, in *The New York Times*, 20 Oct. 1985, quoted in *Webster's II New Riverside Desk Quotations*, ed. James B. Simpson (Boston: Houghton Mifflin, 1992), 260.

16   Robert Frost, in *The New York Times*, 7 Nov. 1955, quoted in *Good Advice on Writing*, ed. William Safire and Leonard Safire (New York: Simon & Schuster, 1992), 179.

16   Joan Didion, quoted in *Writers on Writing*, ed. Jon Winokur (Philadelphia: Running Press, 1986), 103.

16   Susan Sontag, interviewed in *Conversations with American Writers*, ed. Charles Ruas (London: Quartet Books, 1984), 186–87.

16   Anne Sexton, quoted in *Writers on Writing*, ed. Jon Winokur (Philadelphia: Running Press, 1986), 73.

16   Maya Angelou, in *Writers at Work: The* Paris Review *Interviews*, 9th Series, ed. George Plimpton (New York: Penguin, 1992), 180.

16   Edward Albee, quoted in *Good Advice on Writing*, ed. William Safire and Leonard Safire (New York: Simon & Schuster, 1992), 220.

16   Gore Vidal, *The New York Times*, 24 Feb. 1976, quoted in James B. Simpson, *Simpson's Contemporary Quotations* (Boston: Houghton Mifflin, 1988), 317.

17   E. B. White, in *Writers at Work: The* Paris Review *Interviews*, 8th Series (New York: Viking, 1988), 12.

17   Thomas Griffith, *How True: A Skeptic's Guide to Believing the News* (Boston: Atlantic Monthly Press Book, 1974), 61.

20   Anne Lamott, *Bird by Bird: Some Instructions on Writing and Life* (New York: Anchor, 1994), 22.

21   Stephen Spender, "The Making of a Poem," *Partisan Review*, Summer 1946.

22   Betty Sue Flowers, "Madman, Architect, Carpenter, Judge: Roles and the Writing Process," *1979 Proceedings of Conference of College Teachers of English of Texas*, LXIV, Sept. 1979, 7–10.

23   John Mason Brown, *Dramatis Personae: A Retrospective Show*, Compass Book ed. (New York: Viking, 1965), 458.

23   Wendell Berry, "Some Thoughts I Have in Mind When I Teach," *Writers as Teachers, Teachers as Writers*, ed. Jonathan Baumbach (New York: Holt, Rinehart, 1970), 23.

29   H. L. Mencken, quoted in William H. Nolte, *H. L. Mencken: Literary Critic* (Middletown, CT: Wesleyan University Press, 1966), 33.

36   George Bernard Shaw, "Epistle Dedicatory" prefacing his play *Man and Superman*.

41   Rudolf Flesch, *The Art of Plain Talk* (London: Collier, 1962), 97 ff.

43   Bergen Evans, "But What's a Dictionary For?" *Atlantic Monthly*, May 1962.

44   Lucas, *Style*, op. cit., 39–40.

48   Donald Hall, *Writing Well* (Boston: Little Brown, 1973), 42.

48   Sydney Smith, quoted in Lady Holland, *A Memoir of the Reverend Sydney Smith*, vol. 1 (New York: Harper & Brothers, 1856), 333.

51   Theodore M. Bernstein, *The Careful Writer: A Modern Guide to Usage* (New York: Atheneum, 1965), 14.

53   Mina Shaughnessey, *Errors & Expectations: A Guide for the Teacher of Basic Writing* (New York: Oxford U.P., 1977), 85.

53   Mark Twain, *Selected Shorter Writings of Mark Twain*, ed. Walter Blair (Boston: Houghton Mifflin, 1962), 226.

53   Elizabeth Taylor, *Elizabeth Taylor: An Informal Memoir* (New York: Harper & Row, 1965), 124.

53   John W. Aldridge, *Time to Murder and Create: The Contemporary Novel in Crisis* (New York: David McKay, 1966), 169.

53   T. S. Eliot, *On Poetry and Poets* (New York: Farrar, Straus and Cudahy, 1957), 111.

54   Theodor Seuss (Dr. Seuss), quoted in Murray, *A Writer Teaches Writing*, op. cit., 237.

54   Ray Bradbury, "Seeds of Three Stories," in *On Writing, By Writers*, ed. William W. West (Lexington, MA: Ginn, 1966), 48.

54   Oliver Wendell Holmes, *Over the Teacups* (1890), quoted in *Writers on Writing*, ed. Thomas H. Brennan (Jefferson, NC: McFarland, 1994), 103.

54   Ford Madox Ford, *Joseph Conrad: A Personal Remembrance* (London: Duckworth, 1924), 197.

54   Nolte, *H. L. Mencken*, op. cit., 55.

55   Dwight Macdonald, *Against the American Grain* (New York: Random House, 1962), 192.

55   Charles W. Ferguson, *Say It with Words* (New York: Knopf, 1959), 57–58.

55   H. L. Mencken, *Prejudices: First Series* (New York: Knopf, 1919), 12.

56   Brown, *Dramatis Personae*, op. cit., 99.

56   Joseph Conrad, "Preface" to *The Nigger of the Narcissus*.

56   John Updike, "Upright Carpentry," in *Assorted Prose* (New York: Alfred A. Knopf, 1965), 77.

57   Paul Gallico, "A Large Number of Persons," *Vanity Fair* magazine, 1931.

58   Blaise Pascal, *Pensées*, trans. W. F. Trotter (New York: Dutton, 1958), Section I, #29.

58   Robert Frost, "Preface" to *A Way Out* in *Robert Frost: Poetry and Prose*, ed. Edward C. Lathem and Lawrance Thompson (New York: Holt, Rinehart, 1972), 272–73.

59   Anne Lamott, op. cit., 26, 28.

59   Dorothy Allison, *Skin: Talking About Sex, Class* & *Literature* (Ithaca, NY: Firebrand Books, 1994), 165–66.

62   George Orwell, "Politics and the English Language," *Shooting an Elephant and Other Essays* (New York: Harcourt, Brace, 1950), 85, 87.

63   James M. McCrimmon, *Writing with a Purpose* (Boston: Houghton Mifflin, 1972), 410.

63   Porter G. Perrin, *Writer's Guide and Index to English*, 3rd ed. (Chicago: Scott, Foresman, 1959), 15–20.

63   Maugham, *The Summing Up*, op. cit., 38.

64   Bonamy Dobrée, *Modern Prose Style*, 2nd ed. (Oxford: Clarendon, 1964), 218.

64   Hesketh Pearson, *G. B. S.: A Full Length Portrait* (New York: Harper & Bros., 1942), 111. Reprinted as *George Bernard Shaw: His Life and Personality* (New York: Atheneum paperback, 1963), 130.

66   Evans, "But What's a Dictionary For?", op. cit.

67   Gregg Hopkins, letter to the author.

68   Rudolf Flesch, *The Art of Readable Writing* (1949; reprinted Collier Books ed., 1967), 97.

69   Witold Rybczynski, *Home: A Short History of an Idea* (New York: Penguin, 1986), 212.

69   Stewart Brand, *How Buildings Learn: What Happens after They're Built* (New York: Viking, 1994), 138.

70   Ron Suskind, *A Hope in the Unseen: An American Odyssey from the Inner City to the Ivy League* (New York: Broadway Books), 17.

70   Voltaire, quoted by Rudolph Flesch, *The Art of Plain Talk* (London: Collier- Macmillan, 1951), 91, and by Arthur Schopenhauer, "On Style," in *The Art of Literature*, trans. T. Bailey Saunders (London: George Allen, 1891), 29.

70   Mark Twain, "Pudd'nhead Wilson's Calendar," *Pudd'nhead Wilson*, Limited Editions Club edition (Avon, CT: Cardavon Press, 1974), 28.

70   Mark Twain, letter to D. W. Bowser dated 20 March 1880, cited in http:// www.twainquotes.com/Writing.html.

71   Brand, *How Buildings Learn*, op. cit., vii and 114.

71   Henry Thoreau, *Walden, Where I Lived, and What I Lived For*, in *Walden and Other Writings of Henry David Thoreau*, ed. Brooks Atkinson (New York: Modern Library, 1950), 82.

71   W. Somerset Maugham, quoted in Cyril Connolly, *Enemies of Promise*, rev. ed. (New York: Macmillan, 1948), 35.

71   Hemingway, "Advice to a Young Man," op. cit., 153.

73   Rybczynski, *Home*, op. cit., 222.

74   Paul Graham, *Hackers & Painters: Big Ideas from the Computer Age* (Sebastopol, CA: O'Reilly, 2004), 31.

74   Mark Bittman, "The Way to Italy's Heart," *Travel Holiday* magazine, July/August 1999, 74.

74   Lucas, *Style*, op. cit., 132.

76   E. E. Cummings, *E. E. Cummings: A Miscellany*, ed. George J. Firmage (New York: Argophile, 1958), 13.

76   Gloria Steinem, "A New Egalitarian Lifestyle," *The New York Times*, 26 Aug. 1971.

76   Donald Lloyd, "Snobs, Slobs, and the English Language," *The American Scholar*, XX (Summer 1951), 279.

79   Evans, "But What's a Dictionary For?," op. cit.

80   Robert Frost, "Introduction" to *King Jasper* by Edward Arlington Robinson.

81   Wayne Booth, "The Rhetorical Stance," *College Composition and Communication*, 14 (October 1963), 141.

81   Theodore M. Bernstein, *Miss Thistlebottom's Hobgoblins: The Careful Writer's Guide to the Taboos, Bugbears and Outmoded Rules of English Usage*, Noonday edition (New York: Farrar, Straus & Giroux, 1973), 189.

81   William Strunk Jr. and E. B. White, *The Elements of Style*, 3rd ed. (New York: Macmillan, 1979), 70.

82   Nora Ephron, *Wallflower at the Orgy* (New York: Bantam edition, 1980), viii.

83   H. W. Fowler, *A Dictionary of Modern English Usage* (Oxford: Clarendon, 1960), 457–58.

83   Sir Winston Churchill, quoted in Richard Lederer, *Conan the Grammarian: Adventures of a Verbivore* (New York: Simon & Schuster, 1994); reprinted in *The Best Writing on Writing*, vol. 2, ed. Jack Heffron (Cincinnati: Story Press, 1995), 210.

85   George O. Curme, *Syntax* (Boston: D. C. Heath, 1931), 459.

85   Bernstein, *Miss Thistlebottom's Hobgoblins*, op. cit., 174.

85   Robert Selph Henry, *The Story of the Confederacy*, rev. ed. (1931; reprinted Gloucester, MA: Peter Smith, 1970), 11.

86   John Dewey, *Experience and Education: The 60th Anniversary Edition* (Indianapolis: Kappa Delta Pi, 1998), 48.

87   Jerome Frank, "The Speech of Judges: A Dissenting Opinion," 29 Va. L. Rev. 625 (1943); rpt in *The Scribes Journal of Legal Writing*, vol. 6, 1996–1997, ed. Bryan Garner (Scribes—The American Society of Writers on Legal Subjects: Dallas, 1998), 99.

88   Brendan Gill, *Here at The New Yorker* (NY: Random House, 1975), 161.

88   Peter Goldman, taped conversation with 325M student Ben Dean, in his 325M course paper "An Interview with Peter Goldman," Fall 1981.

88   Somerset Maugham, *The Summing Up* (Garden City: International Collectors Library American Headquarters, 1938), section xiii, 42-43.

88   H. L. Mencken, "Literature and the Schoolma'm," *Prejudices, Fifth Series* (New York: Knopf, 1926).

97   H. L. Mencken, "The Poet and His Art," *Prejudices, Third Series* (New York: Knopf, 1922), 147–148.

101 Tommy Thompson, "Nonfiction Books: The New Bestsellers," *Writer's Digest*, Aug. 1977, 21.

101 Raymond Chandler, *Selected Letters of Raymond Chandler*, ed. Frank MacShane (NY: Columbia U.P., 1981), 79.

102 Barbara Tuchman, *Practicing History: Selected Essays* (New York: Knopf, 1981), 16.

102 Tuchman, *Practicing History*, 17.

102 Tuchman, *Practicing History*, 16-17.

103 Dr. Samuel Johnson, "Preface to Shakespeare" (1765), *Johnson: Prose and Poetry*, ed. Mona Wilson (Cambridge, MA: Harvard U.P., 1963), 495.

104 Malcolm Gladwell, *Outliers: The Story of Success* (New York: Little, Brown, 2008), 299.

107 Anne Fadiman, *Ex Libris: Confessions of a Common Reader* (NY: Farrar, Straus and Giroux, 1998), 39.

108 Joseph Epstein, "The Crime of a Happy Childhood," in *The Middle of My Tether* (NY: W. W. Norton, 1983), 234.

108 James Dickey, source unknown.

109 Robert Frost, "The Mountain," *The Complete Poems of Robert Frost* (NY: Holt, Rinehart and Winston, 1949), 59.

117 Ernest Hemingway, interviewed by George Plimpton in *Writers at Work: The* Paris Review *Interviews*, 2nd Series, ed. George Plimpton (New York: Viking, 1965; rpt. Penguin, 1977), 222.

118 Donald H. Ross, *The Writing Performance* (Philadelphia: J.B. Lippincott, 1973), 24.

121 Rudolf Flesch, *The Art of Plain Talk*, op. cit., 108.

121 Fran Lebowitz, quoted in "And Other Amusing People" by Allison Silver, *The New York Times*, 28 Feb. 1982.

122 Adlai Stevenson, quoted in *The Forbes Book of Business Quotations*, ed. Ted Goodman (NY: Black Dog & Leventhal, 1997), 84.

123 Alexander Pope, *An Essay on Criticism* (1711), lines 362–63.

124 Mark Twain, "Autobiography," *The Portable Mark Twain*, ed. Bernard DeVoto (New York: Viking, 1968), 619.

124 Twain, "Pudd'nhead Wilson's Calendar," op. cit., 35.

124 Leon Edel, "Literature and Biography," *Relations of Literary Study: Essays on Interdisciplinary Contributions*, ed. James Thorpe (New York: Modern Language Association, 1967), 62.

125 Eric F. Goldman, *The Tragedy of Lyndon Johnson* (New York: Knopf, 1969), vii.

126 Robert Frost, in *Writers at Work: The* Paris Review *Interviews*, 2nd Series, ed. George Plimpton (New York: Viking, 1963); rpt Penguin, 1977, 30.

127 *Words into Type*, by Marjorie E. Skillin et al., 3rd ed. (Englewood Cliffs, NJ: Prentice Hall, 1974), 184.

135 Charlie Chaplin, interviewed in *Life* magazine, 10 March 1967.

135 H. L. Mencken, quoted in Nolte, *H. L. Mencken*, op. cit., 50.

135   C. S. Lewis, *Letters of C. S. Lewis* (New York: Harcourt, Brace, 1966), 127.

136   Melvin Maddocks, in a review of *Max Jamison* by Wilfred Sheed, *Life* magazine, 15 March 1970, 13.

136   Gale Hickman, letter to the author.

136   Sammy Davis, Jr., with Jane and Burt Boyar, *Yes I Can: The Story of Sammy Davis, Jr.* (New York: Pocket Books, 1966), 130.

136   Mark Twain, *A Treasury of Mark Twain*, ed. Edward Lewis and Robert Myers (Kansas City, MO: Hallmark, 1967), 48.

136   Peter Mayle, *A Year in Provence,* Vintage edition (New York: Random House, 1991), 75.

136   J. William Fulbright, *The Arrogance of Power* (New York: Random House, 1966), 5.

140   Twain, *A Treasury of Mark Twain,* 17.

141   Yul Brynner, widely attributed. Specific source unknown.

141   Joseph Wood Krutch, *If You Don't Mind My Saying So* (New York: Sloane, 1964), 128.

141   Woody Allen, *Getting Even* (New York: Warner Paperback Library, 1972), 19.

142   Jo Coudert, *Advice from a Failure* (New York: Stein & Day, 1965), 156.

142   Barbara Tuchman, "Can History Use Freud? The Case of Woodrow Wilson," *Atlantic Monthly,* February 1967, 44.

142   Corey Ford, "The One and Only W. C. Fields," *Harper's*, October 1967.

142   Spender, "The Making of a Poem" (1946).

142   Eliot Fremont-Smith, review of *Language and Silence: Essays on Language, Literature, and the Inhuman* by George Steiner.

145   See, for example, Annabel Davis-Goff, "Reading *War and Peace* to William Maxwell," in *A William Maxwell Portrait: Memories and Appreciations*, ed. Charles Baxter, Michael Collier, and Edward Hirsch (NY: W. W. Norton, 2004), 179.

145   Elmore Leonard, *Elmore Leonard's 10 Rules of Writing* (NY: William Morrow, 2007), 33, 31.

147   Gorham Munson, *The Writer's Workshop Companion* (New York: Farrar, Straus, and Young, 1951), 269.

147   Twain, *A Treasury of Mark Twain,* 59.

147   Twain, *A Treasury of Mark Twain,* 6.

147   Orwell, "Politics and the English Language," 91.

148   James Thurber, quoted in *Writers on Writing,* 91.

148   Raymond Carver, in *Writers at Work: The* Paris Review *Interviews,* 7th Series, ed. George Plimpton (New York: Viking, 1986), 315–16.

148   Robertson Davies, *The Merry Heart: Reflections on Reading, Writing, and the World of Books* (New York: Penguin, 1996), 240.

149   H. L. Mencken, quoted in Nolte, *H. L. Mencken,* 49.

149   John Updike, in a commentary written for *On Writing, By Writers,* ed. William W. West (Lexington, MA: Ginn, 1966), 121.

150 Oscar Wilde, *The Importance of Being Earnest*, Act I.

150 H. L. Mencken, *The Vintage Mencken*, ed. Alistair Cooke (New York: Vintage, 1955), 233.

151 Ken Macrorie, *Telling Writing* (New York: Hayden, 1970), 250.

152 Fulbright, *The Arrogance of Power*, 3.

152 Schjelderup-Ebbe, quoted in Anthony Storr, *Human Aggression* (New York: Atheneum, 1968), 25.

153 Larry McMurtry, *Atlantic Monthly*, March 1975, 30.

160 H. L. Mencken, quoted in Nolte, *H. L. Mencken*, 62, 102.

160 Jacques Barzun, *Teacher in America*, Anchor Book ed. (Garden City, NY: Doubleday, 1959), 47.

161 Mme. Geoffrin, quoted by Charles Saint-Beuve in "Madame Geoffrin," *Sainte-Beuve: Selected Essays*, trans. Francis Steegmuller and Norbert Guterman (Garden City, NY: Doubleday, 1963), 154.

162 Ray Bradbury, *Zen in the Art of Writing*, essay titled "The Joy of Writing."

163 "An Interview with Ernest Hemingway," ed. George Plimpton, *The Paris Review*, vol. 18, Spring 1958.

165 Ezra Pound, *ABC of Reading* (New York: New Directions, 1951), 32.

165 Bernstein, *The Careful Writer*, xv.

166 Bernstein, *The Careful Writer*, 95.

166 Quentin Crisp, interview with Jeanne Claire van Ryzin ("In the Profession of Being") in the *Austin American-Statesman*, 15 July 1998, E7.

172 Anna Quindlen, "Enough Bookshelves," *The New York Times*, 7 Aug. 1991, 26.

173 Ernest Hemingway, quoted in *The Writer's Quotation Book: A Literary Companion*, ed. James Charlton (New York: Pushcart Press, 1980), 48.

173 Sidney Jourard, *The Transparent Self*, rev. ed. (Florence, KY: Van Nostrand, 1971), 62.

Index

abbreviations, 163–164
accommodate, 165
accurate nouns, 70
Act, in plays, 159
active verbs, 50, 52
active voice, 52
actor, grammatical subject and, 50
A Dictionary of American Usage
    (Evans), 66n
adjectives, 70
adverbs, 70–71
aesthetics, axiom in, 67
affect–effect, 165
A Hope in the Unseen (Suskind), 70
"A Large Number of Persons" (Gallico), 57
Albee, Edward, 16
    Who's Afraid of Virginia Woolf?, 18
Aldridge, John, 53
Alexander, Shana, 136
Allen, Woody, 14, 54, 141
Allison, Dorothy, 59–60
all right, 166
a lot, 166
ambiguity, commas and, 131–132
American Heritage Dictionary, 147
The American Mercury, 89
analogy, 30–31, 55, 56, 69, 107n, 109
and, beginning a sentence with, 73, 74, 78–80
and/or, 166
and or *but*, 73–74
Angelou, Maya, 16
anticipating reader response, 9
Antony and Cleopatra, 36

"appreciations," 13
"A&P" (Updike), 69
Architectural Digest, 95
arguments
    classification of, 32
    sequence of, 33
    signposting, 39
    summaries in, 71
    support for, 33, 34
artful presentation, 101
    attractive formatting, 102–107
    dramatic plotting, 109–112
    example, 112–116
    interesting phrasing, 107–109
artful writing, 53
The Art of Plain Talk (Flesch), 41
art of thinking, 96
assertions, 42
assigned topics, 14–15
Associated Press Stylebook, 73, 156
Assorted Prose (Updike), 56
assure–ensure–insure, 167
Atlantic Monthly, 43, 66, 79
attitude, verb choice and, 53
audience
    collaboration with, 111
    identifying the, 31
    identifying with, 20, 36
    sense of, 31, 33
authentic manner, 58
authorities, to support argument, 34
axiom in aesthetics, 67
Axthelm, Pete, 124–125